DICKENS STUDIES ANNUAL

Robert B. Partlow, Jr., *Editor*

DICKENS
STUDIES
ANNUAL

VOLUME
5

Edited by

ROBERT B. PARTLOW, JR.

SOUTHERN ILLINOIS UNIVERSITY PRESS

Carbondale and Edwardsville

FEFFER & SIMONS, INC.

London and Amsterdam

COPYRIGHT © 1976 *by* Southern Illinois University Press
All rights reserved
Printed in the United States of America
Designed by Andor Braun
International Standard Book Number 0-8093-0765-0
Library of Congress Catalog Card Number 78-123048

Contents

Preface

ROBERT GIDDING'S article in the June 1975 issue of the *Dickens Studies Newsletter,* "A Cockney in the Court of Uncle Sam," is enough to give any editor of Dickens scholarship and criticism a serious jolt. As that editor ponders the manuscripts he has selected and published over the last few years, he is forced to do what he perhaps had not time in the rush of events to do before: consider the types of essays he chose, the nationality of the authors, and the balance he sought to achieve in various issues and volumes. Some of our most brilliant and foresighted editors have, indubitably, definite and fixed policies governing such matters; others take the easier path and simply publish the best that is on hand when a deadline is reached, a policy which has at least the merit of Arnoldian approval and the additional merit of appealing in some measure to readers of several critical persuasions. But Mr. Giddings makes one wonder if such a procedure is not wrongheaded, if not downright blind and evil.

In his essay he divides Dickens scholars and critics into two major classes: those who are going at the novels in the right way, with the right values and assumptions, and those who are not. Among the most esteemed of the sheep are Edmund Wilson, Hillis Miller, the New Critics, Warrington Winters, Charles Feidelson, Marshall McLuhan, Dorothy Van Ghent, Taylor Stoehr, and a dozen or more Americans. Prominent among the goats are Dr. Leavis (preeminently), Humphry House, John Butt, Kathleen Tillotson, A. O. J. Cockshut, Angus Wilson, Philip Collins, Barbara Hardy, and another dozen or so British critics. In effect, Mr. Giddings finds only good in American and wrongness in British treatment of Dickens and his novels, an attitude pleasing, no doubt, to those who believe that the war between Great Britain and her colonies never quite ended.

Mr. Giddings does, to be accurate, insist that "the great strength of British Dickens scholarship is . . . largely historical" and that the Pilgrim edition of the letters and K. J. Fielding's edition of the speeches are definitive and useful. But he is constantly undercutting the British achievements of the last forty years, primarily by his insistence that these achievements are not worth anything, at least as compared with American efforts to understand Dickens and to enrich our reading of his novels. He quotes with approval Hillis Miller's dictum that the tendency of those like T. A. Jackson and Philip Collins is "to dissolve Dickens' novels into the context of the social and political history of his time," not noticing that the psychoanalytical-mythopoeic approach he considers valid may dissolve Dickens' work into case histories. Giddings speaks scornfully of the terrible stranglehold on the universities by the Oxbridge elite, who have encouraged "a narrow academic view of Dickens which is actually against life," which ignores Freudian psychology and Marxist sociology, insists that literature be judged according to the dictates of bourgeois morality, and is guilty of the worst sort of xenophobia. As a result British criticism has never come to terms with Dickens' novels either as works of art or as documents about life as it is really lived.

American scholars fare much better—though one may wonder if they will be entirely pleased with Mr. Giddings' explanation of the reasons for their superiority: a kind of pleasing primitivism. He posits two quite different traditions dominating the literary establishments of Britain and the United States: the logical/classic and the transcendental/symbolic. Whereas Britain forfeited the "great symbolic-metaphoric tradition of respect for the scriptures" in favor of Newtonian physics, the sceptic-empiricism of Locke, Berkeley, Hume, and the Utilitarians, the Americans retained the older tradition brought over by the first British settlers and never lost it—we Americans are "a kind of cultural Lost World," a vast cultural-lag society untouched by Augustanism (which is apparently every intellectual development since about 1660). The British, therefore, unlike their American cousins, fear the occult, psychology, and sociology; they see little of the comedy, poetry, fable, fairy tale, myth, or "hidden power"; they are unable to see Dickens as a poet and visionary dreamer with a deep understanding of the ways in which vatic power can be communicated. Conversely, American critics use the assumptions and techniques of analysis approved by Mr. Giddings: Marxist, anti-Establishment, psychological, sociological, mythic, symbolic, linguistic—all which strike one as rather precocious for a cultural Lost World untouched by Augustanism. The most praiseworthy Dickens critics are, therefore, those like Taylor Stoehr, Hillis Miller, and Steven Marcus.

Mr. Giddings is certainly entitled to his opinions about the current state of Dickens studies and the reasons therefor, his division of critics into sheep and goats, and his selection of a particular set of assumptions and techniques as the only proper way to approach and comprehend Dickens. But just as certainly one is entitled to ask if he is not being simplistic and reductionary.

Any competent, trained, alert reader knows that the act of reading involves a complex interaction of the author, the work being considered, and the reader himself. Each element in this "equation" is filled with ambiguities, unknowns, contradictions, and difficulties, essentially because the materials of literature are human, largely nonobjective, and verbal—and all the difficulties are multiplied if the author and work are of a different culture and/or era from the one on which the reader exists. It can be truthfully said that almost all the literary works we read are contemporary, otherwise they would be mere artifacts worth little except antiquarian attention. But in another, deeper sense, *no* literary work is contemporary: even one's most extensive knowledge of the present time is not adequate to comprehend the total experience of every author; there are always more or less wide areas of ignorance, lack of experience, shallowness of knowledge (consider, for example, a British student reading modern American black novels or an American student reading the novels of Lord Snow). The critic's task is to bring whatever expertise and delicacy of response he has to bear on the novels so that he may elucidate them and enrich the understanding of more ordinary readers.

Put the case another way: the perfect critic would be the one who could not only re-create, even come to be, the author and be inside him as he creates his novel, but would also bring to that novel the added insights and techniques of a later age not available to the author. This perfect critic would have a thorough knowledge of the life and times of the author (biographical and psychological, political, social, economic, intellectual, religious, and the like, in so far as the author was involved in them) because every man writes out of himself within the interlocking environments we call history. The more complete the reader's understanding of Victorian London, the more vivid will be his re-creation of *Oliver Twist.* The fuller his grasp of mid-Victorian social customs and prejudices, the keener will be his grasp of the satire in *Dombey and Son, Little Dorrit,* and *Our Mutual Friend.* A biography like Forster's or Edgar Johnson's will make innumerable nuances within the novels available to the reader; so will studies supplementing the biographies, such as those of Collins on crime and education, and Trevor Blount on the background of *Bleak House.* An author, with his peculiar genetic and developmental history, is embedded in a complex of matrices: familial, psychological, literary, political, historical, sociological, and so on, which influence him in various ways and to varying degrees, and which are necessarily incorporated into his fictions, either consciously or unwittingly—there is no escape. These are the raw materials of his art, to be modified and shaped to fit the aesthetic pattern of a given fiction. The average American reader of *Great Expectations* misses a great deal unless he has a guide: he has never seen the Cooling marshes; he has never seen modern London, let alone Victorian London; he knows little of the changing Victorian concepts of the gentleman, the value of money, or class structures; not knowing Dickens, he cannot know why he wrote *this* novel at this particular moment, or why he created Biddy and Estella, Joe and Jaggers and Wemmick, Magwitch and Compeyson, in their particular forms, or why Miss Havisham appears as she does. This reader may be able to grasp the basic plot, the superficial psychology of the characters, and the more obvious elements of the meaning, but even here there are weaknesses, unsound or distorted understandings, because the novel is being read as if it were contemporary—and it is not contemporary, but a Victorian statement which still has something to say to twentieth-century readers.

Similar problems affect the trained critic. He too is embedded in an interlocking series of historical matrices, but they are rarely the same as those of the author; perhaps this is a partial explanation for the anguished claims that X is reading his own meanings into a given text—and so he probably is. How fully does a devout atheist enter into the religious meditations of a Dostoievski? What can a dedicated Marxist do with Dickens? The very human tendency is to force an admired author into one's own image, to see in him what one wants to see, and to ignore or explain away those parts of the work not approved—even to see meanings which are demonstrably not present. And this is true of readers and critics who are trying to be objective, not impressionistic or propagandistic. Thus a critic oriented toward Freudian or Jungian psychology, in his assumption of the universal truth of those systems of thought, will read characters and events in terms of the insights and categories of those systems, rather than in terms of the psychology Dickens was using. A radically oriented critic like T. A. Jackson will find that Dickens is very much like T. A. Jackson, except, of course, that the earlier radical is rather old-fashioned. Hence the many, and contradictory, readings of Shakespeare, Shelley, and Dickens, among many others. This is not to say that all interpretations save mine and thine are illegitimate or wrongheaded. Coolly considered, it is one of the major glories of literary criticism that it is *not* exact, mathematical, scientific, but a human endeavor embracing many "disciplines," a mansion of many rooms. The ideal reader-critic would be expert in such disciplines as philosophy, history, psychology, linguistics, religion, as well as literature, and would be able to bring all these disciplines to bear on a single text. One who assumes that only one approach, or a limited cluster of approaches, is valid and that all others are to be cast into the outer gloom has posited a philosophy of impoverishment.

If we define art as the imposition of order, form, and meaning on the raw materials of experience, both objective and subjective, and if we note that each art has its peculiar modes of expression, then we can define literature as a verbal structure embodying certain aspects of human experience. The subcategory, the novel, can be defined as a structure of words referring to people and their problems, written by a single person and hence the product of a unique mind at a given point in history. It follows, then, that the novel is:

1. Historical: bound to a definite time and place in terms of the author, the means of production and distribution, the audiences, as well as the contents. *A Tale of Two Cities,* for example, is, among other things, Dickens' mid-Victorian version of an eighteenth-century event read initially by his contemporaries but now being criticized by a French critic (Sylvère Monod) for the benefit of twentieth-century American students.

2. Social: concerned with the relationships of individuals and social groups to other individuals, social groups, codes of conduct, class structures, current behavioral patterns, and so on. Even when a novel concentrates heavily on an individual (for example, *Mrs. Dalloway* or *Ulysses*), he must be considered part of a social group, involved in group values, interacting with other people and institutions. Even a Robinson Crusoe is more than minimally social: he carries with him the concepts of a trueborn Englishman of the early eighteenth century, he establishes a "culture" modeled on what he has been taught at home, he creates relationships with Friday and the savages. Social matrices are operable even when not obviously present.

3. Moral: concerned with, indeed stemming from, values and value structures, either explicit or implicit, embodied in the characters, events, and social patternings in the novel. Morality is literally impossible to ignore either by the author or the critic; in an important way morality *is* the novel: the choice and presentation of heroes and villains, the sympathetic or despicable characters, the selection of problems held significant enough to be embodied, the ways in which problems and conflicts are resolved are all value judgments. There are obvious examples (such as *Crime and Punishment* and *Middlemarch*), but even an avowedly amoral novel (say by Robbe-Grillet) or one which mounts an attack on conventional morality is, paradoxically, moral in that it posits a set of values counter to accepted standards of the moment. The novel is therefore didactic in that the author promulgates a set of values for the consideration of the reader, whether openly or not. At the very least every novel is didactic in that it presents the reader with vicarious experience, teaches him something he had not previously known so well.

4. Psychological: a complex interaction of the mind-workings of

the author, his process of creation, his created characters, and the reader's own mental operations in the presence of a given novel plus his knowledge of contemporary psychology (Freudian, Jungian, Rankian, or whatever) and the psychology available to the author (for example, Sterne and Fielding). Biographical and psychoanalytical information is here necessary but hard to secure with accuracy, especially for authors of the past, and difficult to interpret even when available.

5. Formal: a structure of words, a rhetorical structure, a strategy of presentation, a pattern of verbal symbols having reference to the world outside the structure of words. Hence we have analyses of such matters as images and image patterns, symbols, irony, coherence, tension, and so on, with and without reference to the world outside the novel. Formal theories most often see literature as a self-contained activity, an autonomous universe with its own procedures and ends, with its own self-consistency (Baumgarten), showing "purposiveness without purpose" and the object of disinterested contemplation (Kant), having a value distinct from any instrumental value (Bradley), or a self-contained mythic structure (Frye).

Each of these only partially-separable categories has its counterpart in one or more critical theories and approaches, and each critical theory has its own rationale. Each has its merits, and each its built-in dangers. Formal theories, seeing literature as a more or less autonomous realm and thus concentrating on those elements that make up the verbal structure and texture of the unique artistic experience, can reduce literature to insignificance: rhetoric is the strategy, not the war, the plans, not the goal; the reader can admire the elegance of the battle plan, but he really wants to know what the fighting is all about. Theories other than the formalistic are eventually concerned with literature as one more human activity; they are most concerned with the novel, for example, as a product of and a contribution to life, considering that no activity, including the aesthetic, can be divorced from that life, that nothing save God alone is a *Ding an sich*. The danger here is that literature may disappear as a separate field and become merely a series of documents to be used for historical, sociological, psychological, or other purposes. What is needed—and what obtains in most actual critical practice—is a dialectical process, an interaction between moral and formal considerations, a dynamic synthesis of the two within the same critical essay or among a series of essays. The critic of novels is especially committed to this reasoning: the novel is, almost by definition, not a pure form, not like a string quartet. The novel has been committed to a presentation of human life at a particular moment in time in the best possible form for that presentation.

The policy of the *Dickens Studies Annual* has always been that of The Dickens Society: to study the life, times, and work of Charles

Dickens, without prejudice or a bent toward any one "school" of criticism or any local social or political philosophy. The editors practice this policy not because of their innate humility or their insistence on democratic principles, but because of the internal logic of the critical process. Any type of analysis which enlightens the reader is valuable; any technique of analysis which is effective is pragmatically acceptable; any opinion or assumption which can plausibly be supported by reference to the data of the novel must be given at least a hearing; conclusions, even those varying widely from the currently accepted, should be permitted a hearing, on Areopagitic reasoning.

A collection of essays by different hands, especially one spreading over many years, may be dominated by one philosophy, one type of approach or analysis, or one area to be investigated; for example, Leonard Manheim's psychologically oriented *Hartford Studies in Literature* and Edmund Epstein's *Language and Style.* It seems to me, however, that such self-limiting orientations are possible only if the subject matter be as diverse as possible, if specific authors and works are not named as a precondition for publication. If a single author is the only given subject, then a single narrow avenue of approach and analysis will not do; it is just not enough to provide the range of insights and facts demanded by that subject. Nothing more stultifying can be imagined than a seventy-year run of *The Dickensian* devoted to nothing but biographical or psychological information. The first four volumes of the *Dickens Studies Annual* have therefore offered a variety of different types of studies in an attempt to explore the range of possibilities; at least one example of each of the major critical approaches has so far appeared—a procedure which fully satisfies no one but offers perhaps one or two articles per volume which a reader finds new, interesting, worthy of being quoted or used in his own investigations.

This present Volume 5 continues our practice. Leonard Manheim's essay, for example, entitled "Dickens' HEROES, *heroes,* and heroids," is a kind of summary of work he began as long ago as 1952 in the *American Imago* and continued in earlier volumes of the *Annual,* work that has never been given the credit it deserves (as Mr. Giddings points out in speaking of the publications of Warrington Winter in the same general area). As a leader of the application of psychoanalytic theory to literature, especially Dickens' novels, he has greatly enlarged our understanding of the ways in which Dickens incorporated with increasing explicitness his personal fantasies and defenses into his fictions. In this article he points out that, if we are able to understand the various configurations in the novels, we should be able to look at the whole cycle as if it "constituted a single *roman à clef,*" and that the most significant of these configurations is the hero-pattern, that is, the hero of myth according to Otto Rank, the hero who is a product of the writer's unconscious, the hero as a fantasy-formation which compensates for the author's mundane life, the hero who may be an attempt at self-analysis and self-therapy.

Manheim's psychological approach is paralleled by other articles in this volume, notably by Christopher Mulvey's "*David Copperfield:* The Folk-Story Structure," which also investigates the significance of the hero-motif in a single novel. Mulvey selects the key word in the first sentence, "hero," and goes on to analyze the themes, motifs, and conclusions of the novel which derive from fairy tales, folk stories, and Jungian archetypes. But, whereas Manheim's intention seems often to be to use the novels as a means of uncovering the real, hidden nature of Charles Dickens and the ways in which that nature sought outlet in his fictions, Mulvey's intention is more to explain not only the inner meanings of a realistic Bildungsroman but also the power of a mid-Victorian re-creation of a part of our collective unconscious, one which evokes half-understood, but deeply moving, identifications.

Stanley Tick's essay is likewise akin to that of Manheim in that it is a study of the ways in which Dickens' guilt complex, deriving from compulsive secrecy about the blacking-warehouse episode, is expressed in hidden forms in the novels. Jaggers-Wemmick is taken as Dickens' supreme effort at expressing his "dominant theme" of secrecy and guilt, but Tick traces that theme back into the earlier novels and offers a persuasive reading of the biographical matrix and the "autobiographical" elements Dickens built into his creations. Like Manheim, Tick assumes that each novel is not only an artistic unity in itself but is at the same time a part of the massive writing-out of the author's secret, private life.

At first glance Nina Auerbach's essay on "Dickens and Dombey: A Daughter After All" might seem to be a case of special pleading, another piece of Women's Lib propaganda masquerading as literary criticism, but it is not quite that, even though she does read the novel primarily as a conflict between the male and female principles, between hardness and liquidity, between authority and sympathy. She regards Dombey's outlook as more fundamentally sexual than monetary, and considers that the mission of Florence is to make the stiff and erect into the spreading and diffuse. She acknowledges that the railroad and the sea are the two major symbols: the railroad is "the sphere of the mechanical and masculine," embodies phallic force, and progresses linearly; the opposing sea is natural and eternal, ebbs and flows like the female cycle, and is mindless and implacable. Implicit throughout are Professor Auerbach's distaste for the role women were forced to play in the mid-Victorian age and a counter-taste for androgyny. Such an essay could have been as ludicrous as *Dickens' Sexual Props:* it could have seen dark phallic significance in curving railroad tracks and upright church pews—but it does not. This reading of *Dombey and Son* is firmly based on some of the best modern scholarship, demonstrates the author's thorough understanding of her subject, and imposes twentieth-century concepts on an 1846 universe of values and emotions with the requisite care. The essay is especially valuable in that it analyzes passages and events too often ignored by more conventional critics. I suspect that "Dickens and Dombey" will provoke politely acidulous debate in Dickens seminars for many years.

The title, "The Intelligibility of Madness in *Our Mutual Friend* and *The Mystery of Edwin Drood,*" by Lawrence Frank is rather misleading: one might assume that the author meant to describe, classify, and analyze the types of aberration in these two novels according to some Freudian or other psychological system and then demonstrate that these fools and madmen are meaningful in some sense. Instead, this article is a long meditation on Dickens' handling of Gothic motifs in his later works. "The London of *Bleak House* and *Our Mutual Friend* is a Gothic castle haunted by incubi and grotesques of various kinds, expressing the social and psychological terrors of Victorian society. The Cloisterham of *Edwin Drood* is that analogue of the haunted castle, the monastery of the Gothic tradition." Frank is most effective in showing that Dickens' Gothicism was used as a means of exploring the nature of unconscious forces, and then applying his insight into the reading of the major characters. He is especially persuasive in his discussion of the Wrayburn-Headstone double and the transfer of that double into the single consciousness of John Jasper—perhaps the most provocative discussion of those characters yet written.

H. L. Knight's "Dickens and Mrs. Stowe" defines the relationship between the two authors in terms of psychological, biographical, and literary analysis. On the surface the essay is a study of the literary and personal reactions of Dickens to the American writer, a standard category of criticism—for example, Dickens and Thackeray, Dickens and Marryat—and here Knight ably summarizes earlier work by other investigators. More significant for Dickensians, however, is his exploration of the reasons for Dickens' growing dislike of Mrs. Stowe, grounded, according to Knight, in Dickens' guilt feelings, guilt deriving from the discrepancy between his real-life treatment of his family and his taking of a mistress, and his centrally-important treatment of marriage and the family in his fictions, growingly at odds with each other and in danger of exposure by the statements and positions of Mrs. Stowe.

The other essays in this volume are not at all or only partially psychologically oriented. Joseph Butwin's "The Paradox of the Clown in Dickens" is an interesting opening discussion of a subject that needs more extensive consideration than even Garis, Axton, and Hillis Miller have given: Dickens' knowledge of and involvement in the world of the pantomime, the circus, and the stage. As Butwin points out, the "clowns" from the *Sketches by Boz* and the introduction to the memoirs of Grimaldi down through the whole corpus are not simple figues of amusement or comedy but are complex human beings in their own right, richly symbolic, often ironic comments on the other characters, certain modes of conduct, and certain moral values. James Marlow's "Dickens' Romance: The Novel as Other" is an ambiguous title until he defines "Romance" as the counter of "novel" and proceeds to a study of Dickens' theory of fiction, deriving this from the novels themselves, the letters, notes, journalistic practices and comments, prefaces, and a consideration of what Dickens learned from such critics as Coleridge and Hazlitt. Perhaps the most useful conclusion Marlow reaches is that Dickens' fundamental aesthetic axioms stem from his moral purpose, much like that of George Eliot: the desire, even the demand, that the novel devote itself to the development of human understanding and sympathy in the reader, that the novel strive to break the bell jar of selfness and to counter materialism and apathy. Edward Evans in his "The American Episodes of *Martin Chuzzlewit*" also concerns himself with the moral and historical aspects of Dickens' work. This essay covers the ground more passingly observed by Barbara Hardy, Harry Stone, and Hillis Miller, with enough detail to make the presentation persuasive, especially in its careful linking of the novel with *American Notes,* Dickens' personal reactions to America in 1842, and the artistic demands of the novel. Most significant is Evans' explanation of Dickens' moral distaste and growing disillusionment as he observed the shocking disparity between the appearance of freedom and justice and the actual greed, hypocrisy, and dehumanization in both United States and England, the two parts of the novel, so that one is merely the other writ larger and more crudely.

This volume of the *Dickens Studies Annual,* then, like previous volumes, offers what Mr. Giddings deplores: a combination of "English" and "American" types of scholarship and criticism.

Carbondale, Illinois   *Robert B. Partlow, Jr.*
August 1975

Notes on Contributors

NINA AUERBACH, Assistant Professor at the University of Pennsylvania, is presently doing research on a grant from the Ford Foundation at the Radcliffe Institute. She has published articles on Jane Austen, Charlotte Brontë, and *Alice in Wonderland*.

JOSEPH BUTWIN, Assistant Professor at the University of Washington, has published reviews and articles on Oscar Wilde as martyr-clown and on the French Revolution. He is presently completing a biography of Sholom Aleichem for Twayne Publishers.

EDWARD J. EVANS, a Lecturer at Dalhousie University, appears here in print for the first time. As Killam Fellow in his university, he is completing his doctoral dissertation on mythology in the Victorian period.

LAWRENCE FRANK, Assistant Professor at the University of Washington, has previously written on Esther Summerson in *Bleak House* for the *Dickens Studies Annual* and is now at work on articles on the double in *David Copperfield* and on parricide in *A Tale of Two Cities*. In addition he is finishing his book-length study of the double in Dickens' fictions.

H. L. KNIGHT, Associate Dean at the Golden Gate University, is completing two major projects: a book on *Communication for Justice Administration,* with Walter Stevenson, scheduled for publication early in 1976; and a dramatization of *Uncle Tom's Cabin* to be presented as part of the University of California at Berkeley Bicentennial American Theater Season.

LEONARD F. MANHEIM, now Emeritus Professor of the University of Hartford, is the well-known doyen of psychoanalytical studies of Dickens. He is perhaps most noted as the founder and editor of *Literature and Psychology,* from 1951 to 1967, and as founder and editor of *Hartford Studies in Literature,* from 1968 to date. Besides his numerous reviews and articles, he has been coeditor, with his wife, of *Hidden Patterns: Studies in Psychoanalytic Literary Criticism* and is coeditor and contributor to the forthcoming *A New Anatomy of Melancholy: Studies in the Writer and Suicide*. His influential criticism of Dickens is listed in the notes to his article in this issue of the *Annual*.

JAMES E. MARLOW, Assistant Professor at Southeastern Massachusetts University, has published on Carlyle and on Dickens in *Nineteenth-Century Fiction,* the *Dickens Studies Newsletter,* and the *Victorians Institute Journal*. He has two research projects under way: a comparative study of Dickens and Dostoievski, and an analysis of the language of *Coriolanus*.

CHRISTOPHER MULVEY, Assistant Professor at The City College, is engaged in a study of Anglo-American relations in the nineteenth century.

STANLEY TICK, Professor at San Francisco State University, has published widely on Conrad, James, and Faulkner, as well as on Dickens. He is also joint editor of *The Writer in the Modern World*. The major project now on his desk is a study of *A Tale of Two Cities*.

Dickens Studies Annual

Leonard F. Manheim

DICKENS' HEROES, *HEROES*, AND HEROIDS

AT THE outset I should explain the terms in my title. By the HERO I mean the hero of myth, the hero of fantasy; hence the hero image which is the product of the Unconscious in the individual's life. The pattern was systematically set forth by Otto Rank in *The Myth of the Birth of the Hero.*

> The hero is the child of the most distinguished parents, usually the son of a king. His birth has been preceded by all manner of obstacles (such as parental abstinence, long sterility, or secret union of the parents). During his mother's pregnancy or even earlier there occurs an annunciation (a dream or oracle) concerning his birth, which often threatens the father with grave danger.
> Because of this prophecy the new-born child, usually at the behest of the father or of some person who occupies the position of the father, is destined to death or to exposure; as a rule he is placed in the water in a small chest.
> He is rescued by animals or by very humble people (shepherds), and he is nursed by a female animal or by some very simple woman.
> Attaining manhood, he finds his distinguished parents again, after a most devious pursuit; he revenges himself upon his father, and is then recognized and achieves greatness and fame.[1]

As indicated in the notes, there are other similar syntheses, some of which quite naturally stress the HERO's "Virgin Birth."

By the *hero* I mean to designate more than the male character who is the source of the reader's dominant interest in a novel, more than the ego-ideal through which the author hopes to hold the interest of the reader as a means of fulfilling wishes of both author and reader. The *hero* is—at least for Dickens—rarely a single character. He (or she, or both he *and* she) is usually a multiple projection (psychological decomposition, "doubling") of the author's dynamic drives onto a number of characters, some of whom, let it clearly be noted, are the very opposite of ego-ideals. Here I quote from Thomas Mann's analysis of this pattern in his 1938 "Lecture on Goethe's *Faust.*"

> Weislingen in *Götz von Berlichingen,* Clavigo, and Faust are the three characters through whom Goethe does poetic penance for his betrayal of love. At the same time he uses the dramatic form to defend himself. Remember the masterly and in their way incontrovertible speeches in which Carlos convinces Clavigo of the necessity of deserting Marie Beaumarchais. Clavigo and Carlos are one and the same person in a division of roles for the purposes of the play. So likewise are Tasso and Antonio, Faust and Mephistopheles: a dialectic separation into two parts of the poet's personality. . . . But indeed the relation of self-deception to truth is far less opposed in the poet's mind than in an ordinary human being's. What a poet can give himself, what he can make of himself, that is his, that is himself; and in the Homeric "poets ever were liars," the last word has a different and stronger sense than it has in common life.[2]

And when I use the word "heroid" I am guilty of a highly personal neologism. At one time I was writing in a somewhat ironic tone of "the heroic Tom Pinch." A finger slipped; I struck a *d* instead of a *c;* my wife cried "Stet!" and the damage was done; a "Freudian slip" had created a useful new term. The *OED* will not help, for the term has nothing to do with the *Heroides* of Ovid; but any ordinary dictionary will make it clear that the suffix *-oid* has the significance of "like; resembling; having the form of." It seems to me that it is often more useful than "semiheroic."

My next preliminary should be to indicate the extent to which this study covers various aspects of patterns throughout the novels. I must omit full treatment of those aspects which I have treated elsewhere and refer my reader to those other treatments for a more systematic account of the pattern than can be obtained from this essay alone.

First there are my studies of individual novels. The first and most important of these is "The Personal History of David Copperfield," which I published in 1952.[3] My other study of a single novel is "A Tale of Two Characters," published in this *Dickens Studies* series.[4] I dealt with one aspect of the hero pattern in several of the novels in "The Dickens Hero as Child." [5] Papers which do not deal directly with the hero pattern, but which do touch on that pattern peripherally, are my "Floras and Doras: The Women in Dickens' Novels" [6] (which deals in part with the heroine-as-hero), "Thanatos: The Death Instinct in Dickens' Later Novels," [7] and, to a very minor extent, "The Law as 'Father.' " [8]

Bearing in mind these necessary omissions, let us examine the three aspects of the hero-pattern which I have set forth, in a number of novels. The treatment will be, so far as it is possible, fairly systematic, but the order will not be chronological nor will there always be an attempt to isolate, rigidly or dogmatically, the three designated aspects. The order of treatment will follow connections by association, some obvious, others more obscure.

— *I* —

The HERO, as the fantasy formation which compensates, in fantasy, for the hard lot which the commonplaces of mundane existence force upon everyone, is always to be recognized by some variant of the Rank pattern. One of the earliest characteristics by which we can recognize the HERO is the unusual circumstances surrounding his birth. Now it is rarely possible for the hero of a nineteenth-century novel to be "the child of most distinguished parents, usually the son of a king." Yet no one can fail to notice how partial nineteenth-century novelists, Dickens included, were to the plot device of the long-lost parent, the long-lost child, the long-lost brother or sister. Even this device, however, will not account for an "unusual" parentage for many of the characters; hence Dickens uses an even simpler system. He simply eliminates parents for most of his leading characters and many of his minor ones.

Pickwick Papers will generally be recognized as the novel which was written at the period of its author's most satisfactory psychological adjustment and freedom from obvious signs of emotional tension. Yet few characters in *Pickwick* itself (excluding the more ominous interpolated tales) have a full complement of parents. Mr. Wardle, for example, has an aged mother but no father. We would hardly expect to be told much about Mr. Pickwick's parents—although he may be a perennial infant, blessed with a most satisfactory "guardian," but no other member of the traveling committee has any parent, except Mr. Winkle, who is belatedly endowed with a very businesslike father. Sam Weller himself has a father—very much of a father—and a stepmother.

Barnaby Rudge, although it was published in *Master Humphrey's Clock,* had its origin in the *Pickwick* days. In it Dolly Varden alone has a full quota of legitimate parents, a very pleasant father and a most unpleasant mother. Barnaby has a sweetly pathetic mother but, to all intents and purposes, no father except as a sinister, unknown persecutor. Joe Willett, Edward Chester, and Emma Haredale have unpleasant fathers and no mothers. Hugh is the bastard son of a mother who was hanged in his infancy and a rightful father who disowned and persecuted him. To move ahead for a moment to a novel which *was* written in a period of stress, we find *Martin Chuzzlewit* dealing specifically with family interrelationships, yet with its hero, young Martin, an orphan with no parent substitute except a grandfather, and Tom Pinch, raised by a grandmother. Mary Graham is, of course, an orphan, and both Jonas Chuzzlewit and the Pecksniff sisters are and, it would seem, always were motherless.

Dickens' first true HERO is to be found in the full panoply of his timeless being in the first novel of the first period of great stress. Oliver Twist comes about as close as any Dickens hero, or for that matter as any hero of modern fiction, to being the product of a virgin birth. He is a posthumous child, to all intents and purposes fatherless. Whatever grossness might ever have been inherent in the sexuality through which his shadowy mother must have conceived him is purged away by her death in childbirth, and we find Oliver firmly established as the standard HERO of myth. Every fantasy of extraordinary birth may now be indulged in by the author who identifies himself with the myth-figure he has created. Needless to say, the HERO ultimately reaches his apotheosis and comes into his rightful heritage. He charges endlessly against a series of grotesque, evil "fathers" and sibling-rivals. Again and again they go down like ninepins before his meekness and humility (for he is of the Jesus-type rather than of the Hercules-pattern), yet the battle is never ended until the author decides that his hero has suffered sufficiently and is purified and worthy of his great destiny. There are intervals in which the nightmare merges into a sweet dream of idyllic parental protection, but soon the ideal loveliness is swept away and the HERO goes forth once again to defy the images which are destined to be defeated, but only after manifold tribulations. The dream-quality and the wish-fulfillment mechanisms of the novel are exhibited in the unabashed use of outrageous coincidences, and in incidents like the semimortal illness of Rose Maylie, which enables the dreaming author to bring back to life his own newly lost virgin incarnation (Mary Hogarth).

In *Oliver Twist* we must constantly keep in mind the author's own mental anguish. In addition to his inner emotional conflicts, indeed as partial compensation for the pain they cause him, we find evidence of pride to the point of vanity, pride in the success he is achieving in the world of literature. He turns to his old parent-bugaboos and exclaims, "See! You did not appreciate me. You have failed, for you see that I have succeeded, just as my boy-hero succeeds despite all the obstacles which you and your kind attempt to put in his—and my—way." If the Unconscious of an author wants to say all that, it will keep him on better terms with his family and with his Victorian readers if he says it in regressive fantasy-form in a novel.

There was nothing of all this in *Pickwick Papers*. There the hero-figures are clad in the robes of the glorified parents or are humanized by amiable weaknesses such as characterize Winkle or Snodgrass. The specific pattern by which we shall come to recognize the Dickensian hero is only slightly adumbrated by such slanting references as the direct mention of the brand of shoeblacking which Sam used at the *White Hart* (120) or Tony's depreciation of poetry as something that "no man ever talked . . . 'cept a beadle on boxin' day, or Warren's blackin' . . . or some o' them low fellows" (452) [9]

Sam Weller as hero tends to be objective rather than subjective. His early lack of education and his experience with the "two-penny ropes" and with the vagabonds who slept under bridges and in the open has resulted in remarkable self-adjustment and social adjustment, with drives seemingly directed toward normal adult goals. His instinctual overflow is admirably sublimated rather than repressed, and he enjoys the role which he assumes, of fatherly protector to the semi-infantile Mr. Pickwick and as hero of humble life in his own right. Yet even he shows oblique traces of resentment against his jovial father. Sam has certainly not had a very happy childhood, and the beloved Tony is, from the viewpoint of his system of child rearing, a rather unsatisfactory father: "I took a great deal o' pains with his eddication, sir [Tony boasts]; let him run in the streets when he was wery young, and shift for his-self. It's the only way to make a boy sharp, sir" (271). But the momentarily contented author isn't very much exercised over such neglect. He merely thinks, "Well, that's what my parents did to me, and it has certainly made *me* sharp." Perhaps it would be well to say as little as possible about Tony's attitude toward his grandson and namesake in the ghastly resurrection of the Wellers in *Master Humphrey's Clock.* Old Tony is now engaged in "showing off" young Tony in the same way as John Dickens had used young Charles as a public entertainer. The best we can say is that young Tony, like young Charles, probably enjoyed it.

Sam is a natural untutored philosopher, to be sure, but Dickens indicated rather obliquely that he has had access to *some* books, in fact, books by the very authors whom Dickens read in his childhood. He shows a remarkable and unexpected familiarity, for example, with Laurence Sterne's *Sentimental Journey,* for he sagely remarks to Mr. Pickwick that "no man never see a dead donkey, 'cept the gen'l'man in the black silk smalls as know'd the young 'ooman as kep' a goat; and that wos a French donkey, so wery likely he warn't wun of the reg'lar breed" (715). Sam Weller, sired by the actor Sam Vale, born with the assistance of infant memories of Mary Weller, is always a hero rather than a HERO, and there is no other like him.

Even in the interpolated stories in *Pickwick* the hero-figure does not assume so ominous an aspect as does the father-image. We should, perhaps, note a certain idyllic romance ("Story of the Parish Clerk,"

[xvii]) which is attributed to the pen of Mr. Pickwick, turned author under the stimulus of an attack of rheumatism. The hero, one Nathaniel Pipkin, is a homely and humble schoolmaster who raises his eyes above his station to one *Maria* Lobbs, daughter of a wealthy tradesman. His suit, difficult to begin with, is made doubly so by the teasing of her cousin *Kate*. Nathaniel finds out, to his sorrow, that Maria is using him merely as a pretext to meet the young man whom she really loves. Nathaniel is discovered by the irate father, is about to take the handsome lover's blame upon himself, then retires gracefully from the field. That is as far as Dickens goes in *Pickwick* in disposing of a youthful chagrin which he now thinks he is forever over and done with.

It is between these two extremes—the turgid, nightmarelike myths of *Oliver Twist* and the benign jollity of *Pickwick*—that the moods of the earlier novels vacillate. Within most of these earlier novels the individual hero-figure does not undergo much change, for Dickens as caricaturist is the master of static rather than dynamic character portrayal, and even in the novels of development like *Nicholas Nickleby, Martin Chuzzlewit,* and *David Copperfield,* the changes which the heroes go through are jerky and sudden rather than subtle and natural. This trait, like many others, tends to become less and less marked in the increased facility of the later novels like *Great Expectations* and *Our Mutual Friend.*

— 2 —

As the novels follow each other after *Oliver Twist,* the pattern of the HERO's personality becomes more and more complex, and the characters which embody his real and ideal phases (like those which stand for the father, unregenerate or penitent) tend to be more and more split up, yielding more and more fragmentary caricatures, each bearing within himself one of the varied phases of the author's increasingly complex conflicts. In *Martin Chuzzlewit,* for example, the major projections of the author-as-HERO are to be found in Martin the younger, in Tom Pinch, and, to a lesser extent, in melancholy Augustus Moddle, in "manly" John Westlock, and in schizothymic Mark Tapley. In Jonas Chuzzlewit we find a specimen of a type of negative hero-figure which will be at its peak in Uriah Heep. The word *negative* should be taken in its photographic sense, for these characters are black where the hero would be white, and white where he might be black.

Dickens' constant plaint about his "bad" upbringing is again voiced through the character of young Martin, a model of selfishness (until he is redeemed by his contact with the noble Tapley). But Martin's selfishness is not innate; it is the product of his upbringing at the hands of his grandfather and namesake, just as Jonas' vices are the product of *his* upbringing by old Martin's brother, Anthony. Young Martin recognizes the vice in his grandfather, but not in himself, and his comments in a conversation with Tom Pinch furnish an interesting example of his (and his author's) facility in projection.

> "I have been bred and reared all my life by this grandfather of whom I have just spoken. Now, he has a great many good points; there is no doubt about that; . . . but he has two very great faults, which are the staple of his bad side. In the first place, he had the most confirmed obstinacy of character you ever met in any human creature. In the second, he is most abominably selfish."
>
> "Is he indeed?" cried Tom.
>
> "In those two respects," returned the other, "there never was such a man. I have often heard from those who know, that they have been, time out of mind, the failings of our family; and I believe there's some truth in it. But I can't say of my own knowledge. All I have to do, you know, is to be very . . . careful that I don't contract 'em." (93–94)

Later the author brings the accusation home to old Martin through the firm but respectful utterances of Mark Tapley: "There was always a great deal of good in him, but a little of it got crusted over, somehow. I can't say who rolled the paste of that 'ere crust myself . . . but I think it may have been you, sir. Unintentional I think it may have been you. I don't believe that neither of you gave the other a fair chance" (798).

Having thus disposed of the hereditary defect of "selfishness" which his hero has been able, thanks to noble guidance, to shake off, Dickens now needs a character upon whom he can bestow those positive qualities of goodness and kindness which he most desired to see embodied in a heroic conception of himself. He could always obtain satisfaction by vicarious introjection from a creation such as Tom Pinch. Normally we should spend little time on Tom, for he is so virtuous, so noble, so much like an adult verion of Kit Nubbles that he rivals the *feminanities* in bland dullness. Yet Dickens devotes a great deal of time and attention to him; and, what is even more remarkable, he approved as the frontispiece to a novel which dealt with the Chuzzlewit family a cluttery and prolix illustration which deals to a great extent with Tom Pinch. Whether the conception of that frontispiece originated with Dickens or with Phiz is not really important in the light of Dickens' approval of the finished product. The whole matter of the genesis and development of detail in illustrations can be left to experts like John Harvey, John Reed, and Michael Steig.[10] Still the psychologically revelatory frontispiece must be allowed to speak for itself—after careful examination.

Our first impression is of Tom playing a two-manual organ, probably not at a church service but in a lonely practice session. Figures pour out of the organ and out of the sheet music, figures that represent the acme of unbridled fantasy. On the console are suspended young Martin and his bride, Tom's secret love, Mary Graham. They are in marionettelike postures, and Mary seems to be conducting the symphony while Tom plays, gazing fondly at her. Above the organ, and extending upward into the mass of cloudlike figures beyond, is an angelic female figure supporting the head of Tom Pinch; another, in the hands of a crotchety black deveil, holds the grinning head of Pecksniff. From both hang trailing garlands. A tiny female figure with a lugubrious face, bearing in its arms a large black cat, sits on a ledge before a casement window opened upon a full moon. She suggests the rueful last picture of Charity Pecksniff.

Throughout the whole garland of sketches—some of them merely music-note stick figures—the theme of happily wedding couples is repeated over and over, with representations of Martin and Mary, John Westlock and Ruth Pinch, Mark Tapley and the landlady of the Blue Dragon. Mark and the landlady are again shown dancing with a merry-looking dragon between them, smoking a pipe. Mrs. Gamp, who can be identified only because the huge bandbox which is her head bears her name upon it, dances off with a saucy teapot and milk jug past a dim crowd of nightcapped patients, looking miserable. Poll Sweedlepipe dances with a birdcage on his head and other cages grouped tenderly about him, while his right hand leads a wig stand, capped with a wig and swathed in a barber's shaving cloth. Bailey Junior looks on with approval.

The uppermost panel shows Mary in the village church with Tom mooning around hopelessly in the background. Then we see Tom at work at his drawing board while Pecksniff contemplates his own portrait bust. Pecksniff stands upon two huge volumes which insolently bear Christopher Wren's motto, "Si monumentum requires, circumspice," backed by another huge book labeled "Sic vos non vobis [mellificatis apes]." In another scene Tom mounts a stile after knocking down Jonas. Lower down, Jonas crouches on the ground, devil-ridden, while a crowd of snaky-locked Furies pursue him, and ghostly draped figures offer him poison cups and daggers. Again, Tom walks through the Pecksniff living room with a huge drafting book under his arm, reading to himself out of another book, to the horror and amusement of Cherry and Merry. As we reach the bottom of the garland, fantasy runs riot. Pecksniff is suspended from a huge mason's tripod, waiting to be set in place as a cornerstone. Below him dividers, trowels, hods, and hammers dance madly. The attending mason looks on from behind a giant T-square. Jonas looks into a ring of mirrors, each of which is provided with arms holding moneybags. Last, at the very bottom, the dream-picture is completed, showing Pecksniff in terror, surrounded by four Pecksniffs, three of them allowing their vicious countenances to be seen behind masks of hypocrisy, the fourth showing the mask of hypocrisy in position, while the "true" face peers through the thorax and abdomen. A discarded mask, with closed eyes, lies nearby. Thus does Phiz qualify for charter membership in the school of surrealists, and thus do we see the fantasy formations which play so large a part in the depiction of the heroid Tom Pinch by both author and illustrator.

To qualify him for this heroid status, Tom Pinch's birth is taken care of by the usual elimination of parents and the suggestion that his nobility of character is so much at variance with his humbleness of birth that his parentage must have been higher than he suspects. His very appearance causes the sun to shine on a cloudy, snowy day. Yet "poor Tom," as the author calls him so frequently and so patronizingly, has one weakness. He *will* believe in the nobility and honesty of the patron who took him on as a penniless apprentice and "was a father to him when he had none of his own." In spite of evidence that would have convinced the dullest jury, he holds on to his faith in Pecksniff, takes Pecksniff at his "face" value. He sees John Westlock depart in anger and remains loyal, he sees Martin cast forth ignominiously, and he manages to keep faith with both Martin *and* Pecksniff. It is only when Pecksniff's unwelcome wooing of the beloved Mary becomes known to him that he rebels—and then discovers that "there never was a Pecksniff."

And now the full agitation and misery of the disclosure came rushing upon Tom indeed. The star of his whole life from boyhood had become, in a moment, putrid vapor. It was not that Pecksniff, Tom's Pecksniff, had ceased to exist, but that he never had existed. In his death Tom would have had the comfort of remembering what he used to be, but in this discovery, he had the anguish of recollecting what he never was. For as Tom's blindness in this matter had been total and not partial, so was his restored sight. *His* Pecksniff could never have worked the wickedness of which he had just now heard, but any other Pecksniff could; and the Pecksniff who could do that could do . . . anything and everything except the right thing all through his career. From the lofty height on which poor Tom had placed his idol it was tumbled headlong, and

> Not all the king's horses, nor all the king's men,
> Could have set Mr. Pecksniff up again.

Legions of Titans couldn't have got him out of the mud; and serve him right! But it was not he who suffered; it was Tom.

His compass was broken, his charts destroyed, his chronometer
had stopped, his masts were gone by the board; his anchor was
adrift, ten thousand leagues away. (493–94)

For him whose father ideal has been destroyed, for the hero who has
placed too much trust in the father who is destined to deceive and
abuse him, security is lost forever!

If we pass lightly over the heroid character named John Westlock,
whose most interesting facet is that, as an independent young bachelor,
he occupied ideal bachelor chambers in the same Furnival's Inn in
which Dickens as bachelor and young benedict had resided, we come to
two characters in semiheroic mold whose marked feature is their schizothymia. Schizothymia is a perversion of emotional response which
might easily be the hypocrisy which Pecksniff personifies throughout
the book. Dickens seems, at first, to feel that Mr. Mould, the under-
taker, must be a consummate hypocrite, intent on having his clients
express their grief in terms of showy funerals. Later, however, the author shows a greater degree of insight when he finds Mr. Mould in the
bosom of his cheerful family, with young daughters who spend their
childhood playing at "berryings" with the coffins in their father's shop.
An even greater degree of schizothymia is implicit in Mrs. Rodgers'
description of her melancholy boarder, Mr. Moddle. He was bad
enough at expressing his delight in being in Merry's company even
before she married Jonas Chuzzlewit. After she has broken his heart,
however, and convinces him that everybody seems to be "Somebody
Else's," he strives to solace himself by taking his landlady to the theatre
"to an extent . . . which is . . . beyond his means; [with] tears a-stand-
ing in his eyes during the whole performance—particularly if it is anything of a comic nature" (507–18). Here it is that Mr. Moddle, hitherto
merely described as "the youngest boarder," comes into his own as a
distinct Dickensian characterization.

To find schizothymia of the most mechanical and artificial sort,
however, we need only examine the entire characterization of Mark
Tapley. He reminds us of that character in the fairy tale who had the
peculiar faculty of freezing in a hot fire and perishing of heat in the
dead of winter! Certainly he is of service to hero-Martin in almost exactly the same fashion as was that odd servant in the legend. He takes
delight in seeking out uncomfortable situations in order that he may
obtain "credit" for being jolly. He sees through the perfidy of Scadder,
Eden's rascally real estate agent; yet he makes no real effort to turn
Martin back even when his peril becomes all too imminent. It is at this
moment that the author attempts to give us an inkling as to Tapley's
motivation. Martin, overcome by the misery of his desperate situation,
falls to the ground in tears, and Mark cannot endure it.

"Lord love you, sir," cried Mr. Tapley, in great terror; "Don't do that! Don't do that, sir! Anything but that! It never helped man, woman, or child, over the lowest fence yet, sir, and it never will. Besides its being no use to you, it's worse than of no use to me, for the least sound of it will knock me flat down. I can't stand up agin it, sir. Anything but that!" (379)

Mark, then, is that type of philosopher who "laughs at any mortal thing so that he may not weep." He must have strongly self-aggressive, propitiatory tendencies for which he overcompensates by "jollity," always living in fear, however, that the hated melancholy will some day overcome him, and always testing his endurance, as one bites down on an aching tooth. To Dickens he must have seemed another incarnation of Sam Weller, but he is never as successful as his earlier avatar, for the author was never again to be the man who could create Sam. He seems to share Sam's attitude on education (a component of the author's ambivalent feeling concerning his own educational background), for he insists that he was educated in the only way that really counts, through experience and "hard knocks." He convinces old Martin that he is more truly educated than either the old man or his grandson; yet he displays a wistful yearning to show his book learning when Tom Pinch orders him to sit down or (jokingly, of course) threatens to swear at him.

"Well, sir," returned Mr. Tapley, "sooner than you should do that, I'll com-ply. It's a considerable invasion of a man's jollity to be made so partickler welcome, but a Werb is a word as signifies to be, to do, or to suffer (which is all the grammar, and enough, too, as ever I wos taught); and if there's a Werb alive, I'm it. For I'm always a-bein', sometimes a-doin', and continually a-sufferin'." (733)

— *3* —

We have devoted considerable time to the analysis of the hero in his fivefold guise in *Martin Chuzzlewit*, for it is in that novel that he occupies the most central position in the picture and is developed more fully in each of these guises than in any novel until *David Copperfield*. Yet the various patterns tend to recur in the other works as well. Is not Martin, after all, a picture which we find again in David and Pip; Mark the same sort of humble hero whom we found in Sam Weller; Pinch, the Kit Nubbles type in slightly more adult form; Westlock, the same sort of casual hero that we find from Mr. Trundle to Herbert Pocket; and Moddle, the somewhat distorted reproduction of the same sort of thing as Mr. Toots?

It is true that some of the novels of the middle period seem to be provided with a plethora of heroes, semiheroes, and antiheroes. There are others, however, particularly among the novels of the period of early emotional stress following (but not wholly caused by) the death of Mary Hogarth, which seem to have a supply of antiheroes but no real hero at all. Quilp and Sampson Brass may well qualify as antiheroes, but can we really find a HERO, a *hero,* or even a semihero in *Old Curiosity Shop?* Can Dick Swiveller possibly fill the bill?

Mr. Swiveller is undoubtedly one of Dickens' great originals, one of the most successful combinations of the realistic hero and the comic genius. J. B. Priestley, whose own writings owe much to the semipicaresque travel-narrative of which *Old Curiosity Shop* is an outstanding nineteenth-century example, places Dick in the immortal company of Ancient Pistol.[11] Yet Dick does not come into the work too auspiciously. He is the boon companion of Frederick Trent, and the tool in the latter's plot to get hold of the alleged fortune of Trent's grandfather.[12] It is only when Frederick and the Shop both slide out of the story that Dick comes into his own. His relations with Quilp, except for the employment which Quilp procures for him in the law office of Brass and Brass, are unconvincing, although there is one good scene in which Swiveller and Quilp are returning from an evening of carousal in Quilp's miserable tavern rendezvous. Dick is once more bemoaning his sad fate as a neglected orphan, but he indignantly repudiates Quilp's claim to be "a second father" to him.[13] Dick's talent for drinking, both alone and in the company of the "Glorious Apollers," is not a little reminiscent of Bob Sawyer and Ben Allen—yes, and Mr. Winkle, too. Dick, until his employment by the Brasses, lacks all means of support other than the remittances he receives from his sorely tried aunt. He reaches his supreme moments in his meetings with the Marchioness. Dickens makes it clear that, whatever other vices he may have had, Swiveller was far too honest to become a lawyer in real earnest. One of the best scenes is that in which Dick, appalled by the female dragon in whose company he has to work as Sampson Brass' law clerk, is hard put to it to control the aggressions which prompt him to physical violence upon the sister of his employer. His device for sublimation, through covert swipes at her headdress, has its interesting points, although it is not to be recommended as a general procedure.

Dick is not a "good" character in the Dickens categories of virtues; we will probably have to view the illness which almost puts an end to his life as a sort of punishment for his dallying with the law and his even more dastardly dallying with the affections of Little Nell. Yet, in the last analysis, he is just what Dickens says he is at the close of the book, "a literary gentleman of eccentric habits, and of the most prodigious talent in quotation," in other words, a frustrated novelist. His humor arises from that sort of inconsequentiality which is at the root of the comic spirit. Dick is just as much an arrant pretender in the field of letters as Winkle was in the field of sports, but just because his pretensions are along literary lines, his amiable weaknesses are not unmasked as Mr. Winkle's were—and he has at least as much success in his choice of a wife as the sporting gentleman had.

After all of the time we have spent on Tom Pinch, it would be useless to devote much more to Kit Nubbles. Despite the detailed relation of his virtues, trials, joys, and triumphs, he never comes to life for a moment. He is the only person of alleged masculinity whose adoration of Little Nell the author can tolerate, but this is because, as Kit himself explains to his pretty fellow servant Barbara, a real girl, "I have been used, you see . . . to talk and think of her, almost as if she was an angel" (520). Kit is fatherless, of course, but he has no cause for complaint about his upbringing by his poor but honest and hardworking mother. The very enjoyment of life of the Nubbles family serves to mitigate some of the horror which pervades the rest of the tale. We need not believe in them, however, any more than we need believe in the goodness of Mr. and Mrs. Garland and their superson, Abel. Indeed, if we dwell on some of the elements of Abel's upbringing, which the author seems to hold up as a model, the Garlands may fill us with a horror such as only Quilp could otherwise inspire. Mrs. Garland boasts of Abel's family ties in this fashion—

> "You see, Mr. Witherden, . . . Abel has not been brought up like the run of young men. He has always had a pleasure in our society, and always been with us. Abel has never been absent from us, for a day: has he, my dear?"
>
> "Never, my dear," returned the old gentleman, "except when he went to Margate on Saturday with Mr. Tomkinley that had been a teacher at that school he went to, and came back upon the Monday; but he was very ill after that, you remember, my dear; it was quite a dissipation."
>
> "He was not used to it, you know," said the old lady, "and he couldn't bear it, that's the truth. Besides, he had no comfort in being there without us, and had nobody to talk to or enjoy himself with." (111)

Poor Abel!

— *4* —

Our search for heroes should surely include the novels written in the first person: *David Copperfield, Great Expectations,* and the Esther Summerson chapters of *Bleak House.* It is true that I have already written rather extensively on the first and last of these (see nn. 3, 6), but the study of *David Copperfield* was published over twenty years ago, in a journal which may not be readily available to Dickens scholars (I know that I have had to supply at least two of them with offprints of the article). It is therefore proper for me to recapitulate some of my findings at this time, for I have not found it necessary to alter many of these findings over the passing years.

Our first point of interest is in the novel's title. Dickens had composed expanded titles for novels like *Martin Chuzzlewit,* for example, but usually with a satiric purpose. Here the title is possibly ambiguous in intent, but direct enough in its wording: *The Personal History, Adventures, Experience, & Observation of David Copperfield the Younger of Blunderstone Rookery. (Which He never meant to be Published on any Account.)* Yet the biography-novel opens with the words, "Whether I shall turn out to be the hero of my own life, or whether that station will be held by anybody else, these pages must show."

The effect is a little dizzying—like the novel-within-a-novel technique in Gide's *Les Faux-monnayeurs.* For the opening words are those of Dickens' "most autobiographical" novel, and they are also the openings words of an account of David's life, which seems at the outset to be a novel, but which is said to be "intended for no eyes but mine." David, like Dickens, has rejected the idea of writing direct autobiography. Yet, while he was in Switzerland during his short time as a young widower, he lived in a country where he might perhaps have met one Charles Dickens, engaged in writing *Dombey and Son*—but let David use his own words: "I wrote a Story, with a purpose growing, not remotely, out of my own experience, and sent it to Traddles, and he arranged for its publication very advantageously for me; and the tidings of my growing reputation began to reach me from travellers whom I encountered by chance" (816).

As David continues to write, in an unusually rapid and condensed style, in this and the following chapter, dealing with his return to England and the revelation of his reunion with Agnes, the expurgations which mark the conversion of self-revelation into fiction continue to be more and more apparent. For, while the novel throughout does give evidence of the author's facility in projection (and multiple projection), the similarities in the two "lives" are really quite superficial. The point has been made before, and by others, but some of the details will bear repetition.

Dickens was said to have felt great surprise when it was first pointed out to him that David Copperfield had the initials C. D. in reverse. Yet D. C. would have been born at about the same time as C. D. and had apparently reached about the same age as C. D. at the time he was writing his "secret" autobiography. He had read the same books that C. D. had read; he had attended a school which had some points of similarity with, but was really far worse than, the academy at which C. D. completed his formal education. He had worked as an adolescent under conditions he had considered degrading, but which were far less traumatic than the task of pasting labels in the exposed window of a blacking-factory. D. C. had had experience in the law, but as an articled clerk in a proctors' office which was far more "aristocratic" than that of the solicitor to whom C. D. had been an office boy and nonarticled law clerk (D. C. was like Richard Carstone when he dallied with the idea of entering legal practice, and C. D. like Mr. Guppy of the office of Kenge and Carboy). Each of them had learned shorthand and had earned his living by reporting parliamentary debates; each had used newspaper connections to further his ambition to become a writer, and each had become a successful writer and a traveler on the Continent. But C. D. could never have said that his reputation in England preceded his return from the Continent while he was halfway through his "third work of fiction" (817). Neither D. C. nor C. D. is willing to "expose" his own real-life history without fictional elaboration!

The expurgation becomes apparent at the outset, for David insists that, in a circumstance reminiscent of the HERO-pattern, the major trauma of birth has been mitigated for him. "I was born with a caul," he says, and makes much of the circumstances relating to such a birth. The HERO is not "drawn from the waters" by his birth; he is delivered in a way that brings the "waters" into the world with him, and is then "reborn" by being delivered from the state of prenatal omnipotence when he is, paradoxically, already "in the world." The very superstition connected with the caul, which was saved and afterward raffled off as an amulet, indicates its mythological connotations; it is supposed to insure its owner against *drowning.* (There is no evidence which I know that Dickens had been born in a caul, but it is an interesting note that Sigmund Freud, for whom Dickens was a favorite author and *David Copperfield* a favorite novel, had been the product of such a semimiraculous birth.)

Other aspects of the HERO pattern may be cursorily recapitulated. David has the usual panoply of MOTHERS characteristic of the HERO. Like Oliver Twist, he has a "real" mother who is as nearly virginal ("a mere baby") as a mother can possibly be in a nineteenth-century novel. He has a humble foster mother (who shares Clara Copperfield's Christian name) and a fairy godmother who takes umbrage and repudiates him at his birth, only later to accept him, adopt him, give him a new name, a new home, and an upper-class education, watching over him all through both of his lives as a married man. He undoubtedly had a father-progenitor who is really nonexistent, a cruel stepfather (aided and abetted by a cruel stepmother, who doubles the traditional stepparent by being the stepfather's sister, but who is, so far as David is concerned, his stepfather's wife); and he is surrounded by a whole panoply of father-figures who are as ineffectual as they are well-meaning: Mr. Micawber, Mr. Dick, Mr. Wickfield, Dr. Strong, even Daniel Peggotty.

He descends into the pit of financial deprivation, marital unhappiness, and bereavement, but he is redeemed through suffering so as to be worthy of the patient Griselda who has long waited for him. (Very long, indeed, for he discovers his "real" love for her in the sixtieth of sixty-four chapters, then marries her, begets alleged children of his own, and lives happily ever after—in the last chapter of all.)

As far as the characteristic multiple projection of the author-as-hero is concerned, it will be sufficient if I repeat the schematization I have previously made:

$$\text{Ham} \rightarrow \begin{array}{c}\text{Tommy}\\\text{Traddles}\end{array} \rightarrow \text{David} \rightarrow \text{Steerforth} \rightarrow \text{Uriah Heep}$$

$$\begin{array}{c}\text{Unreal}\\\text{Virtue}\end{array} \rightarrow \begin{array}{c}\text{Practical}\\\text{Virtue}\end{array} \rightarrow \text{Neutrality} \rightarrow \begin{array}{c}\text{Attractive}\\\text{Vice}\end{array} \rightarrow \begin{array}{c}\text{Repulsive}\\\text{Vice}\end{array}$$

— 5 —

At this point, before I refer rather briefly to the hero-figures in the later novels, I should try to present my long-standing contention concerning *David Copperfield* and the novels which directly preceded and followed it. To my mind they are clearly related from a dynamic viewpoint, and together they serve to separate the earlier novels from the later ones. And, in order to make that point even sketchily, I shall have to try to relate the novels to the available biographical data.

I have always contended that *David Copperfield, Dombey and Son,* and *Bleak House* constitute three phases of an attempt at self-analysis and therapy. In *Dombey* the aim was to come to terms with and comprehend the Father; in *Copperfield* the analytic process concerned itself with the Hero, and in *Bleak House* the analytic aim concerned itself with the heroine, as HERO-and-virgin, and as mother-ideal. It is fitting, therefore, that the ramifications of the hero-pattern should be most clearly evidenced in *Copperfield,* for neither *Dombey* nor *Bleak House* has any real HERO or hero, either singly or in multiple projection. Little Paul may be a variant in terms of the Child-as-hero, and I have discussed that elsewhere (see n. 5). I have also discussed the Lady of the Summer Son as a substitute hero in another study (see n. 6). And without these who is left? Walter Gay is absent for too long a time from the stage of *Dombey* for the reader to develop the kind of interest in him which a hero should engender. Practically the same thing would have to be said about Allan Woodcourt. Hence the only novel of the analytic period to present the various phases of the hero is the novel which is specifically devoted to self-analysis through attempted analysis of the hero, *The Personal History of David Copperfield.* And once more mounting my hobby, I contend that this novel is not only one of the most popular but also the one which came as close as possible to achieving the therapy which it sought.

But, alas, the therapy could not succeed. The analytic impulse was doomed to failure at the outset. One cannot come to terms with a father-image by creating an ogre (Dombey *père*) whose motivation is never plumbed with any conviction. One cannot come to terms with Esther, the virgin mother, by trying to project oneself in her person and then summarily having to give up that attempt by the necessities of a third-person narrator in the solution of a mystery. This clearly deserves more elaboration than I can hope to accomplish here, and my next step will be even more damaging to my critical reputation.

For despite all the attempts at rehabilitation and defense, I still hold to the old opinion that the novel which followed the analytic struggle, *Hard Times,* constituted an artistic debacle. Let me put a theoretical question to its defenders: what would be your evaluation of Dickens as a novelist if the only novel he had written had been *Hard Times?* I cite only one opinion to support mine. It is that of a gentleman who had great distinction in academic circles and who also achieved literary eminence in a quite unrelated field. He could not be considered a scholarly critic of literature, and as a Dickensian he was prone to critical judgments that were at times sheer idolatry. Yet Stephen Leacock would write: *"Hard Times* has no other interest in the history of letters than that of its failure. . . . The book is . . . an amalgam of Jack the Giant Killer, Ricardo's *Political Economy,* and the Sermon on the Mount: the whole of it intermingled with a comic strain which fails to come off." [14]

The psychoanalytic critic is tempted to try and find possible causes in personal conflicts to account for such abrupt falling-off. He thinks he has found some such circumstances in an account which Dickens himself wrote under cover of an amiable anonymity which deceived no one, but which enabled him to mingle fact and fantasy. One of the last papers in *The Uncommercial Traveller* bears the intriguing title "A Fly-Leaf in a Life" and begins as follows:

> Once upon a time (no matter when), I was engaged in a pursuit (no matter what), which could be transacted by myself alone; in which I could have no help; which imposed a constant strain on the attention, memory, observation, and physical powers; and which involved almost an almost fabulous amount of change of place and rapid railway travelling. I had followed this pursuit through an exceptionally trying winter in an always trying cli-

mate, and had resumed it in England after but a brief repose. Thus it came to be prolonged until, at length—and, as it seemed, all of a sudden—it so wore me out that I could not rely, with my usual cheerful countenance, upon myself to achieve the constantly recurring task, and began to feel (for the first time in my life) giddy, jarred, shaken, faint, uncertain of voice and sight and tread and touch, and dull of spirit. The medical advice I sought within a few hours was given in two words: "instant rest." *Being accustomed to observe myself as curiously as if I were another man,* and knowing the advice to meet my only need, I instantly halted in the pursuit of which I speak, and rested. [Emphasis is mine.][15]

Some of the symptoms sound like those which appeared acutely during the reading tour in America and finally led to the abrupt termination of his readings, but that occurred in 1867–69, and *The Uncommercial Traveller* appeared in installments during 1860. Furthermore, "A Fly-Leaf in a Life" goes on to compare the (alleged) public reaction to this collapse with the fictional reactions of the public to the physical, moral, and financial collapse of Mr. Merdle in *Little Dorrit.* That novel first started running in December of 1855: the last installment of *Hard Times* appeared in August of 1854. During the interval two Christmas numbers ("The Seven Poor Travellers" and "The Holly Tree Inn") appeared; Dickens traveled to Paris and Folkestone, presided at a dinner for Thackeray, gave readings for charity, and acted in Wilkie Collins' *The Lighthouse.*

I think I may be permitted the speculation that Dickens was depicting in "A Fly-Leaf in a Life," more or less accurately, the state of "battle fatigue" which accompanied and followed *Hard Times.* I will go further and hazard an opinion (for which I have had some informal psychiatric corroboration) as to the therapy by which Dickens overcame the neurasthenia, anxiety, somatic hallucinations, and delusions of reference which followed the unsuccessful attempt at self-analysis in the three "analytic" novels. It was a real psychological battle, which had been going on in conscious form for over eight years, which extended in its unconscious implications for many, many years before that, and which was to resume its irritating effect upon his psyche for years to come, even after he had come to terms with his immediate symptons and had found a way to live with his neurosis since he could not find a way to live without it.

The mode of therapy which Dickens achieved was a sort of depersonalization, something like what he refers to in the italicized words in the quotation above. He has learned to stand outside himself, to view himself objectively (so he thinks), to view the characters which he creates with greater conscious objectivity. They are *in* him but no longer *of* him, so far as he is concerned. This is the new *modus vivendi* by which he becomes once again able to live, even precariously, with himself. The old motivations crop up again in the dreamlike episodes which recur in the postanalytic novels, but the therapy requires a renewed and increasing round of activity, and it carries with it an attitude toward his characters (not to mention his friends and relations) which is markedly aggressive. And this aggressivity is ultimately turned inward to result in the self-aggressive drives of the "chronic" suicide which I have also described elsewhere (see p. 2 and n. 7).

— 6 —

Let us then consider the configurations of the hero patterns during this later period. First, the characteristics of the HERO of myth no longer stress to the same extent as in the earlier novels the earlier years of the HERO'S life. Instead we have a preoccupation with what Jungian analysis calls the "Night Journey," a descent into the Pit, followed by a resurrection which is not always joyous, nor even complete. The instances come to mind at once. Stephen Blackpool falls into a real as well as a symbolic pit, from which he does not return for more than the final moments of his life. Arthur Clennam follows William Dorrit into the pit of imprisonment from which the latter has been, incompletely, rescued. Arthur's rescue comes from his beloved Amy and his benefactor Doyce, for he can and, seemingly, will do nothing to help himself. The dual HERO of *A Tale of Two Cities* goes so far toward the terror of Death that one of his "persons" can only be rescued by the death of the other (see n. 4). So much has been written about the fall and rise of Pip that I need not labor the point here. In *Our Mutual Friend,* where the symbol of both birth and death is water, both John Harmon and Eugene Wrayburn are, in mythic terms and almost in reality, drowned and reborn. George Silverman can never manage to clamber out of the pit despite his best efforts, and, of course, we know that Edwin Drood has travelled the road to the Land of the Dead so far that we can never be certain that he will ever return.

In the projections of the author-as-hero we find two newer trends. First, we find heroes who are middle-aged rather than in young manhood or even childhood. When Dickens reached forty he seems to have decided that there was no reason why the hero should not also be in his forties and yet be rewarded with the dream virgin. Yet Arthur Clennam really differs very little from the younger Dickens heroes. And when he is finally united with his *bien-aimée* we know that he, like David, may live happily ever after, but that for his creator, the dream virgin will still be lurking just around the corner.

There is an interesting sidelight on ages when we examine *A Tale of Two Cities.* Carton and Darnay both begin young, of course, though they do age by the mystic seventeen years during the course of the story. But their age plays no great part in the pattern. What seems to me to be most striking is that the character who had reached about the same age as Charles Dickens when we first meet him is Dr. Manette! Here again I shall have to refer to my previous study of this novel (see n. 4).

Pip grows as he grows up, of course, but there is no really complete image of him in middle age, the point where we leave him at the end, no matter which ending we accept. The really older, mature hero-figures are to be found in the final novels. John Harmon, Eugene Wrayburn, and Septimus Crisparkle may not actually be as old as Arthur Clennam, but they do give the impression of being mature men. It seems odd, but I always think of John Jasper as being an older man, although Dickens stresses the fact that he is barely older than his nephew.

And that suggests a glance at the father-as-hero, often a foil or double for the father-as-enemy, but sometimes a hero projection in his own right. From Mr. Pickwick to John Jasper, by way of Mr. Brownlow, the Cheerybles, Master Humphrey in the role of The Single Gentleman (the old-man-whose-name-is-not-Trent simply will not do), Gabriel Varden, Bob Cratchit, old Martin from the time of his discovery of Pecksniff's perfidy through the great moment of his unmasking of the arch-hypocrite, Captain Cuttle, and Mr. Peggotty (to choose the most attractive of the galaxy of benevolent fathers to David)—all of the ideal fathers, and father-ideals, exist to reassure the hero (and the reader) that there is always someone who will help to make things right at the end. But after *Bleak House* he seems to disappear. Can Mr. Sleary atone for the shortcomings of Mr. Gradgrind and Teacher M'Choakumchild? Frederick Dorrit means well, but he is a victim rather than a rescuer. So, too, is the most complete of father-heroes, Dr. Manette. So is mild Reginald Wilfer. The only fathers really to qualify as fortresses of strength in time of need are Joe Gargery and Mr. Grewgious. And how little either of them really manages to accomplish on behalf of the hero!

Another change in the pattern of the *hero* in the later novels is the attenuation of the practice of multiple projection. In part this is due to the skill which the later Dickens has acquired in the creation of developing rather than static heroes. The most significant doubling, of course, occurs in the Carton-Darnay picture. In *Great Expectations* we might find a scheme something like that in *Copperfield,* but the progression

Pocket → Pip → Orlick

is really quite different. Herbert Pocket is a character in his own right, not really an insipid heroid; Pip can bear the burden of a number of characteristics of the hero figure in the process of his development, and Dolge Orlick is a stick figure, a black villain of melodrama who cannot be compared to the Heep of Infamy. In the last novels Dickens is so secure in his art and so free of the earlier infantilism of multiple projection that there are, in *Our Mutual Friend* at least, two completely developed independent heroes and an extraordinarily well motivated counterhero: John Harmon, Eugene Wrayburn, and Bradley Headstone. In *Drood* there might have been some interesting interplay involving Edwin, Neville Landless, and the idyllic Lieutenant Tartar, but we do not have enough of the novel to judge the final outcome; we do have John Jasper as both father-enemy and counterhero, though, and that is almost enough to compensate for the others.

The idyllic heroid is also notably missing from the later novels. We could make some interesting comparative points between The Reverend Frank Milvey and The Reverend George Silverman. But enough is enough.

I have cited the Rank synthesis of the HERO pattern earlier in this essay; in the note to that quotation I have mentioned Karl Menninger's parallel account of man's persistent fantasies.

In the later editions of *The Human Mind* Dr. Menninger contented himself with a listing of these fantasies, with a brief statement showing the narrative pattern involved in each. In the first edition of that influential work, however, Menninger undertook a statement of the entire life story embodied in these fantasies.[16] Very little adaptation of that general fantasy narrative is needed to make it apply to the specific pattern of Dickens' psychological makeup. It would run something like this—

> Behold me! I am the Inimitable, the procreator and the creator, the father of a family and the father of the even larger family of children I have created, unaided, in my works. I am at least the equivalent of these heroes to whom I have given birth, unassisted. I eschew all women except virgin mothers, for whom I have only reverence, sacred love, and devotion. The common earthly parents whom I have come to know were surely not my own, and I therefore despise them—my egotistical, improvident supposed father and those who undertook to fill his place, and the horrid, laughter-provoking female persecutor who called herself my mother. I must rid myself of them and of the very thought of them. Yet to have such terrible wishes, to express such wishes in the name of creation is a

sin, perhaps the unpardonable sin. My very wishes have surely brought about the unhappy deaths of these poor creatures. I must absolve myself; I must take my punishment. I must see with my own eyes and feel in my own heart all of the woes and miseries that people suffer everywhere. I must see it all and I must write of it all, for such is my redemption.

But this is not enough. I still suffer from the injury and infection which life has dealt to me. I will flee from it; I will seek solace where and with whom I may. But am I never to be purified: I must seek and find once again that happier time in life before the world and its vileness had sullied me and my pure loved one. By the power which will restore my youth I am made invincible. Perhaps I have lost the Magic Wand, but I shall find it—I must find it again. I escape into a haven of refuge, the very womb of my true MOTHER, my earliest and my latest paradise. There I remain, to return when I have finished my purgation.

The pattern is indeed fantastic, but it is the fantasy with which the Unconscious clothes all shoddy, unrewarding reality. In all lives its existence is implicit; in the life of a great artist it tends to be more and more explicit. The very quality of Dickens as a man and an artist makes it quite obvious to those with the clues to its configurations, the key to the code which hides it. With it we ought to be able to look behind the whole cycle of novels as if they constituted a single *roman à clef*. This, in some measure, is what I have attempted to do.

James E. Marlow

DICKENS' ROMANCE

The Novel As Other

WITH A few exceptions,[1] twentieth-century criticism has given little serious attention to Dickens' theory of fiction. We know that Dickens took his role as artist seriously, for he criticized Thackeray's "pretense of undervaluing his art, which was not good for the art that he held in trust."[2] We know that he felt that the craft of fiction required "patience, study, punctuality, determination, self-denial, training of mind and body, hours of application and seclusion."[3] We know of his copious allusions to fairy tales, to the *Arabian Nights,* and of his interest in precursors like Fielding and Goldsmith and in the stage. We can readily see that he continued experimenting in technique throughout his life. But Dickens left no systematic theory of art; we have only the evidence of his practice in his novels, some running notes made during the composition of the novels, some ideas conveyed through his journalism, the occasional (in both senses) comments in his prefaces, and the few specific suggestions he made to other writers in his extant editorial and personal correspondence. However, these editorial comments are operational rather than theoretical; the prefaces, because he "was on the defensive," give "a misleading impression of his concept of fiction";[4] and the running notes and the novels are often ambiguous. Consequently, rather than attempting to formulate Dickens' theory of literature, most criticism has tended to stop with Forster's report that Dickens hoped "that his books might help to make people better."[5]

We know, however, that Dickens had access to many of the best English theorists. There is evidence that he knew, among many others, the work of Wordsworth, Coleridge, and Dr. Johnson; he knew both Leigh Hunt and Lord Jeffrey of the *Edinburgh Review* personally; and he owned no less than thirteen books by William Hazlitt. No one would deny that to "help to make people better" is the first priority of his art, nor that this mission is to be accomplished through "delight." But his knowledge of critical theory debars us from seriously believing Dickens to "warble his native wood-notes wild." To consider him naïve would be

[23

to begin with a distorted view of Dickens' artistic integrity. In order not
to distort Dickens' world more than necessary, it is important to uncover, if possible, a consistent set of principles behind his operational
decisions.

I propose to draw, so far as I am able, a hypothesis about Dickens'
theory of literature from his practice and his criticism. Of course the
hypothesis will require testing and revision, but the advantage of having a frame of reference within which to argue conflicting critical opinions is sufficient that the present construction, however rickety, should
be risked. It has been said that a poetics of the novel has been impossible to formulate because the novel has been in continuous change, indeed, that the novel is by definition ever new. Dickens' own practice
was continuous experiment: one need only read the first paragraph of
the unfinished *Edwin Drood* to see major innovation in his technique.
However, though we risk sometimes making Dickens' poetics a product
when it truly was always in process, I believe that there is enough con-
sistency behind all his "tricks and manners," as David Masson said of
his style in 1859, and all his technical innovations to allow us to grasp
the powerful intention which animated his work from first to last.

The desire to "help to make people better" is of course the first
axiom of Dickens' aesthetic theory. The corollary of this desire is the
unique relation he had with his public. Publication by monthly parts
provided him, in the numbers sold, with a sensitive register of the pref-
erences of the public. However, merely to cater to the public's taste
could scarcely be, especially for a man of Dickens' urgent temperament, a realistic attempt to make people better. It seems quite evident
that his sales meant to him more in terms of hearts listening than in
terms of shillings paid. As he wrote one of his numerous correspondents, "believe me that your expressions of affectionate remem-
brance and approval, sounding from the green forests of the Missis-
sippi, sink deeper into my heart and gratify it more than all the
honorary distinctions that all the courts of Europe could confer." [6] He
often mentioned that he felt personally loved wherever his work was
read. If his audience was moved to a personal affection for the "implied author" of his novels, was that affection not itself part of the author's aesthetic purpose?

"If I could ever learn that I had happily been the means of awakening within him any new love of his fellow-creatures, . . . I should
feel much pleasure from the knowledge." [7] The pleasure is, I suggest,
that of the artist, not the man. For, in awakening love of his fellow in
men, Dickens succeeds in what he proposes in "A Preliminary Word" to
do in *Household Words:* "to bring the greater and the lesser in degree,
together, upon that wide field, and mutually dispose them to a better
acquaintance and a kinder understanding." Dickens is here proposing

to change his readers, to make them, by means of his art, more conciliatory, more open to their fellowmen, and thus to the world. If a novel can cause an affection for its author, the reader has been enlarged; thus it may be possible for Dickens to bring opposites together, and to "mutually dispose them to . . . a kinder understanding." Dickens' choice of words here indicates that he felt that such acquaintance and such understanding would not occur without the help of his art: he clearly saw that he must break through the circle of Selfhood around each man. Hence, the first priority of the critic is not to study changes of heart in characters, for these are only means, and often not primary means, but rather to study the change of heart in the reader, for this is the end of Dickens' art.

The essence of Dickens' art, Forster rightly says, is that it brought "all things within human sympathy." The single human element which could connect members of opposing classes or sects or ideologies was for Dickens the imagination, or the fancy as he generally preferred to call it. Philip Collins rightly says of Dickens, "He did not, however, habitually differentiate between the two terms, as Wordsworth and Coleridge had done." [8] Although the fancy is a faculty of the mind, through bad education and false ideals it can be stifled or perverted: Headstone and Quilp represent these two possibilities. Fancy, "according to its nurture, burns with an inspiring flame, or sinks into sullen glare, but which (or woe betide that day!) can never be extinguished." [9] Quilp's fancy was unrestrained, and Headstone's was too much repressed; proper nurture of their fancies might have salvaged them as human beings. As Headstone represents those human beings who conform to the false ideals of society at all costs, Quilp represents those outside society. "All people," wrote Dickens to Miss Coutts on 15 November 1848, "who have led hazardous and forbidden lives are, in a certain sense, imaginative; and if their imaginations are not filled with good things, they will choke them for themselves, with bad ones." [10] Individuals, in other words, who are cut loose from the norms of society have by their very condition nurtured the faculty of fancy. The connection between freedom and fancy is apparent. But in order that the appetite of the fancy does not lead to license, it must be fed with a diet which will succeed in relating the individual to his fellowmen. Inadequate fare for the fancy will leave the individual outside the human community but still inside his own desiring self. An example of what Dickens conceived to be adequate sustenance for the fancy—Dickens supported heartily endeavors, such as those by his friend Macready, to bring Shakespeare and other good drama back to the theaters: "There are not many things of which the English as a people stand in greater need than sound rational amusement. As a necessary element in any popular education worthy of the name; as a whole incentive to fancy, depressed by the business of life; as a rest and relief from realities that are not and never can be all-sufficient for the mind,—sound rational public amusement is very much indeed to be desired." [11]

On the other hand are the human beings who, through indoctrination or Self-will, have sought to attenuate their fancies: a fancy is an aberration, materially caused, "a fragment," says Scrooge, "of an underdone potato." Essentially, they are denying that the fancy is a faculty of the mind. "Scrooge," for example, "had as little of what is called the fancy about him as any man in the city of London"; like Marley, he was wearing a chain he had forged in life, "of my own free will [I] wore it." But under the powerful influence of the Christmas season, Scrooge's fancy revives sufficiently to save him from Marley's fate. We see, therefore, that it does not matter whether, in England, fancies have been misfed or starved, nor whether deprived by exterior circumstances or by personal will, whether found in the Nation of the Poor or the Nation of the Rich—the task of the artist is the same: "to open their shut-up hearts freely," to quote the *Carol,* and the key to this "shutupness" is the fancy.[12]

Before we can determine *how* people may be made better, let us consider further *why* people need being made better. Dickens' world view needs a great deal more study than it has yet been given; however, two elements in it seem well established. These are the primary dangers which Dickens saw attacking the spirit of man. The first is that the earth from which man has sprung exerts its pull on him. This is the "Clay-given mandate" of Carlyle, "Eat Thou and be Filled." Watching out for "number one"—as Lowten says in *Pickwick Papers*—can take innumerable forms, such as the family pride of Dombey, the spiritual pride of Mrs. Clennam, the cupidity of Smallweed, and the primitive lawlessness of Bill Sykes, but the result is always the same: an increasing divorcement from the spiritual reality of the world. To become earth or clay, ironically, is to be less concrete. What is concrete, as Kierkegaard defines it, is a synthesis of the finite and the infinite. For both him and Dickens, worldliness is unreality. For Dickens, to pursue apparent worldly good creates not security and satisfaction but ever growing insecurity and dissatisfaction with reality.

The second primary danger comes from the other direction: the intellect. It comes from the belief that man can ameliorate his condition through abstract principles and legal prescriptions. Mr. Filer in *The Chimes* and of course Gradgrind are examples of this belief. For Dickens, the collection of related ideas known as positivism, realism, materialism, utilitarianism does not improve but rather loosens man's grasp on full reality. By eliminating wonder and delight, these ideas would deprive man of those pleasures that are at once the goal and the incentive of life. Hence, from the mandate within and such counsel without, men are incited to withdraw from concrete interaction with the world and their fellowmen, incited to reside in a Selfhood growing ever more abstracted and apathetic. Dickens believed art could counter, on the one hand, man's materialism, and, on the other, his apathetic abstraction; indeed, to do this is the "trust" of the artist. By appealing to the fancy and not the understanding, art could bring the feelings alive, and it is these feelings which can break down the defensive walls the Self erects between itself and the world. So, with this generalization, let us turn to the specific methods Dickens uses to restore man to his world, and spirit to man—which dual restoration he called "Romance."

— 2 —

On 13 April 1855 Dickens advised W. H. Wills, on a novel his good friend and reliable assistant editor had attempted, that "if the scene, where the woman who dies is lying in bed, were truly done, the conversation between the heroine and the boy would belong to it—*could* not do violence to it—and whatever it might be about, would inevitably associate itself in the reader's mind with the figure on the bed, and would lead up to the catastrophe that soon happens." Here "truly" takes more of an affective than a normative meaning. Everything "truly" done, even when seeming to contrast or ignore the reader's chief object of interest, will inevitably "lead up" to it. This is because, as Dickens goes on to tell Wills, "whereas if the scene were truly and powerfully rendered, the improbability more or less necessary to all tales and allowable in them, would become a part of a thing so true and vivid, that the reader must accept it whether he likes it or not" (*NL*, II, 653). Clearly what Dickens is expressing here is his recognition that the aesthetic response depends upon the reader's perceiving a definitive Gestalt, which other details will revolve around and inevitably reflect. The "thing" does not mildly enlist the reader's attention, it possesses him. Nor does it matter whether this Gestalt, this "thing," is rendered fancifully or realistically. When it is "vivid and true" the conventional orders of propriety and credibility are simply bypassed. Leigh Hunt had already countered the standard positivistic objection that, however vivid, such impressions are fictitious: "Whatever touches us, whatever moves us, does touch and move us. . . . We can only judge of things by their effects."[13] For Dickens, too, what moves men is real, and literature is therefore at least as real as Gradgrindian facts.

For Dickens the goal of literature was not realism. Though he occupies a "middle ground between the romantic and the realistic,"[14] realism for its own sake was never an aim simply because mere realism may not inscribe an adequate Gestalt upon the reader's mind: "It does not seem to me to be enough to say of any description that it is the exact truth. The exact truth must be there; but the merit or art in the narrator, is the manner of stating the truth. . . . And in these times . . . the tendency is to be frightfully literal and catalogue-like—to make the thing, in short, a sort of sum in reduction that any miserable creature can do in that way." [15] The value of the literary object, then, derives from the art of the narrator; its value depends not upon statistical probability nor upon deductive regularity but simply upon the impression that it makes. Dickens of course did not disregard probability, or even verisimilitude. Early in his career he was grateful to Forster for recognizing the essential reality of Nancy in *Oliver Twist*. His response to questions of the probability of Nancy's behavior was a flat: "IT IS TRUE." He wrote to young Wilkie Collins, 20 December 1852, "I think the probabilities here and there require a little more respect than you are disposed to give them" (*Letters*, I, 294). The point is, that in ignoring probability, the impression, the affect, could be broken. Dickens knew that probability was a genuine part of the reader's interest.

But because he believed that coincidence and accident, not strict probability, were the conditions of human life—and that they were certainly more interesting—he did not hesitate to include these elements in his fiction. "I am not clear," he wrote Edward Bulwer Lytton on 5 June 1860, "and I never have been clear, respecting that canon of fiction which forbids the interposition of accident in such a case as Madame Defarge's death" (*NL*, III, 162–63). For, "the ways of Providence" are only "to *suggest,*" he had written Collins, and "art is but a little imitation." Monroe Engel is right when he says of Dickens, "He wanted to leave in his fiction some of the interest of life itself—chance, surprises, unpredictability, even within the necessary order of consequences." [16] A following out of statistical probability by a novelist would, to use one of Dickens' favorite metaphors, merely serve to grind the reader, that is, to turn him into dust—with all the spiritual implications of that word. Dickens had, in Madame Defarge's death at the hands of Miss Pross, "the positive intention of making that half-comic intervention a part of the desperate woman's failure, and of opposing that mean death . . . to the dignity of Carton's wrong or right; this *was* the design, and seemed to be in the fitness of things" (*NL*, III, 163). Opposing, or contrasting, the one death with the other was a certain way of making a striking effect. Such an effect, though in the "fitness of things," is addressed not to the understanding but to the fancy. In arguing that Krook's spontaneous combustion could be substantiated by medical authority, Dickens obviously deprecated having his fictive action undercut by the charge of improbability. Indeed, Krook's demise was carefully shown to be the probable consequence of his habits. But in both examples we can see that Dickens chooses his action not for the sake of probability but for the sake of impression.

If verisimilitude has little necessary connection with what is "vivid and true," even less has sensationalism. For every murder scene in Dickens there are numerous scenes, equally memorable, whose tone is gentle pathos or humor. Even were a succession of sensational or violent scenes able to render art "true," Dickens was perfectly conscious that his readers appreciated the lighter touches quite as much. "I am inclined to suspect," he wrote Wilkie Collins on 31 October 1861, some twenty years after the fact, "that the impression of protection and hope derived from Nickleby's going away protecting Smike is exactly the impression—this is discovered by chance—that an audience like most to be left with" (*To Collins,* 106). Along the same lines Dickens could advise Wills on 13 May 1854 about a story for *Household Words,* "An alteration occurs to me—easily made—which I think would greatly improve it, in respect of interest and quiet pathos, and a closing sentiment of pleasure to the reader" (*NL,* II, 559). The simple insertion into the story of a picture of a faithful old lover, Dickens felt, would bring about this valuable "quiet pathos." From these comments we may see that by "vivid and true" Dickens does not mean the loud or the egregious. He seems to have recognized that aesthetic perception is not geared to such quantitative factors. Aesthetic responses, like feelings, he would probably agree with Hazlitt, "evaporate in so large a space— we must draw the circle of our affections and duties somewhat closer— the heart hovers and fixes nearer home." [17]

Affects from art which do not hover and fix near home Dickens consistently deplored. The term he uses to designate such inartistic affects is "severity." Severity may occur in any part of a novel, but especially in characterization, action, and diction. A character—no matter how ethical—can easily weary a reader by his too assiduous purpose. "It seems to me," Dickens wrote Collins on 24 January 1862 (*NL,* III, 282), "that great care is needed not to tell the story too severely. In exact proportion as you play around it here and there, and mitigate the severity of your own sticking to it, you will enhance and intensify the power which Magdalen holds on to her purpose. For this reason I should have given Mr. Pendril some touches of comicality . . . and humour as those with which you have irradiated the private theatricals." Hence, we realize that even humor is used functionally by Dickens, used with an eye to the total impression. In the notes he prepared as he wrote *Our Mutual Friend* he wrote: "More books, and the misers, and about hidden wills." Under that he added: "Relieve by making Wegg as comic as possible." [18] Humor can be used, also, around such unmitigatedly good and innocent characters as Dickens' own earlier

heroes and heroines for relief, both in the sense of lessening the reader's discomfort and in the sense of creating a prominence by means of
contrast.

Earle Davis has pointed out that "Dickens always felt the need for
contrast," [19] but, precisely, this contrast is not so much an objective one
as a rhetorical one, not so much in content as in attitude: the contrast is
essentially between a reader's sense of constriction, whether demanded
by the morality or the logical succession of the story, and the reader's
demand for respite, for *not* being made to stick to it. Even a focus on
moral obligations may alienate the reader in the same way that too
severe an exposition of a character being crushed by the forces of
necessity will alienate him. Hazlitt well describes why the reader is
alienated by the common moral tale "George Barnwell": "The mind, in
such cases, instead of being deterred by the alarming consequences
held out to it, revolts against the denunciation of them as an insult offered to its free-will, and, in a spirit of defiance, returns a practical answer to them, by daring the worst that can happen." [20] Dickens understood this reaction and therefore insisted that the reader always be
given a strong impression of going where he likes. Thus Dickens tries
to objectify not only in thought or event but also in the *rhetorical rhythm*
man's personal sense of freedom. Unless a reader felt this sense of
freedom, Dickens felt, he would not read on. His real attitude toward
the public is revealed in a letter to Wilkie Collins 7 January 1860: "You
know that I always contest your disposition to give an audience credit
for nothing, which necessarily involves the forcing of points on their attention, and which I have always observed them to resent when they
find it out—as they always will and do" (*Letters*, II 110).

If a "good" character may be presented too severely, clearly, a
"bad" one may be. "It is remarkable," Dickens wrote to Percy Fitzgerald
on 27 July 1864, "that if you do not administer a disagreeable character
carefully, the public have a decided tendency to think that the *story* is
disagreeable, and not merely the fictitious person" (*Letters*, II, 217). The
reader must always have something to be interested in, something, in
other words, which appeals to the sympathetic imagination, not the understanding. Interest may be maintained by comedy or satire or even
stylistic spectacle, or by desire for the well-being or punishment of
characters, or by curiosity about the denouement—by any aspect of the
three kinds of interest defined by Wayne Booth.[21] One example of
Dickens' method of creating interest may be seen in his advice to Collins on 9 January 1866 (*To Collins,* 132–33) concerning the dramatization of the latter's *Armadale:* "You could only carry those situations on a
real hard wooden stage, and wrought out (very differently) by real live
people face to face with other real live people judging them—you could
only carry those situations *by the help of interest in some innocent person*

whom they placed in peril, and that person a young woman. There is no one to be interested in there." On stage, without the possibility of stylistic means of relief, Dickens felt the audience had to be given a "Practical" interest, a character who hovers near home. Bella, Dickens writes in the running notes to *Our Mutual Friend*, "says she is mercenary and why. *But indicate better qualities.*" He adds, on the next line, "Interest the reader in her." In other words, Dickens enjoins himself to add qualities which enable the reader to sympathize with Bella despite her own faulty understanding. In whatever part of fiction he focused on, Dickens always sought to interest the reader and so involve him freely.

George Ford has keenly observed that "Dickens' method is to make such 'strongly marked' black characters probable by greying them not with virtues but with humor." [22] This is often true, and as often true of "good" characters as "bad" ones; but Dickens' purpose is more prehensile than this description implies. By greying his "flat" characters with humor his intention is not to make them merely probable. His intention is to make them *tolerable* to man's soul, and not tolerable in themselves but as contributing elements in the impression made by their entire context. He warns himself in a memorandum to *Dombey and Son* "not to make too much of the scene with the father, as it may be too painful." Too painful, the scene may cause the reader to snatch back his psychic commitment to a character or indeed to the entire narrative. It is useless to speak of siding with the underdog; prolonged and unrelieved injustice to Florence would alienate most readers. Whether his characters are flat, greyed with humor, or fully rounded, Dickens' object is the reader's engagement. Therefore, we must not seek a consistent theory of characterization. For character is subordinate in Dickens—not to action but to the impression of the context as a whole. Characters may be rounded and probable (for mimesis may sustain reader interest, especially if the reader discovers something new), or "greyed" and tolerable, or caricatures, or merely sticks upon which to hang the other kinds of rhetorical interest—just as the case seems to require. But above all is the impression: no severity, simply interest the reader.

"Severity" may occur in other ways than in the treatment of character and the dramatic scene. On 25 December 1861 Dickens advised Bulwer Lytton, "But then I would soften the scene where Nature and Death are, for this reason—because as it stands, it seems to me to be more laboriously symbolical than the other parts of the book, and consequently to be not quite in keeping with them" (*NL,* III, 270). Explicit symbolism tends to appeal to the understanding rather than the fancy. Thus it draws away from the reader the sense of the living presence of the fiction and calls in concepts. For concepts may often be, we know— and it will be seen how this is important to Dickens in a moment—but stolid defenses of the self. Dickens wanted the reader immersed in the vivid effect, thus on a perceptive plane, beyond concepts. He wrote to Charles Knight, a contributor to *Household Words,* on 27 July 1851 (*Letters,* I, 259–60):

> Will you look carefully at all the earlier part, where the use of past tense instead of the present a little hurts the picturesque effect? I understand that each phase of the thing to be *always a living present before the mind's eye*—a shadow passing before it. Whatever is done, must be *doing.* . . . These shadows do not change as realities do. No phase of his existence passes away, if I choose to bring it to his unsubstantial and delightful life, the only death of which, to me, is *my* death, and thus he is immortal to unnumbered thousands.

Although Dickens is speaking about the particular literary "shadow" named Robinson Crusoe, this advice to Knight amounts to one of his most extended theoretical statements. Even so small a change as that of tense may be sufficient to engage the reader's attention, to make the verbal description a living present before him. The reader, says A. A. Mendilow in *Time and the Novel,* "if he is engrossed in his reading translates all that happens from this moment of time onwards into an imaginative present of his own." [23] Dickens' advice seeks to facilitate this translation; the engrossment of the reader by whatever means is his goal.

Our soul draws its circle near home, and always the artist's task is to penetrate that circle. The problem is how. Dickens wrote a writer on 20 February 1866: "Then, unless you really have led up to a great situation like Basil's death, you are bound in art to make more of it. Such a scene should form a chapter of itself" (*NL,* III, 461). Had the writer led up to the death scene in detail, apparently a short one would have been sufficiently vivid; not having done so, she is "bound in art" to make the scene a chapter in order to make it more striking. Later, in the same letter, Dickens counsels, "also, taking the pains to sit down and recall the principal landmarks in your story, you should then make them far more elaborate and conspicuous than the rest." This stressing of chosen scenes is not, he insists, "a meretricious adornment, but positively necessary to good work and good art." Publishing by installment complicated the problem of making the "landmarks" striking, and even so experienced a writer as Elizabeth Gaskell received advice from Dickens upon how to divide the novel *North and South* most effectively. "I do not apologize to you," he writes in June of 1854, "for laying so much stress on the necessity of its dividing well, because I am bound to put before you my perfect conviction that if it did not, the story would be wasted—

would miss in effect as it went on—*and would not recover it when published complete*" (*NL*, II, 562). Even so little considered a technique as dividing into chapters and installments can, if improperly done, deprive the novel of its power to create a strong impression and so to penetrate. Proper division, of course, means the proper articulation of parts: but our lesson once again is that Dickens judges the parts by the whole. The difficulty of designing *Our Mutual Friend*, he says in the Postscript, "was much enhanced by the mode of publication; for it would be very unreasonable to expect many readers, pursuing a story in portions from month to month through nineteen months, will, until they have it before them complete, perceive the relations of its finer threads to the whole pattern which is always before the eyes of the story-weaver at his loom." The author naturally wants each installment to be striking, but his decisions are ultimately determined by the desire that the work should not "miss in effect as it went on."

— *3* —

From this cursory view of Dickens' practical criticism, we may risk inferring three basic principles behind his artistic choices. The first is: do not alienate the reader. Ernst Cassirer has said, "Like the process of speech the artistic process is a dialogical and dialectic one." [24] This statement summarizes the very essence of Dickens' aesthetic theory. When the readers find the author out, when they discover that they have been written down to and so had their understanding coerced, they will rebel against the author and dissolve any involvement with the work of art. To "force points on a reader," Dickens knew, when cognitive interests are "too elaborately trapped, baited, and prepared" (*To Collins*, 75), makes the reader the dupe, and the writer a tyrant. Intrusions by the narrator, which Dickens rarely committed with serious intentions, also alienate the reader. As A. A. Mendilow says, "Lamb objected very strongly to the attitude of superiority implied in these intruded comments of the author. Reprimanding the weakness in Wordsworth he wrote: 'An intelligent reader finds a sort of insult in being told, I will teach you how to think upon this subject.' " [25] Lamb's point, like that of Hazlitt quoted earlier, is that an attitude of superiority, whether moral or intellectual, whether conveyed through authorial intrusions, tone, or otherwise leaving the author's thumbprint in the plot, causes the reader to withdraw commitment and to defy the intended significance, and to miss the intended feeling. An author defied by his audience obviously cannot help to make people better. Thus inartistic effects prevent (except, ironically, by stirring the free will) a work of art from doing what, according to Dickens, it was meant to do. In order to feel beauty, Cassirer has said, "one must cooperate with the artist." [26]

Dickens approaches the same idea from the other direction: it is the task of the writer not to alienate the reader.

The second principle is: at all times make a figure stand out from its ground. Any aspect of the narrator's art, for example dialogue, can constitute this figure. "I have been trying other books," Dickens wrote Forster from France in 1865, "but so infernally conversational, that I forget who the people are before they have done talking, and don't in the least remember what they talked about before when they begin talking again!" [27] As Forster comments, this is an extreme contrast to Dickens' own art. The tag lines and the elocutionary habits of his own characters were perhaps necessary mnemonic techniques in novels published over the course of a year and a half. But these techniques also succeed in making the characters striking. What only matters is that the literary figure be effective enough to win through to the reader.

In a letter to Collins on 7 January 1860 (*Letters*, II, 110–11), Dickens points to a failure to create an adequate figure in diction: "Perhaps I express my meaning best when I say that the three people who write narratives in these proofs have a DISSECTIVE property in common, which is essentially not theirs but yours." Unless the figures are sufficiently articulated to arouse an active response in the reader, they are inartistic, for, as "Alain" says in writing of Dickens' techniques, "to the extent that a novelist has not imbued with feeling a certain point of focus, he takes us everywhere in vain; nothing is real. His images are vapid, and we recognize their unreality." [28] Dickens expressed much the same idea when he linked "vivid and true"—as did Hazlitt when he discussed "Gusto." The impact may come from character, image, plot, diction, or thought, any one of which can win through to the reader, gain access to the fancy. In reading Dickens, in fact, one senses that even too exclusive an emphasis on any one of the fictive parts would be considered "severity." In his larger novels we find a constant alteration of parts emphasized, sometimes character, then plot, then diction, and so on. This fact leads to the realization that Dickens had always in mind the pattern underlying and unifying all of the vivid parts.

The third principle is: treat the work of art as a whole, to which the fancy and the soul of the reader can freely respond. Essentially, this idea does not differ from the Romantic notion of the work of art as an organic unity. It is a single Gestalt, that is, a unified configuration which has properties not derived from its parts. "A work of art," says Susan K. Langer, "is a single, individual symbol, although a highly articulated one." [29] In advising his correspondents to make their principal landmarks more conspicuous than the rest, Dickens was clearly seeing the artistic work as an articulated but indivisible whole. Dickens had grown increasingly impatient with critics who doubted that he concerned himself sufficiently with the design of the whole novel. "I was occupied," he says in the Preface to *Little Dorrit,* "with this story, during many working hours of two years. I must have been very ill employed, if I could not leave its merits and demerits in a whole, to express themselves on its being read as a whole." The identical disposition against instructive prefaces is evident when he wrote Collins on 20 December 1852, "I have no doubt that the prefatory letter would have been better away, on the ground that a book (of all things) should speak for and explain itself" (*Letters,* I, 294). Of course a book that succeeds as a symbolic whole will speak, and to the fancy. In the Postscript to *Our Mutual Friend* Dickens speaks of the "whole pattern which is always before the eyes of the story-weaver at his loom."

The very use of the term "pattern" suggests why Dickens was interested in "quiet pathos" and similar effects and was not the purveyor of sensational effects that some critics have accused him of being. He knew an unrelieved succession of lurid incidents will inevitably become all ground; the brightest orange does not stand out against equally bright reds and yellows. "There are dark shadows on earth," he says at the conclusion of *Pickwick Papers,* "but its lights are stronger in the contrast." A pattern, a whole, will interweave both. Sensational events may wholly lack aesthetic value because such value is relational and not inherent in any part or phase.

Moreover, a concatenation of sensational events tends to coerce the reader—a feeling which the soul must eventually repudiate. The soul, says Hazlitt, "clings obstinately to some things and violently rejects others." [30] Dickens knew that the reader would always reject any technique that treated him as a passive observer of a mechanically connected train of events, no matter how lurid. For the soul "violently rejects" all rhetorical effects that smack of epistemological determinism. "I think the business of art is to lay all that ground carefully, not with the care that conceals itself—to show, by a backward light, what everything has been working to—but only to *suggest* until the fulfillment comes" (*NL,* II, 125). In this view, the reader sees an open-ended perspective, and actively projects his own views. Therefore, Dickens attempts to create whole patterns, ones which the reader feels himself to be freely working out. For, unless sensing himself free and creative, the reader does not employ the faculty of fancy. And only through the fancy, Dickens knew as legatee of the great Romantics, does art provide spiritual benefit, that is, help to make people better.

Dickens was well aware that literature was a spiritual reservoir. In *David Copperfield,* we recall, it is eighteenth-century novels which sustain David's spirit during the oppression by Mr. and Miss Murdstone. Dickens knew that once the reader's fancy was involved, art could carry him out of himself and out of his situation in the world and so refresh and restore him. The gift that the artist holds "in trust" for mankind is the capacity to arouse the fancy.[31] How does the artist employ it? Edward Wagenknecht points out that Dickens used his own personality as a basis for his art. In the "Preface" to *A Tale of Two Cities,* Dickens states: "A strong desire was upon me then to embody it [the story] in my own person. . . . Throughout its execution, it has had complete possession of me." What Dickens is testifying to is not merely that he used his own personality but that he created in *ekstasis* (Sartre's term) from his own personality. This accounts for his remark to Mrs. Brookfield in a letter of 20 February 1866, "My notion always is, that when I have made the people to play out the play, it is, as it were, their business to do it, and not mine" (*NL,* III, 461). His own word for this creative ecstasy is "metempsychosis." [32] Clearly, this state can account for his animism, his pervasive ambiences, such as the fog in *Bleak House,* and the strength of his so-called eccentric characters. But, as we have seen, every technique is subordinate to his larger purpose: to engage the fancy of the reader. The goal of this creative ecstasy, is to create, through the fancy, an ekstasis in the reader.

Thus, the faculty of fancy supports no less than the very possibility of self-transcendence in the world. Appeals to the reason or to self-interest cannot bring men in the world together; vague utilitarian first principles satisfy no one in the long run—not even John Stuart Mill—and are easily corrupted in practice; sectarian religions divide rather than unite mankind; politics and political economy only lend support to the idea that this is a Hobbesian world and that no man cares for nor dares trust his brother. But Dickens follows Hazlitt in holding that the faculty of fancy can bring men together. Hazlitt argues in his *An Essay on the Principles of Human Action* (1805) that through the imagination man can genuinely enter into his fellowman's interests. "The imagination, by means of which alone I can anticipate future objects, or be interested in them, must carry me out of myself into the feelings of others by one and the same process by which I am thrown forward as it were into my future being, and interested in it." [33] It is no wonder that Hazlitt was proudest of this work, for it strikes blows simultaneously against the solipsistic tendencies of idealistic philosophy and against the tendencies in materialistic philosophy to rule out the possibility of free will. In stating that "our self-love and sympathy depend upon the same causes" (68), Hazlitt short-circuits the apologists for laissez faire capitalism. If it is possible to care for others, man need not rely on the secondhand morality available in the idea that in helping oneself one is helping others. Through imagination, then, man may enter the interests of others and so nullify the idea that life is only "nasty, brutish, and short," that his "lot is not necessarily a moody, brutal fact," as Dickens expressed the idea in "A Preliminary Word."

As it is possible, then, to care for others—indeed, to escape the shell of the ego—the first requirement for society is incentive. Hazlitt points out, "The only reason for my preferring my future interest to that of others must arise from my anticipating it with greater warmth of present imagination. It is this greater liveliness and force with which I can enter into my future feelings, that in a manner identifies them with my present being" (140). Dickens could not have agreed more: a priority of his fiction, as we have seen, is liveliness and force, to make things vivid and true. By presenting characters and situations which excite the fancy, Dickens could nourish the primary source of good in man. Feelings deeply aroused, even by fiction, bring men to project themselves out of their present concerns, out therefore of their selfhood. They enter the interests of others, including those of the "implied author," with the "warmth of present imagination." As Hazlitt said in *The Plain Speaker*, "But I could not wish a better or more philosophical standard of morality, than that we should think and feel towards others as we should, if it were our own case. If we look for a higher standard than this we shall not find it; but shall lose the substance for the shadow." [34] Neither Hazlitt nor Dickens argues for a vague do-goodism; their argument is thoroughly grounded on the premise that man is capable of planning his own future, from which the consequences follow that man is therefore capable of achieving ekstasis and therefore must be able to enter others' interests as well as his own. Moreover, it is the faculty of the fancy which makes this ekstasis possible, and since the writer appeals directly to this faculty, literature can directly foster sympathy for others. Indeed, it seems to follow that aesthetic impact and moral benefit exist in a direct relationship.

This universal faculty of fancy, then, is the ground, "that wide field,", upon which Dickens proposes to bring divided society together through art. In *Our Mutual Friend* there is an effective symbol of what fiction can do. The story of the murder of John Harmon was going from mouth to mouth, though it was in fact a falsehood. The "Harmon Murder," Dickens writes, "—as it came to be popularly called—went up and down, and ebbed and flowed, now in the town, now in the country, now among palaces, now among hovels, now among lords and ladies and gentlefolks, now among labourers and hammerers and ballast-heavers" (31). Even false gossip provides a kind of nexus between the classes and between individuals; how much more so may literature, which is written to be "vivid and true"?

Dickens, in the tradition of Leigh Hunt and Hazlitt, did not stumble on his techniques of imbuing images with feeling. For him this was the very object of art. It is not so much that Dickens was "aware that his flair is the distinctive fantasy which he casts over everything," [35] but rather that this distinctive fantasy is the desideratum of his every effort.

It was his duty as an artist. For, above all, he wanted an active response from the reader. So, it may be said, do all writers. But Dickens' method is founded on the belief that, in Hazlitt's words, "the heart is the centre of my moral system, and the senses and the understanding are its two extremities." [36] In striving to create a literary object which would excite the reader's heart, no man could always succeed, but Dickens was continually forging new techniques, continually widening and deepening his characterizations, tightening his plot construction, extending the scope of his language, in order to penetrate to the reader's fancy, which in turn would create ekstasis, thus extending sympathy beyond the self.

I use the word "penetrate" because Dickens knew that men surround themselves with the idols of the cave, the theatre, and the tribe in order to dominate the world around them and secure their own sense of well-being. Podsnap is the epitome of this subtly proprietary relation to the world, but it is shown by scores of Dickens' characters, for example Dombey, Murdstone, Magwich, and John Jasper. Rather than engaging fruitfully in harmony or mutuality in the world, such characters wish to "know" and thus to assimilate the world. This desire is of course born in fear—fear of the threatening aspect of the world. Most men have to some degree what R. D. Laing calls "ontological insecurity." If they succeed in distorting the world, they have to their own satisfaction dissolved the otherness of the world. They have reduced it and absorbed it. Like the schizoids who develop what Laing calls a "false-self system," they retire from the world, substituting their own notions for the world. "The isolation of the self is a corollary, therefore," says Laing, "of the need to be in control." [37] To Dickens, this retirement and its sponsoring urge to control require primarily the silencing of the heart, the aborting of feelings. Consequently, because, as Hazlitt says, in knowing "what one man feels, we so far know what a thousand feel in the sanctuary of their being," the goal of art is to make men feel. If we feel, Dickens believed, we cannot elude our essential mutuality with others.

Feeling is for Dickens always a prelude to action, that is, interaction with the world. As action without feeling—as in "Telescopic Philanthropy" in *Bleak House*—is only a mask for manipulation by the self, so genuine feeling manifests itself as interaction between souls. Therefore, ignoring the realists, the utilitarians, and the apologists for established religion, Dickens sought to make men better by presenting in his art vivid representations which would stir their fancies and, in the consequent ekstasis, reestablish their links with the world. His fiction can be wholly understood on no other ground. As an artist, his duty was "to show to all, that in all familiar things, even in those which are repellent on the surface, there is Romance enough, if we will find it out." This "fantastic fidelity," as Forster termed it, may perhaps satisfy neither the realists nor the mythologues. But Dickens' art is addressed not to the intellectual conceptions of these schools but to the elementary faculty which every human being possesses: the fancy.

— *4* —

We have seen that the possibility of art making people better inheres for Dickens in the fancy. Through the fancy men's feelings are revived and they are thus enabled to see the interests of other men with as much warmth as they see their own interests. Essentially, for Dickens, this is "Romance." To foster Romance, Dickens sought first to engender active response; second, to create vivid parts and relate these parts so that maximum interest is generated; and third, to create a whole, organic work of art. Recollecting Dickens' first, moral, axiom, I think we may go beyond these aesthetic priorities to isolate not only the agency—fancy—by which Dickens hopes to make people better but also the consistent element in every aspect of his Romance.

It may be said that in the first aesthetic priority Dickens sought to create enticing figures of humans and situations upon the ground of our ordinary consciousness; in other words, to draw the reader's attention from his habitual perception of the world. We take interest in Aunt Betsy and Mr. Micawber because they dash our comfortable stereotyping, and so generate fresh attention. The second priority, it may be said, is to articulate action which by its significance and internal coherence stands out against the ground of the perceived world, which refuses to vouchsafe us manifest forms. The fictive world therefore becomes an alternative to and even a paradigm for the real world. The third priority contrasts with the second in the sense that, instead of providing man form where before he could perceive none, it means to give men who do not intend for the world to have form an undeniable manifestation of form. In other words, where men have so arranged their world that only Self and its instruments exist, Dickens raises up over against this solipsistic Self the figure of the Other. What I am proposing is that Dickens sought in his art to lay the imprint of the Other upon the consciousness of his readers. As the fancy is the agent, the Other is the material of that movement from Self I have called, after Sartre, ekstasis.

The first mode of otherness derives from that with which this essay has been primarily concerned: the choice and treatment of fictive parts. The fact that we do not readily identify (to use this inaccurate but common term) with Dickens' characters but rather enjoy them suggests the way Dickens induces us to receive otherness. To identify, after all, is not to experience ekstasis: it is to absorb others into the system of the

Self. But, in taking Sam Weller and Mrs. Gamp into our hearts we never believe that we absorb them. They have been called caricatures, distortions of reality; the truth is that they are effective simply because they cannot be readily fitted into our usual perceptual categories, and so explode our own caricature of the world. Caricature, when made a charge against Dickens, reveals more about the critic than the character. (Of course some fictional caricatures are bland and fit into our a priori schematizations.) Furthermore, we do not tend to take kindly to those which do not fit because we are being made to re-view, literally, our world. But the pleasure of fiction induces us to open ourselves. We do not so much make Weller and Gamp ours as they make us theirs.

There is another side to the effect of this first mode of otherness— as there is to each of the three modes. Although we must "decreate" our perceptual forms, we are also being fascinated, enchanted, by the vivid presentational phenomena. Therefore, while we momentarily recoil from the pain of new vision, we are attracted beyond it to, won to a new interest in, the world, which had heretofore been merely assigned a passive role in what Beckett calls "the boredom of living." Dickens is, after all, in this mode simply revealing an aspect of the world, showing "to all, that in all familiar things, there is Romance enough"—he is simply, on the one hand, making familiar things wonderful again, and on the other making us comfortable with the threatening world so that we do not recoil from it entirely. The clay-given mandate, after all, speaks in the voice of fear and in the language of the ego. By removing causes for fear and by eliciting a projection of our interest, Dickens hopes to quiet the clay-given mandate in us.

The second mode of otherness is that of the fictive *whole* over against the appearance of our world. Here there are again two distinct effects. This alternative world provides us, first, with an escape from the world whose "brutal Fact" threatens to overwhelm us. We never long doubt that the fiction is fiction, but, after the respite provided by our reading, we are able, Dickens felt, to renew our wonder at and interest in the world, or, at the very least, to renew our strength for our struggle against the influence of the world on our spirit, to resist being absorbed into worldliness.

The second effect is that the alternative world seems complete and coherent: during the experience of the work of art we are given substantive cause for Hope: the world, implies the work of art by its very being, may not be as inchoate as quotidian experience often leaves us believing. We derive therefore a new willingness to encounter the world again, a new faith that the machinery of necessity which the world seems to support requires only the proper context to be melted away, and that the free spirit of man is the ultimate fact in the world. Art, we may hence say, reconciles man to his world. Dickens in laying out the ground plan for contributions to the frame story entitled "The Wreck of the 'Golden Mary' " has perhaps summarized best what it is art may do for man-in-the-world: "The captain remembering that the narration of stories had been attended with great success on former occasions of similar disasters, in preventing the shipwrecked persons' minds from dwelling on the horrors of their condition, proposed that such as could tell anything to the rest, should tell it. So the stories are introduced." [38] Thus, the work of art is an alternative psychic environment for shipwrecked modern man.

The third mode of otherness is the novel as a whole work of art with, as Cassirer calls it, its own teleological form. It may be that the upsurge of the original Self and Other is simultaneous; but, after the Self has deprived the world of otherness, this must be resurrected by art. Suzanne K. Langer says of fiction, "Virtual life, as literature represents it, is always a self-contained form, a unity of experience, in which every element is organically related to every other," and, she goes on to point out, "actual experience has no such closed form." [39] Such organic form is not as susceptible to being reduced to comfortable notions as the actual world seems to be; it is more resistant to the categorizations with which we insulate and isolate the Self. Whereas the second mode of otherness functions to restore man to his world, this third mode functions to preserve the world from man. It is the organic wholeness of a work of art which defeats man's rationalizing habits; no work will be exhausted by any system the reader attempts to analyze it by; the work stubbornly resists us, and forces us at last to admit that we are confronting a thing which, like another human being, limits us and thus preserves us from drowning in our phantastical omnipotence, a phantasy that robs us of all power to operate in the concrete world. [40]

Because aesthetic satisfaction depends upon the degree to which we have taken in the "significant form," we are incited by our very desire for aesthetic pleasure to take in and harbor this otherness. Pleasure in art, Cassirer advises, is "not the enjoyment of things but the enjoyment of forms." But since this is a form of the Other, our pleasure, paradoxically, entails the dissolution of our own manufactured and fail-safed "reality" and the movement of the Self out of this false selfhood into a fresh reality of relationship with an Other. The very act of adjusting to a new form may cause movement of the spirit. The individual is confronted by an alien but undeniable object, which demands new relationships, new orientations; thus, in Beckett's terminology, a "perilous zone in the life" of the reader is created, from which a more valid self can grow.

It may be objected that these modes of otherness are factitious, that they are not more than hallucinations and so—as G. H. Lewes followed Taine in suggesting of Dickens' effects—symptoms of madness.

If so, they are of course mere nothings. As such, it follows they cannot bring about true sympathy. Phenomenologically—as we saw Hunt point out above—fiction is as real as the data of sense-perception because it moves us as much. Moreover, if the novel is an hallucination, it is not that of the reader. Therefore he is exposed to that which he is not.

After all, as we have noted, the world itself is often ground down into one's own conceptions of it and absolutely deprived of otherness. For example, to Mr. Podsnap the world, like the arts, conforms to his expectations: "Elsewise, the world got up at eight, shaved close at a quarter past, breakfasted at nine, went to the city at ten, came home at half-past five, and dined at seven" (*Our Mutual Friend,* 128). If the elements of the world, including the arts, do not conform to Podsnap's expectations of them, he flourishes them away. But a novel which has moved the fancy succeeds, paradoxically, in establishing its irreducible otherness, for the fancy is not stimulated by that which the reader has already known and committed to the possession of the Self. Even a realistic copying of the world was for Dickens simply more of what everyone knew. What the artist must therefore give the reader is what the reader is not and has not: the Other.

In experiencing the aspects of otherness that is the content, the form, and the being of the novel, man is prepared to apprehend Kant's categorical imperative. When art defies our instrumentalizing, men are opened at last to the possibility of sympathy, and with this to *concrete* freedom in the world. Thus, in providing us with "Romance," Dickens is providing us with the experience of different modes of the Other. Here we have come full circle: the essential way in which Dickens helps to make people better is his creation of what he calls "Romance," of *the novel as Other.*

H. L. Knight

DICKENS AND MRS. STOWE

THOUGH MRS. STOWE was a Dickens reader some fifteen years before she wrote *Uncle Tom's Cabin*,[1] it was only upon receipt of her novel that Dickens became aware of the American writer-reformer. A chronicle of their subsequent relations, along with hitherto un-published Dickens letters, has been presented by Harry Stone.[2] His article sets forth what he describes as "a curious and revealing literary and personal relationship." In following the relations of Dickens and Mrs. Stowe as Stone has traced them, we quickly arrive at some problems which deserve further exploration.

Stone begins by reprinting the sole extant fragment of Dickens' 1852 compliments to Mrs. Stowe:[3] "I have read your book with the deepest interest and sympathy, and admire more than I can express to you, both the generous feeling which inspired it, and the admirable power with which it is executed." Stone next recounts the unfortunate consequences of an 1853 pamphlet by Lord Denman which compared *Uncle Tom's Cabin* to *Bleak House* on the question of slavery and the slave trade. Briefly, this pamphlet suggested that Mrs. Stowe, the greater author because the greater reformer, had come out in the open to do what the fashionable but insincere Dickens would not do: attack the problem of slavery for the evil everyone knew it to be. Denman went so far as to call Dickens an enemy of abolitionism because of his carica-tured do-gooder, Mrs. Jellyby, in *Bleak House*. Dickens tried to correct such an impression, without actually answering the attack, by publish-ing an article on "North American Slavery"[4] in *Household Words*. Den-man attacked this article as well, labeling it, in Stone's words, "unrealis-tic and insincere."

Following this episode, Dickens retreated somewhat from his initial enthusiasm for *Uncle Tom's Cabin*. He confided to a friend[5] that he thought Mrs. Stowe had "appropriated" material from his own work. Mrs. Stowe visited England soon thereafter, personally meeting

[43

Dickens and his wife. Dickens' first open hostility toward Mrs. Stowe resulted from her publication of an account of this visit.[6]

As Stone points out, Mrs. Stowe was complimentary in her references to the Dickenses—especially Catherine Dickens—but Dickens chose to take offense. I think Stone is right when he concludes that "Dickens, already unhappy in his marriage, no doubt had reasons for differing with Mrs. Stowe's analysis of his wife's character."

Ten years later Dickens exploded in rage against Mrs. Stowe over her publication in the *Atlantic Monthly* [7] of an account of Lord Byron's separation from his wife which accused the poet of an incestuous relationship with his half-sister, Augusta Leigh. Stone makes the following analysis of this rage: "Thinking about [Mrs. Stowe] he could recall her sudden and challenging popularity, her connection with Lord Denman's damaging attacks upon him and his art, her triumphant progress through England, her unfeminine crusading vigor, her gossipy and 'moony' references to Catherine's size and his youth. And now with her distasteful public exhumation of a great writer's personal secrets, he could hardly escape adding to the unpleasant picture which already clustered about her." [8] A closer look at Dickens' possible motives for suggesting that Mrs. Stowe had appropriated from his own work and an analysis of the content of Mrs. Stowe's essay on Lord Byron yield an even broader understanding of the significance of Harriet Beecher Stowe for Charles Dickens.

In an 1854 letter to Mrs. Richard Watson,[9] Dickens noted "many points in *Uncle Tom's Cabin* very admirably done." But he had a good-humored complaint about the American authoress: "She (I mean Mrs. Stowe) is a leetle unscrupulous in the appropriatin' way. I seem to see a writer with whom I am very intimate (and whom nobody can possibly admire more than myself) peeping very often through the thinness of the paper. Further I descry the ghost of Mary Barton, and the very palpable mirage of a scene in The Children of the Mist; but in spite of this, I consider the book a fine one, with a great and gallant purpose in it and worthy of its reputation." The specific references are to Mrs. Gaskell's *Mary Barton* (1848) and to portions of Sir Walter Scott's *A Legend of Montrose* (1819).[10] The veiled reference seems, from both tone and context, to be to Dickens himself. Harry Stone has asserted this identity as an incontestable fact.[11]

But the question of influence is not the point of repeating these jibes at Mrs. Stowe's sources. Rather, the issue is one of moral sympathies. *Uncle Tom's Cabin* was a work Dickens admired for its social efficacy. His admiration led him to offer it every benefit of the doubt on the question of its artistic merit.

Eventually, the public hue and cry over the novel—and the unfortunate insistence on comparing it with Dickens' work—led him to back away from his initial enthusiasm for the book. Over the years, a series of accidental overlaps in the lives of Dickens and Mrs. Stowe seems to have led him toward a personal distaste for her (as evidenced by his eventually reviling her).

Behind this literary gossip lies a problem basic to Dickens' life: the tension between a veneer of moral compliance and the actuality of unconventional attitudes and adjustments. What makes Dickens' and Mrs. Stowe's relationship particularly interesting and illuminating is that it started out so well, with such a firm identity of concerns and intents, and ended up so dismally. As we shall see, the conflict is revealing about Dickens as a person and about the relations of English and American intellectuals where moral issues are concerned.

For these reasons, tracing the similarity Dickens thought he saw between *Uncle Tom's Cabin* and his own writing will serve to show how really close in sentiment and conviction the two writers were when they first came to mutual notice. We shall here compare the death of Eva in *Uncle Tom's Cabin* with what was surely one of the best known scenes from Dickens' novels at the time Mrs. Stowe was writing *Uncle Tom's Cabin*.[12]

In making such a comparison we must bear in mind George Gissing's observation that "Little Nell struck readers not only as pathetic, but as fresh and original, which indeed she was; overfamiliarity robs us of the delight which was inspired by a new vein of fiction, discovered and worked by a master spirit." [13] Overfamiliarity has also created the false impression that the life and death of angelic maidens such as Nell was the gratuitous stock-in-trade of English and American writers throughout the nineteenth century. This is simply not true. Dickens created a new fictional type in Nell. If Mrs. Stowe's novel of a decade later contains an almost identical maiden, true in every detail to the Dickens formula, then, if one is unwilling to say with surety that Mrs. Stowe got her from Dickens, one must at least be willing to admit that the two writers were remarkably similar in certain of their thoughts and feelings.

In reducing the death of Nell to a "formula" there is no intent to devalue the work. It is assumed that Dickens' creation has as much right to the accolade "inspired" as does any other artistic creation. The sole motive for this structural analysis is to give some objective shape to the comparison with Mrs. Stowe's scene.

The death of Nell can be reduced to seven essential elements: 1. the child's premonition of imminent death; 2. the waning of fear and increase of joy at the prospect; 3. a transitional state in which the child experiences some sort of transcendental awareness; 4. arrival at assurance of salvation; 5. concern for the salvation of others; 6. acceptance by the community as a quasi-saint; and 7. a heartening rationalization of the death by the narrator. Analysis of the texts reveals a remarkable similarity, primarily of structure, but also of imagery, between the two scenes matched to this grid.

In the *Old Curiosity Shop,* Nell's premonition of death is her intense reaction to seeing the house in which she is to die. Nell describes it as "a place to live and learn to die in!" We learn that in her new village home, Nell habituates the graveyard and church crypts, pondering the mystery of death. At such times, she is "filled . . . with deep and thoughtful feelings, but with none of terror or alarm. A change had been gradually stealing over her in the time of her loneliness and sorrow."

Nell soon loses what Dickens describes as "an involuntary chill, . . . a momentary feeling akin to fear." She seems to accept the shortness of her remaining time in her wistful assurance that she will not be likely to see Spring again. When she is not caring for her debilitated grandfather, Nell's time is occupied in conversation with the aged sexton and an infant boy. The sexton is a foil for Nell's ethereal focus on cosmic time, as contrasted with his mundane and ephemeral preoccupations. He is also a partner, along with the schoolmaster, in Nell's musings over the Bible. In her contemplative retreat, Nell gains an assurance of her own salvation which is symbolized by her looking down on the village from the church tower. This assurance is verbalized by the infant boy in his tearful pleading with her to postpone becoming an angel. Nell's concern with the salvation of others is perhaps most succinctly expressed in her comment on the noisy village boys, released from the classroom and frolicking past the church, "It's a good thing. . . . I am very glad they pass the church."

As her end draws near, all the residents of Nell's community—but especially the lowly—share the conviction that she is soon to be an angel. She receives deferential respect and affection each day, but it is intensified on Sunday when she goes to church. After her death, Dickens assures us that, painful to us though such losses may be, they purify and reorient the world of the living.

Little Eva's premonition of death is handled by explicit exposition: "What is it that sometimes speaks in the soul so calmly, so clearly, that its earthly time is short? Is it the secret instinct of decaying nature, or the soul's impulsive throb, as immortality draws on? Be it what it may, it rested in the heart of Eva, a calm, sweet, prophetic certainty that Heaven was near." Should there be any doubt as to how the child responds to this knowledge, Eva speaks directly to the point: "No papa . . . don't deceive yourself!—I am *not* any better, I know it perfectly well,—and I am going, before long. I am not nervous,—I am not low-spirited. If it were not for you, papa, and my friends, I should be perfectly happy. I want to go,—I long to go!"

Despite this seeming readiness, Eva experiences a transitional period of preparation for death. It is at this time that Mrs. Stowe emphasizes Eva's closeness to Uncle Tom by scenes of their Bible reading. It is at this point also that Eva converts Topsy to Harriet Beecher Stowe's particular understanding of Christianity as the religion of Love.[14] Indeed, Mrs. Stowe turned her father's Calvinism on its head when she depicted Eva's assurance of salvation.

> "Dear papa," said the child, . . . "how I wish we could go together!"
> "Where, dearest?" said St. Clare [Eva's father].
> "To our Saviour's home; it's so sweet and peaceful there—it is all so loving there!"

It is this same assurance that informs and supports Eva on her deathbed when she preaches to the assembled slaves: "I want you to remember that there is a beautiful world, where Jesus is. I am going there, and you can go there. . . . But, if you want to go there, you must . . . be Christians. You must remember that each one of you can become angels, and be angels forever. . . . Jesus will help you." Though these may seem cliches, kinds of melodramatic religiosity, to the modern reader, to the Christian reader of mid-nineteenth-century England and America, these were controversial concepts in the tradition of such major innovators as Emerson and the British Romantics.

Eva's death scene stresses her acceptance by the humble slaves as a saint, and reinforces that impression with her handing out her own relics (locks of her hair). When she finally passes on, there can be little doubt in the reader's mind as to the meaning of her death. Eva and Tom have discussed it earlier, eliminating any question of interpretation.

> "Uncle Tom, . . . I can understand why Jesus *wanted* to die for us."
> "Why, Miss Eva?"
> "Because I've felt so, too. . . . I can't tell you; but when I saw those poor creatures . . . and a great many other times, I've felt that I would be glad to die, if my dying could stop all this misery. I *would* die for them, Tom, if I could."

The similarities of imagery are more generalized than those of structure. In point of fact, Mrs. Stowe tended toward flower imagery when she resorted to such subtleties at all, while Dickens, in *The Old Curiosity Shop,* was still working his early vein of weather imagery. The one image pervading both novels is the angel. But this is not original with Dickens, nor does it take any explication to make clear its function.

What is clearer upon examination is the unique, and yet similar, intent with which each writer has constructed the maiden's deathly aura and the scene of her demise.

Each author carefully constructs the room in which the girl will die. Dickens presents a gothic cottage, while Mrs. Stowe presents a French-import boudoir altered to a child's taste and a semitropic climate. But both stress the significance of the scene in terms of a change going on within the maiden who is to die.

Dickens tells us that when Nell was in her cottage home, "The child looked around her, with that solemn feeling with which we contemplate the work of ages that have become but drops of water in the great ocean of eternity." Mrs. Stowe assures us that after Eva became bedridden in the room so carefully pictured for us, "Those little eyes never opened, in the morning light, without falling on something which suggested to the heart soothing and beautiful thoughts."

Nell experiences a gratuitous purification in her cottage, gratuitous in the sense that she has been described throughout the novel as the apotheosis of virtue. Nevertheless, Dickens tells us, "With failing strength and heightened resolution, there had sprung up a purified and altered mind; there had grown in her bosom blessed thoughts and hopes, which are the portion of few but the weak and drooping." Part of what Gissing labeled the freshness and originality of Nell was this return to the primitive Christian association of oppression and salvation, so different from the muscular Christianity of an industrializing society Dickens was to castigate for both its secular and its religious callousness. The tension of city-versus-country in *The Old Curiosity Shop* is given its meaning by this portrayal of Nell. The weaker and more harassed she becomes, the closer she is to the ideal of Christian virtue.

Mrs. Stowe used this same device for making her most telling attack on slavery. She sidestepped all Southern defenses which insisted that only the daily experience of plantation life qualified one for a discussion of the slave system by presenting a dying child, isolated from the world, who *knows*, with the same surety with which she knows she is to die, that the system is wrong.

> She felt, too, for those fond, faithful servants, to whom she was as daylight and sunshine. Children do not usually generalize; but Eva was an uncommonly mature child, and the things that she had witnessed had fallen, one by one, into the depths of her thoughtful, pondering heart. She had vague longings to do something for them,—to bless and save not only them, but all in their condition,—longings that contrasted with the feebleness of her little frame.

Here too, the equation of weakness and rightness is the basic component of the image. The dying child becomes, to use Emerson's phrase, a transparent eyeball through which the reader can see some phase of life significant to the author who presents her.

Both novels reveal a basic tension in the authors' world view. Dickens received an inheritance of Puritan rigidity and Romantic effusion just as important as the collection of eighteenth-century novels which have worked their way into every study of Dickens since they first appeared in *David Cooperfield*. Dickens could accept neither Milton nor Shelley, though his intellectual development bears the impress of both traditions. Dickens shaped a peculiarly Victorian mind to the extent that he helped create an English attitude falling midway between these two extreme—but characteristic—national views.

Mrs. Stowe was also caught between two extremes: Jonathan Edwards and Lord Byron. Kenneth Lynn's essay on *Uncle Tom's Cabin* traces in detail her struggles against both the doctrine of the elect and her fatal attraction to the immoral poet. What Lynn sees as the product of this struggle is *Uncle Tom's Cabin*, only secondarily an attack on slavery, primarily a sermon on the religion of Love. It is certainly true that Mrs. Stowe used her literary skills, as seen in Eva's death, to insist that intellectualization is useless where the true intuitions of love have reached a judgment. This is a doctrine of the sort to which Dickens too was susceptible, even though his mature period is characterized by a more sophisticated approach to such questions. As the recent television dramatization of *David Copperfield* has David conclude, "It is not enough to be loving." However, at the time of writing *The Old Curiosity Shop*, Dickens was neither in his sophisticated phase nor greatly distanced from his work.

The Old Curiosity Shop was written out of desperate need—need to somehow heal over the gaping wound of Mary Hogarth's death. The religion of Love, as it appears in Mrs. Stowe's novel, is the sort of construct which allowed Dickens to regain his hold on the threads of his life. When he read her novel, ten years after his own ordeal, Dickens must have felt a sympathy which transcended any consideration of Mrs. Stowe's having borrowed from his stock of fictional effects. The important thing was that she had spoken out against an abuse with which he too was greatly concerned, and that she had done so from a point of view with which he could sympathize. Such sympathy was, however, short-lived.

In part, Dickens' growing dislike of Mrs. Stowe marks his own maturity. His questioning of man's life in the world went beyond the sureties on which Mrs. Stowe's novel depended. Her maturation took her in a different direction from his. Accenting their differences, and making for repeated irritation, the reappearance of Mrs. Stowe in Dickens' life came at crucial times, and each time with some exacerbating, though inadvertent, criticism.

Because he had initially responded so warmly to her moral sympathies—and because he never completely convinced himself that those standards weren't after all the right ones—Dickens bridled at what he saw as Mrs. Stowe's smug assurances about right and wrong. This irritation came through in his violent, and often unfair, outbursts against her. They make, as a complete story, an interesting comment on the intellectual differences between England and America.

Dickens' own intellectual development was toward moral relativism. Ironically, he arrived at his conclusions internally while his external life was consumed in playing out the role of moral arbiter for a rigidly structured social system. The Victorians who looked toward Dickens as an oracle of the hearth were quite certain that there was a hard-and-fast rule to govern every situation in life. Dickens himself (especially in his later life when he was secretly keeping a mistress) knew this wasn't precisely true. But he only said so covertly and in ways not apparent to his general reader. Like many English intellectuals of his day and after, Dickens was beginning to see the question of morality as perhaps more accurately a question of sensibility.

Mrs. Stowe was also moving away from a rigid system of assessing life's problems, but she was doing so in the belief that the system itself was immoral. If the explicit message of *Uncle Tom's Cabin* is that the South's slave system is inhuman and therefore immoral, the implicit lesson of her religion of Love is that Calvin's election system is inhuman and therefore immoral. Mrs. Stowe never concluded that a question of morals might be a question of sensibilities, though she did seem to conclude that a difference of sensibilities might be at the root of a problem of moral alignment. Thus Mrs. Stowe's discussion of the Byron marriage, with its tone of moral assurance and its assessments of absolute right and absolute wrong, must have rankled Dickens as he evaluated the complexity of motives and perceptions creating the problem over which Mrs. Stowe's prose glided. Ironically, Mrs. Stowe capped her defense of Lady Byron with the suggestion that America housed a moral superiority not completely understood in England: "There may be family reasons in England which prevent Lady Byron's friends from speaking; but Lady Byron has an American name and an American existence, and reverence for pure womanhood is, we think, a national characteristic of the American; and, so far as this country is concerned, we feel that the public should have this refutation of the slanders of the Countess Guiccioli's book." [15]

To read Mrs. Stowe's "The True Story of Lady Byron's Life" (1869) with anything like the associations Dickens himself may have made, we must keep in mind the now well established facts of Dickens' personal life. It is important to stress that these facts were not available to Mrs. Stowe, that they were indeed among the best-kept secrets of the nineteenth century. Despite the publicity surrounding Dickens' separation from his wife, it was not until the posthumous publication of Kate Dickens Perugini's memoirs [16] that the popular image of Charles Dickens as a paragon of domestic virtue and gentle humor received any serious challenge. The subsequent gossip about Dickens' affair with Ellen Lawless Ternan, and the hypothesized 'connections between this liaison and the collapse of the Dickens marriage, were not finally grounded in incontestable fact until seventy-two years after Dickens' death.[17]

It was during the last year of his life, physically ill and emotionally overwrought, that Dickens read Mrs. Stowe's highly suggestive article revealing the scandal concealed in the marital problems of Lord and Lady Byron. By this time, Dickens seems to have grown disillusioned about women, love, and the possibility of finding happiness in a romantic relationship.

Mrs. Stowe began her essay by claiming a social motive beyond the vindication of a dear friend. She wished to thwart a revival of Byron-worship which would do "its best to bring the youth of America once more under the power of that brilliant, seductive genius from which it was hoped they had escaped." While she had some hope of saving the young, she could only lament the sway Byron held over the minds of the older generation—especially the ladies. Mrs. Stowe stressed that while Byron was "setting at defiance every principle of morality and decorum," women all over Europe (by which Mrs. Stowe meant fashionable, intellectual Europe) were seeking "the conversion of this brilliant prodigal son." Though Mrs. Stowe assured her reader that this effort "reflects the greatest credit upon the faith of the sex," her account strongly implied that it reflected little credit on its common sense. Unfortunately, Mrs. Stowe's example of a misguided woman seeking Lord Byron's "conversion" was Dickens' intimate friend, Lady Blessington.

During the years of her friendship with Dickens, Lady Blessington lived at Gore House with Count D'Orsay, her stepdaughter's estranged husband. Rumor labeled this relationship as the same quasi-incestuous adultery of which Dickens and his sister-in-law, Georgina Hogarth, had been accused. Lady Blessington was among the first to receive Dickens as an intimate in the *haut monde*, and her unusual circumstances put Catherine's accompanying out of the question.[18]

The implication of Mrs. Stowe's comments on Lady Blessington is that this aristocratic woman of the world was the dupe of Byron's diabolical attractiveness. To the degree to which Dickens took comfort in Lady Blessington's tacit approval of his private life, he must have felt discomfort at seeing her depicted as anything less than discerning. To suggest that an attractive but immoral man might win her approval was to suggest that a man who won her approval might be attractive but immoral.

Mrs. Stowe's evidence of Byron's manipulating Lady Blessington was a letter, written by Byron to his wife—but never sent. This Mrs. Stowe printed in its entirety in her article. Her evaluation of this letter was that it "was a nice little dramatic performance, composed simply with the view of acting on the sympathies of Lady Blessington and Byron's numerous female admirers." Much of what Byron said of his marriage in that letter echoed what Dickens had said of his own marriage.

Lord Byron wrote that he and Miss Milbank "made a bitter mistake" in marrying, "but now it is over, and irrevocably so." Their antipathies he put down as irresolvable: "For, at thirty-three on my part and a few years less on yours, though it is no very extended period of life, still it is one when the habits and thought are generally so formed as to admit of no modification; and as we could not agree when younger, we should with difficulty do so now." Byron saw their only possibility for equanimity in total separation: "I am violent but not malignant; for only fresh provocations can awaken my resentments. . . . Whether the offense has been solely on my side, or reciprocal, or on yours chiefly, I have ceased to reflect upon any but two things, viz. that you are the mother of my child, and that we shall never meet again."

Compare Dickens, writing in confidence, first to John Forster, and then to Miss Burdett Coutts. To Forster, Dickens confided, "Poor Catherine and I are not made for each other, and there is no help for it. It is not only that she makes me uneasy and unhappy, but that I make her so too—and much more so; . . . we are strangely ill-assorted for the bond there is between us. God knows she would have been a thousand times happier if she had married another kind of man, and that her avoidance of this destiny would have been at least equally good for us both." Like Byron, Dickens felt these antipathies to be irreconcilable—even if a temporary illness were to conceal them: "Exactly the same incompatibility would arise the moment I was well again; and nothing on earth could make her understand me, or suit us to each other. Her temperament will not go with mine."

To Miss Coutts, Dickens wrote, "I believe that no two people were ever created, with such an impossibility of interest, sympathy, confidence, sentiment, tender union of any kind between them, as there is between my wife and me. It is an immense misfortune to her—it is an immense misfortune to me—but Nature has put an insurmountable barrier between us, which never in this world can be thrown down."

Ironically, the policy of public disclosure which Mrs. Stowe deplored in Lord Byron's handling of his marital difficulties is both the policy Dickens himself followed in separating from Catherine and the aspect of Mrs. Stowe's revelations about the Byron marriage which most offended him. Stone tells us that "from his youth Dickens had set himself in sternfaced opposition to those who dug irreverently into the private lives of great literary figures. He castigated the Ballantynes for challenging Lockhart's interpretation of Scott's financial dealings; he trembled lest scholars ferret out the secrets of Shakespeare's domestic life; he spoke with open disgust of the 'unconscious coxcomb' Boswell and compared him to a loathsome jackal." [19] In September 1860, Dickens burned his twenty-two-year accumulation of letters and papers. In a personal letter, he was explicit about his reason for this: "Daily seeing improper uses made of confidential letters in the addressing of them to a public audience that have no business with them, I . . . not long ago . . . burnt every letter I possessed." [20]

Yet irreverent he had certainly been in publishing the secrets of his domestic life with Catherine, and—intentional or not—improper use had most certainly been made of the confidential letter about her first published in the *New York Tribune*. Dickens must have seen some similarity to his own tactics in those of Byron which Mrs. Stowe condemned as predicated upon his wife's silence. Mrs. Stowe was unequivocal in her disgust with what she saw as a one-sided whitewash: "When he discussed her faults publicly it was when public opinion had gone against him, and when he had discovered that her fidelity and mercy, her silence and magnanimity, might be relied on, so that he was at full liberty to make his part good, as far as she was concerned." Perhaps it was this unintended reproach which occasioned Dickens' violent reaction upon first reading the article ("Wish Mrs. Stowe was in the pillory") [21] and his subsequent comments about her to his friend Macready.

> May you be as disgusted with Mrs. Stowe as I am! There is a strong article upon her posthumous scandal, in the current Quarterly. Her 'facts' are as the stock in trade of the old china shop was to the dancing bull. [22]

> I wonder whether you have taken much interest, over yonder, in the Byron scandal! It seems to me that to knock Mrs. Beecher Stowe in the head, and confiscate everything about it in a great international bonfire to be simultaneously lighted over the whole civilized earth, would be the only pleasant way of putting an end to the business. [23]

Mrs. Stowe touched on another theme as well, more secret than the issue of publicity and one which Dickens was even less able to deal with objectively: his feelings for Mary Hogarth. Dickens' love for Mary Hogarth had idealized her purity and virginity. But his nervous collapse upon her death suggests a certain degree of guilt for the closeness with which he approached stronger and more specific desires.

That is, when one has a secret desire for another person—but the desire is a taboo punishable by death—then if the object of desire dies, it is easy to feel guilty about having been the secret cause of that death. Dickens was unable to accept Mary as dead for some time, dreaming a nightly reunion with her. He re-created his own version of her life and death in Nell of *The Old Curiosity Shop*. This allowed him to live with the memory of Mary, but it did not weaken her hold over his perceptions. She is the model for much that is fine in Dickens' women and perhaps as well the source of their unreality. Mary is the positive extreme of a polarity which has the author's mother at its negative end, and between which all the women in Dickens' novels fall. (Perhaps it was Mary whom Dickens sought, and failed to find, in Ellen.)

The other side of this perception is, of course, Dickens' guilt. Characters like Nell are often pursued by demons of sexuality like Quilp. When Dickens made his first major reconstruction of his own life, in *David Copperfield,* he presented not only the formula pursuit of Agnes Wickfield by Uriah Heep, but also the more lifelike and familiar pursuit of Little Em'ly by Steerforth. By the time of the second major reconstruction, *Great Expectations,* these issues had become confused to the point where sexual demons (Orlick, Bentley Drummle) pursue unsympathetic women, more like Dickens' mother than like Mary (Mrs. Gargery, Estella). The subtext of this transition could be that as Dickens matured he began to see the "quest for Mary" as a quest for real girls instead of abstractions of virtue. In doing so he might well have confused his earlier compartmentalization of sex and virtue. These changes would, however, renew whatever guilt he was feeling at the time of Mary's death.

Such a progression might have been part of the disillusionment about women mentioned earlier. Lizzie Hexam in *Our Mutual Friend* and Rosa Budd in *Edwin Drood* are cast from the original Mary-mold, but they lack the purity of percept characteristic of earlier heroines. That is, they see evil more clearly in those around them because it resonates with something dormant, but implicit, in themselves. Dickens' difficulty was that in pitting these heroines against villains more and more like himself (Bradley Headstone, the self-made teacher in *Our Mutual Friend; John Jasper,* the choirmaster in *Edwin Drood*) Dickens suggested a sort of contamination of the good woman by the sort of "brilliant, seductive genius" Mrs. Stowe warned against in her exposé of Byron.

Mrs. Stowe had loved Byron's poetry in her youth, but recoiled from his immorality as an adult. A youthful Dickens had dedicated himself to purity in Mary's name upon her death. A mature Dickens may have sensed something incestuous in his dedication to Mary. Such self-doubts may have been the source of his irritation in reading Mrs.

Stowe's inflamed revelation of what she took to be her irrefutable proof of Byron's incestuous relationship with Augusta. "From the height at which he might have been happy as the husband of a noble woman," Mrs. Stowe wrote, "he fell into the depths of a secret adulterous intrigue with a blood relation, so near in consanguinity that discovery must have been utter ruin and expulsion from civilized society." Dickens too had fallen from the possibility of being happy in marriage to "a secret adulterous intrigue." Ellen was no blood relation, but the matrix for his feelings for this girl was formed by his devotion to his wife's sister. Though Mary was also no blood relation, Mrs. Stowe's emphasis here is on the social consequences of such a union. Had Dickens actually embarked on an affair with Mary and been discovered, the consequences would have been the same for them as would have been discovery for Byron and Augusta.

Mrs. Stowe placed the blame entirely on Byron. In comparing him with his own Manfred, she described his crime as "an incestuous passion which has been the destruction of his sister for this life and the life to come." Beneath Mrs. Stowe's essay on Byron's marital misconduct is the clear message that any man who breaks the marriage vow and indulges himself with another woman is guilty of betraying himself, his wife, the other woman, and God. Mrs. Stowe repeated a comment of Lady Byron which employs an image pervading the deaths of Little Nell and Little Eva. She was asked, "O, how could you love him!" and she replied, "My dear, there was the angel in him." Mrs. Stowe's comment: "It is in us all." For Mrs. Stowe, and for the Dickens who read her essay, it is this angel within whom our transgressions betray.

The source of his guilt was not, of course, that Dickens secretly believed Catherine to possess all the virtue, brilliance, and nobility Mrs. Stowe attributed to Lady Byron. But Dickens' Victorian British understanding of questions of good and evil was still tied to the question of appearances. In his very fictional working out of the theme of discrepancies between the appearance of virtue and its actual existence lies the implicit assumption that in most cases of daily life there exists a causal relationship between appearance and actuality. Without such a given there would have been no issue for his fiction to debate. In her essay, Mrs. Stowe employed a rhetoric of condemnation to attack a man who had set aside his wife and then behaved wantonly with other women. The Dickens who read this essay knew himself to have put aside his wife, the mother of his children, and to have subsequently entered into an unsanctioned union with a girl who had been virtuous and virginal before encountering him (or so, at least, he may well have been led to believe). With the exception of Dr. Strong in *David Copperfield*—the exception proving the rule—older men in Dickens' fiction, and generally in the fiction of the period, related to young girls in only one of two ways: as older brother or father-figure (the good way); or as lecherous seducer (the bad way).

If he received no public condemnation for his affair with Ellen, his very secrecy about it suggests that he feared such attacks. He certainly received a good deal of criticism, both private and public, for his treatment of Catherine during and after the separation. Though intellectually he may not have made any connection between Mrs. Stowe's revelations about Byron and his own guilt about Catherine and Ellen, emotionally he must have responded to sallies such as "Some such hour always must come for strong, decided natures irrevocably pledged, one to the service of good and the other to the slavery of evil. . . . The presence of all-pitying purity and love was a torture to the soul possessed by the demon of evil." [24] Catherine and Dickens were hardly pledged to the opposite extremes of good and evil, and while Dickens had moments when he must indeed have felt "a torture to the soul possessed by the demon of evil," it was not because in facing Catherine he was in the "presence of all-pitying purity and love." Nevertheless, Dickens had come through a marriage in many ways like Byron's and had ended up in a relationship which his society considered, at least officially, as immoral as any of the bad poet's escapades. For Dickens the question must have been how he could escape looking totally evil when he did something even tinged with evil. What may have been even more painful was his inner questioning of the extent to which his sophistries were masking from himself a degradation easily detectable by any unpolluted person. This is certainly the issue around which he built the character of John Jasper in his final work, *Edwin Drood*.

In dealing with the practical consequences of these questions, Mrs. Stowe once again managed to strike Dickens in a sensitive area. With the single exception of the statements about his separation from Catherine, Dickens shielded his private life from public view. I think he acted on the implicit assumption that he could do the most good for a society that revered him if he sustained their belief in his own purity. Whatever inner debate Dickens may have experienced regarding his private conduct, he seems to have concluded, at least pragmatically, that these actions in no way affected his perception of social and moral issues. Mrs. Stowe's essay comes to the opposite conclusion by setting as its purpose to undermine the effectiveness of Byron's poetry by publicizing his misconduct. She puts these issues most explicitly in the mouths of Lady Byron's friends: "Some of Lady Byron's friends had proposed the question to her, *whether she had not a responsibility to society for the truth; whether she did right* to allow these writings to gain influence over the popular mind, by giving a silent consent to what she knew to be utter falsehoods." The point at issue was the forthcoming appearance of a cheap edition of Byron's work—an issue of social consequence with which Dickens could have easily identified.

In coming to his own conclusions about *Uncle Tom's Cabin,* Kenneth Lynn settles on the issue of the American family as crucial to an understanding of the novel and its phenomenal success. In short, Lynn's argument is that American civilization has been characterized by a breakdown of the traditional family structure; that this has been a difficult issue for American writers to treat openly; that Mrs. Stowe made the incredible breakthrough from escapist sentimental literature to a true Balzacian realism in this one novel. His insight, valuable in itself, helps organize the strands of this discussion of Dickens' reaction to Mrs. Stowe and her novel.

While the English mind of the last two hundred years has concerned itself, in its literature, with questions about family organization and the concomitant question of childhood and child-rearing, it has been in America that the greatest changes, in terms of social actuality, have taken place. Americans have lived through greater extremes of—and yet taken a higher moral tone regarding—a problem about which the English have been continually concerned. Mrs. Stowe's account of the total disregard for the black family unit antedates *Hard Times* by two years—years during which Dickens, writing *Bleak House,* focused on a social problem which was in the process of being ameliorated and a pattern of family entanglements suggestive of a power in blood relations which makes itself felt no matter how concealed or disregarded. No one would wish to say that *Uncle Tom's Cabin* is on a level of artistic achievement with *Bleak House,* but Dickens did face contemporary charges, from men like Lord Denman, that he was creating a sterile art in a social vacuum. This is an unfamiliar picture to the modern reader, who thinks of Dickens as the major social-reform novelist of the nineteenth century. It was a totally unacceptable self-image for Dickens himself. Mrs. Stowe, as we have seen, became the vehicle for obnoxious attacks on Dickens' sincerity. Her role in these attacks, though totally passive, colored her later writings for Dickens so that he was quick to take offense at anything he found suggestive of criticism. That Mrs. Stowe could not possibly have known the facts of Dickens' private life does not seem to have mattered.

Her complimentary mention of the Dickenses in her travel memoirs earned her Dickens' derision. Her loyal attempt to clear Lady Byron's name earned her Dickens' fury. In each case, however, Dickens was overreacting: in part because he had once identified so closely with Mrs. Stowe; in part because she accidentally managed to say things terribly implicative to his ear.

If we follow Lynn's evaluation of *Uncle Tom's Cabin* as the starting point of American Realism into our discussion of Mrs. Stowe and Dickens, we can see how much the two initially had in common. After all, no other single issue was as personally and artistically important to Dickens as the family. Through it he dealt with the issue of children and childhood as the most emotionally resonant of themes for him. His attitudes about family colored his social and aesthetic attitudes as well. Moreover, as his personal life became more complex, Dickens' feelings about what family life should be were the source of his most difficult conflicts.

Certainly, Mrs. Stowe's novel appealed to Dickens immediately for its real concern with the preservation of the family unit. In *Uncle Tom's Cabin* the greatest good is the well-fulfilled family role, the greatest evil a perversion of such a role. Mrs. Stowe was initially a kindred spirit on a most intimate level.

The emphasis soon changed, however, to Mrs. Stowe as a challenge on a most intimate level. Dickens' discomfort at her being held up to him as an example of the social reformer he was not soon became irritation as her blatant domestic smugness grated against the inadequacies of his own homelife. When Mrs. Stowe inadvertently described much of Dickens' marital problem in her essay on Lord Byron, Dickens' rage had its source in his own guilt. No rebuke so stings as that which we feel within ourselves to be true. Mrs. Stowe had come so close to Dickens in her concern for the family that when he later felt her to be accusing, he felt that accusation with a pain which only comes where the accuser lies within.

Edward J. Evans

THE ESTABLISHED SELF

The American Episodes of Martin Chuzzlewit

UNTIL VERY recently, a majority of critics would have subscribed to the view put forward by an anonymous reviewer of *Martin Chuzzlewit* in the *North British Review* of May 1845 that

> We must . . . find fault with the American scenes, clever and amusing as they are. These chapters are an unaccountable excrescence, and while they add to the bulk, mar the unity and effect of the book as a work of art. They are, in fact, a book of travels dramatized, and not in the best or most candid spirit; they form a new and more pungent edition of the American Notes, but with only the harshest censures distilled over and concentrated. They have no connexion with the rest of the story.

John Forster, in his biography of Dickens, unintentionally lends plausibility to this view by hinting that the author sent Mark and Martin off to American in order to increase the disappointingly low sales of the monthly installments by capitalizing on the popular success of his *American Notes;* [1] while the apparent vindictiveness of the attack upon American society in itself tends to indicate that Dickens is more interested in unburdening himself of some long-standing grievances than in maintaining the artistic unity of his novel.

A more careful examination of the American episodes of *Martin Chuzzlewit* leads, however, to the conclusion that these chapters, far from being an "unaccountable excrescence," are in fact an integral part of the moral and thematic framework of the novel. As Forster relates, Dickens is in this novel concerned with "the number and variety of humours and vices that have their root in selfishness." [2] Even if it is admitted that the American chapters are improvisations, it can be demonstrated that they do dramatize a number of these vices. They are an almost Swiftian attack upon a society which has given itself over to the pursuit of material wealth and which has, in the process, become a

[59

nullity, an appearance with no substance, an illusion which is often a nightmare.

To come to an understanding of Dickens' portrait of America in *Martin Chuzzlewit,* one must first comprehend his attitude toward that country both before and after his voyage there in 1842. To the radical young Dickens, America was a land of promise. Having overthrown the authority of older European societies, it held forth the promise of a "brave new world," one based upon the equality of the individual and upon social justice—of a society whose members possessed and were allowed to exercise the "inalienable" rights of life, liberty, and the pursuit of happiness. Released from the debilitating influence of an aristocratic class structure, the individual would be free to develop himself fully according to his own resources. Although Mrs. Trollope and other Tory visitors had recorded their impressions of American society in harsh terms,[3] Dickens was convinced that they could not possibly understand the workings of a society which did not possess an aristocratic ruling class. "In going to a New World," he writes, "one must for the time utterly forget, and put out of sight the Old one and bring none of its customs or observances into the comparison." [4] Needless to say, such an intellectual dissociation is nearly impossible to achieve. Moreover, his idealistic view of the kind of culture to be found in America virtually assured Dickens' disillusionment.

This disillusionment did come, but only gradually. His arrival in January of 1842 was greeted with such public adulation that the thirty-year-old author was taken aback in the most delightful fashion. "I can give you no conception" he writes to his friend Mitton, "of my welcome here. There never was a King or Emperor upon the Earth, so cheered." [5] He was lionized wherever he went, and he soon discovered that the "Boz" of *Pickwick* was the most popular author in the United States. The delight which Dickens took in this personal reception was, however, soon overcome by his own critical evaluation of what he considered to be the failure of the American dream. The promise of the new world proved illusory, and in June of that year he was more than glad to set foot once again upon his native soil.

The course and the cause of this disenchantment are graphically presented by Dickens in *American Notes,* published in the autumn of 1842. Although the initial sections of the book praise such things as the gravity and respectability of the legislative assembly at Boston and the enlightened methods of various public institutions, it is as we proceed farther into the work and deeper into the continent that Dickens' social commentary takes on a more caustic tone. American personal habits disgusted him. The national pastime seemed to be spitting, while the standard of personal cleanliness appeared to have been adopted from the pigs travellers discovered on even the most fashionable American streets. Privacy was virtually nonexistent, and freedom of speech was used to license open rudeness.

All these faults Dickens could have forgiven if not condoned. It was in the social and ethical spheres of American society that he saw the greatest disparity between intention and achievement. On viewing the half-built structures of Philadelphia's Girard College, Dickens remarked that "like many other great undertakings in America, even this is rather going to be done one of these days, than doing now" (99). The fact that the college had been left in this condition due to a dispute over who was legally entitled to the bequest adds to its symbolic function. Like the college, Dickens found America to be a land of half-fulfilled promise, a land whose high-minded intentions were belied by a base reality. The land of liberty was also the land in which slavery flourished, where even the makers of the law were lawless in their implacable opposition to the very idea of abolition. A senator for North Carolina openly declared his hostility on the floor of the Senate: "I warn the abolitionists, . . . ignorant, infuriated barbarians as they are, that if chance shall throw any of them into our hands, he may expect a felon's death" (231). Little philosophical profundity is required to detect the perverse morality which underlies such a statement. Dickens felt that the very violence with which Americans maintained their opinions in the teeth of everyone and everything was itself completely inimical to the principle of liberty. Moreover, it led to a narrow-mindedness which tended to perpetuate such strife. Inevitably, American politics became both the end result and the breeding ground of extreme opinion. Dickens recalls a long-winded speech by a "great politician" during his American sojourn which "concluded with two sentiments, one of which was, Somebody for ever; and the other, Blast everybody else! which is by no means a bad abstract of the general creed in these matters" (179).

The most insidious aspect of American society which Dickens witnessed upon his tour was the manner in which the individual, the self, was asserting its authority. Freed from the social conventions of Europe, America had created a whole new set of debilitating circumstances which tended to dehumanize its inhabitants. The use of violence to support personal opinions was simply one aspect of this self-assertion. To Dickens, America became a prime example of what Darwin was later to term the principle of natural selection—of the survival of the fittest. The "Universal Distrust" (245) which he found to be part of the national character was the natural outcome of this desperate need for self-assertion—as were the ravenous eating habits which he encountered on his tour. The love of "smart" dealing (which placed a premium on low business ethics) was simply one further manifestation of this national disease.

Yet, if this self-assertiveness formed one part of the American mentality, Dickens observed a related but contrary aspect. While the members of this society prided themselves upon their individual liberty, they all seemed to subscribe to the same basic values—and these values were not those propounded by their revolutionary forefathers. Sloveliness, inquisitiveness, rudeness, and violence seemed to be characteristic features of the American scene—and they appeared to be characteristics to which no one objected. A licentious press constantly pandered to the adulterated tastes of its avid readers by ignoring the right of privacy and by denying the individual his right to freedom of expression. The general approbation of "smart" dealing Dickens attributed to a "national love of trade" (246). The figure of liberty had been displaced by an effigy of Mammon, an effigy before which an entire nation debased itself—becoming, in the process, a humorless society which valued only utilitarian activities. Dickens wrote that "the people are all alike. . . . There is no diversity of character. They travel about on the same errands, say and do the same things in exactly the same manner, and follow in the same dull cheerless round" (158).

In a sense, Dickens, like Martin Chuzzlewit, underwent a kind of reformation as a result of his American experiences. His bright hopes for a new world founded upon social justice were destroyed by his perception of a reality which bore very little resemblance to this ideal. The unthinking hypocrisy of a number of individuals with whom he came into contact repelled him. The Republic was not what he had imagined it to be; and he felt that, while Americans often boasted that they were immeasurably superior to the English, they were in many ways inferior because of the painful disparity that existed between what they professed to believe in and what they practiced. To Dickens, America was one vast illusion, a polished surface hiding a generally shoddy substance, a fine appearance beneath which one discovered a grim reality.

In November of 1842, Dickens began work on *Martin Chuzzlewit*. A crucial question involved in any examination of the novel is the extent to which the author's American experiences influenced the shape of his work. In this respect, it may be useful to recall that the literature produced by any writer to some degree represents his imaginative extension of personal experience; and it can be argued that the social tendencies which Dickens observed in America provided him with a foundation upon which to base his entire novel. *Martin Chuzzlewit*, although a powerfully comic work of fiction, is also a serious representation of a society devoted to the pursuit of self-interest. Pecksniff is the individual embodiment of such a pursuit, while America is the social incarnation.

Dickens himself stated that his portrait of American society "is an exhibition, for the most part . . . of a ludicrous side, *only*, of the American character" (p. xvi). This should at once alert us to the fact that Dickens was aware of another side of American society which he chose to ignore for artistic purposes; and these purposes can best be understood by an examination of the manner in which the author presents American society, the kind of community which is depicted, and the relationship which these episodes bear with the remainder of the novel.

It is clear that Dickens makes an almost Swiftian attack upon the materialism, violence, and hypocrisy which he detected in the new world. Like Swift's Lilliput, Dickens' America is a utopia, a nonplace, whose origins may be found in an observable reality. Like Lilliput, America is a land of extremes. It is also a world of Yahoos who have founded a society based upon the assertion of self and the worship of money. As in the Lilliput of *Gulliver's Travels,* the very exaggeration of this depiction provides a clue to the meaning of the American episodes of *Martin Chuzzlewit,* for the New World is really the Old World carried to an extreme. It is as though Pecksniff had emigrated to the United States, had been made president, and was deeply revered and faithfully emulated by a sizable majority of the populace. His moral pretence, his acquisitiveness, the hypocrisy which hides his selfishness, and the ultimate vapidity of his nature are observable everywhere. It is singularly appropriate that the first American whom Martin meets upon disembarking is Colonel Diver. The very name "Diver" contains an obvious reference to the biblical Dives, the rich man who used his wealth for selfish ends. In many respects the Colonel is both the representative and the product of his society. He is described as a "sallow gentleman, with sunken cheeks, black hair, small twinkling eyes, and a singular expression hovering about that region of his face, which was not a frown, not a leer, and yet might have been mistaken at the first glance for either. Indeed it would have been difficult, on a much closer acquaintance, to describe it in any more satisfactory terms than as a mixed expression of vulgar cunning and conceit. . . . His thick cane, shod with a mighty ferule at one end and armed with a great metal knob at the other, depended from a line-and-tassel on his wrist" (256–57). Being a gentleman of the press, the cane which he carries is no doubt used to present his editorial opinions in a more forceful manner than that allowed by type and ink. It is the quality of his facial expression, however, which makes him so apt a representative of a large section of his society. The boisterous proprietor of the Rowdy Journal is a visible success, and the moral qualities which manifest themselves in his glance have made him a success. The selfishness which expresses itself as a greed for money must, of necessity, possess a certain amount of low cunning, of what is termed (in Dickens' America) "smartness." "We are a smart people here, and can appreciate smartness," the Colonel tells Martin: " 'Is smartness American for forgery?' asked Martin." " 'Well!' said the

Colonel, 'I expect it's American for a good many things that you call by other names' " (264).

This love of "smartness," however, is just one of the effects of a national preoccupation with money. Material success has become the standard by which all other values are determined: "All their cares, hopes, joys, affections, virtues, and associations, seemed to be melted down into dollars. . . . Men were weighed by their dollars, measures gauged by their dollars; life was auctioneered, appraised, put up, and knocked down for its dollars" (273). In such a society, the individual is free to pursue any course whatever so long as he attains material wealth. The freedom of the individual must necessarily become a matter of continual self-assertion. Thus, the ravenous feeding habits displayed by Americans are but one of the effects of this overpowering necessity. Dining is no longer a social occasion but has been reduced to its simplest utilitarian function as part of the struggle for self-preservation. Personal slovenliness becomes an inalienable right since it allows every man an opportunity to assert his independence from social convention and to establish an equality of filth with his fellows.

The members of such a society are, of course, isolated from one another by their own self-interest. Yet the very unanimity with which they adopt the principles of commercialism inevitably leads to a certain similarity of character. Dickens relates that they "were strangely devoid of individual traits of character, insomuch that any one of them might have changed minds with the other, and nobody would have found it out" (272). Steven Marcus demonstrates that as a community they relate to one another mainly through the cash nexus.[6] Money is the organizing principle upon which this society is built and the value by which all others are judged. Such mutual adherence to a narrow range of values has made Americans a superficial people whose imaginations seldom stray beyond the bounds of their own materialism. Thus, they are too busy to read the "mere notions" contained in books, while at the same time the tedious monotony of their social life (which is, however, now and again relieved by the strong stuff contained in "screamers") finds expression in a certain languid air common to most Americans. Of course, there are the "levees" held occasionally for "remarkable" men. Even these, however, are possessed of a certain sepulchral air: the gentlemen who are to escort Mr. Pogram to the levee held in his honour greet him "in a melancholy voice . . . as if he had been abroad for a twelvemonth in the meantime, and they met, now, at a funeral" (540). Martin's own reception at the National Hotel is well attended literally because it is a gruesome kind of funeral.

This inability to engage in any meaningful social life is allied to another invidious aspect of American society—its public nature. Dickens' America is an illusion, a surface beneath which there is no substance; and because these citizens possess no inner life (or, at least, none beyond the low cunning required for material acquisition), they exist wholly in a public form. Americans do not converse with one another, they make speeches at each other. This kind of oratory plays an important role in establishing and protecting the self. To Americans, everyone is the sum of his words. Since there is no inner substance to sustain the individual, one may establish and maintain an identity through the use of language. All tend to imitate the example of Major Pawkins, who "in trading on his stock of wisdom . . . invariably proceeded on the principle of putting all the goods he had (and more) into his window; and that went a great way with his constituency of admirers" (267). This public self is much more than a mere identity; it forms a smoke screen behind which the individual may hide his true intentions, his real self. Colonel Diver relates that the aristocracy of America is composed "of intelligence, sir, . . . of intelligence and virtue. And of their necessary consequence in this republic. Dollars, sir" (258). As we have seen, in Dickens' America, dollars are the standard by which intelligence and virtue are measured. The colonel is dealing in linguistic perversion to conceal the materialistic grossness of his society. J. Hillis Miller relates this kind of statement to the double-talk and doublethink practiced in Orwell's *1984*.[7] There is an obvious dichotomy between the verbal impression of America propounded by its citizens and the observable reality portrayed by Dickens.

Needless to say, this linguistic perversion is a form of hypocrisy, and hypocrisy is a key element in the America of *Martin Chuzzlewit*. The country founded upon individual liberty and equality now pays lip service to these ideals while simultaneously narrowing their definition. Dickens' description of one of Martin's fellow travellers on the aptly named *Screw* may serve to illustrate this point: "An English gentleman who was strongly suspected of having run away from a bank, with something in his possession belonging to its strong-box besides the key, grew eloquent upon the subject of the rights of man, and hummed the Marseillaise Hymn constantly" (253). The rights of man have been transformed into the liberty of the individual to pursue his own interests at the expense of others, while equality becomes a word which expresses his emancipation from the more limiting aspects of social custom—such as honesty. Hannibal Chollop is, perhaps, the supreme example of American hypocrisy. Newspaper editor, land speculator, and patriot, he is an amalgam of conflicting principles, each of which has been adopted to further his own selfish ends: "He always introduced himself to strangers as a worshipper of Freedom; was the consistent advocate of Lynch law, and slavery; and invariably recommended, both in print and speech, the 'tarring and feathering' of any unpopular person who differed from himself. He called this 'planting

the standard of civilization in the wilder gardens of My country'"
(520). This indeed is freedom—the freedom from any form of restraint
which may become the Hobbesean tyranny of each against all. One
feels that such a life is indeed brutal and short. Opposing opinions are
suppressed violently, while the only operative rule of law is the quick
justice of the mob.

The Norrises demonstrate another aspect of American hypocrisy.
In a society freed from the arbitrary distinctions of an aristocracy of
the blood, they look upon themselves as "nature's noblemen." Yet the
social distinctions which they observe are in every way as arbitrary as
those of the "benighted" Europeans. Mr. Norris has not the honor of
knowing his neighbor because "that person entertained religious opinions of which he couldn't approve" (287); while Mrs. Norris (possessed
of a more egalitarian spirit, no doubt) disapproves of them simply on
the grounds of their lack of gentility. Proud of the fact that America
does not possess a native aristocracy, they continually refer to their
titled acquaintances. The discovery of Martin's impoverished condition
shocks them into insensibility since this hospitality shown toward a dol-
larless stranger jeopardizes their status in the particular "sphere" of
New York society in which they move.

Again, the lack of a native aristocracy by which to differentiate the
individual members of this society has given rise to a new form of her-
aldry. In consequence, there has been a prodigious proliferation of
generals, colonels, captains, doctors, and professors on the principle
that certain individuals are entitled to a greater degree of equality than
others. Those who are nominated as the most remarkable men in their
country prove invariably to be those with the greatest genius for lying,
swindling, and pandering. Thus, social distinction is directly linked to
monetary success—which is, in itself, a direct result of personal dishonesty. On this basis, the American justification of slavery may be easily
adduced. Firstly, and most importantly, it is a profitable investment,
one which produces a maximal return for a minimal input. Secondly, it
is, as the beardless Jefferson Brick suggests, an "ennobling institution"
(263). It is, in fact, a debased form of feudalism. When Brick objects to
the use of the word "master" by Major Pawkins' Irish housemaid, Martin is perceptive enough to reply "All 'owners,' [here] are they?" (266).
Americans have, in a sense, ennobled themselves by substituting an
owner-slave society for the lord-serf relationship of medieval Europe.

This failure of the American dream is again reflected in the New
World's use of language. A number of characters, including Colonel
Diver and Dr. Dunkle, are in the habit of emphasizing the small words
and syllables of their discourse, being of the opinion that "the larger
parts of speech could be trusted alone, but the little ones required to be
constantly looked after" (258). While the appearance of democracy is

carefully maintained (at least verbally), Americans are more than glad to leave the enactment of its substance for future generations. Meanwhile, since there is no firm foundation for American chauvinism, language is a vehicle by means of which a patriot may escape reality in a flurry of exaggerated comparisons. Elijah Pogram describes the vicious Mr. Chollop as a "true-born child of this free hemisphere! Verdant as the mountains of our country; bright and flowing as our mineral Licks; unspiled by withering conventionalities as air our broad and boundless Perearers! Rough he may be. So air our Barrs. Wild he may be. So air our Buffalers. But he is a child of Natur', and a child of Freedom; and his boastful answer to the Despot and the Tyrant is, that his bright home is in the Settin Sun" (534).

It is not difficult to see that logic plays an exceptionally small role in Pogram's oratory, heavily dependent as it is upon false or inconclusive analogies. These tend to establish a patriotic hierarchy which finally transforms Chollop into an American institution, a creature indistinguishable from and, indeed, an inseparable part of the very "Perearers." Any opposing viewpoint may be treated as an act of treason and the offender may be dealt with accordingly—presumably by tarring and feathering. Freedom of speech becomes the freedom of agreeing with the opinions of the verbally talented minority—and of voicing this agreement loudly. This is the reason why Martin is constantly asked how he likes America. Failure to give an almost mechanical answer in the affirmative can be and is taken as an example of European prejudice. A negative answer also provides the inquisitor with important evidence which can be used against the speaker in a most effective manner if he should ever become too critical.

In its extreme form, this twisted language is symbolic of the social and individual nullity which is *Martin Chuzzlewit*'s America by becoming completely devoid of substance and coherence. The ubiquitous Mrs. Hominy and her two L.L.'s (to the uninitiated, translatable as Literary Ladies) are what is called in America "Transcendental." In truth they do transcend the bonds of language by making it a meaningless jumble of high-blown phrases: " 'Mind and matter,' said the lady in the wig, 'glide swift into the vortex of immensity. Howls the sublime, and softly sleeps the calm Ideal, in the whispering chambers of Imagination. To hear it, sweet it is. But then, outlaughs the stern philosopher, and saith to the Grotesque, "What ho! arrest for me that Agency. Go, bring it here!" And so the vision fadeth' " (542–43).

Indeed it does—and that is the very reason for such oratory. Its insubstantial abstraction draws the mind away from a consideration of concrete details. It is a language which has dissociated itself from reality: it is a perfected form of hypocrisy. The Literary Ladies leave an impression of profundity upon their listeners which these listeners, in turn, attribute to the mental superiority of the Literary Ladies. The individual thus creates himself publicly through his words, and these words are accepted as the true reflection of his substance. Yet, since there exists no real substance, all that is witnessed is merely an illusion, a fabric of lies which transforms itself into the irrational and inhuman stuff of which nightmares are made. The individual is self-created and, therefore, holds within himself all standards of authority. In a self-seeking society, these standards will naturally be created by an aggressive minority who will, of course, impose them upon the more pliant majority of citizens. This is the fundamental root of the power held by such men as Colonel Diver, Hannibal Chollop, and Elijah Pogram. Power becomes concentrated in the hands of an active minority which exercises a tyranny over public opinion. Yet the majority of the population accept this tyranny because it works to their advantage. In a land based on the pursuit of self-interest, it would be very awkward should the leadership display any signs of real moral conviction. Slanderous newspapers and corrupt politicians are, therefore, defense mechanisms which protect the self-seeking individual from being punished for his actions—or even from feeling guilty about them. The champion of the American public becomes, thus, the one "who, in the brutal fury of his own pursuit, could cast no stigma upon them for the hot knavery of theirs" (273).

As it is presented in *Martin Chuzzlewit*, America and her society are illusions. They are a democratic, highly moral semblance cloaking a tyrannous, moneygrubbing reality which itself leads to a final nullity. Into this society come young Martin and Mark Tapley; the former seeking riches, the latter desiring "credit." Both are selfish and both labor under a delusion—although they are of differing qualities and extents. Both must be and are reformed by their American experience before they are fit to reenter society as morally healthy individuals. America is the scene of this reformation and is, indeed, its *sine qua non*. As General Choke observes, "What are the Great United States for . . . if not for the regeneration of man?" (349). Dickens clearly meant this to be an ironic statement, and its full meaning emerges as Martin's travels take him deeper into the American continent.

As Mark so aptly puts it, Martin is "a man as is his own great-coat and cloak, and is always a-wrapping himself up in himself" (513). He is an individual who, though basically kindhearted, gauges all things in terms of self. Arrogant, even insufferable at times, he measures every human relationship in terms of its effects upon himself; and, in doing so, he has constructed an illusory world with himself at its center. All things were created especially for his benefit and his is the standard by which all things must be measured. Such an attitude is obviously founded upon an unbounded egoism—which is itself a form of self-assertion. Time and again in the novel, Martin's self-confidence is relentlessly portrayed by Dickens and is shown to be nothing more than an illusion. That this is a dangerously self-destructive illusion becomes increasingly evident as this egoistic self-assurance clouds Martin's judgment. Immediately before his departure for America, he reaches the heights of selfishness by being imperceptive enough not to realize that the diamond ring which he has received as a parting gift from Mary Graham was purchased with what were probably her life's savings. Too proud to accept a gift of money even from the person he loves, Martin is, nevertheless, so obtuse as to mistake the identity of the sender of this portable property. He then has the effrontery to murmur that Mary "is worthy of the sacrifices I have made" (244).

Barbara Hardy contends that Martin's role in America, "as he is lionized like his creator, is to act as spirited and zealous critic of America, given the *ex-officio* wisdom and objectivity of his Englishness." Thus, she feels, "He temporarily drops his [selfish] humour and is humane and zealous as Mark." [8] At first glance, this does appear to be the case. Yet, before ascribing a shallowness of characterization to Dickens, a more careful analysis of Martin's character must be made. Certainly one must admit that Martin is neither stupid nor hopelessly self-centered; and it would require that kind of mentality to remain unconscious of the abuses present in America. His criticism of American society, therefore, does not seem inconsistent with his character—he has, after all, already perceived Pecksniff's hypocrisy. What does seem strange, however, is that after his personal experience with American business ethics, he should still place trust in Zephaniah Scadder and the Eden Land Corporation. Yet even this can be seen as the natural outcome of his egoism. Martin's is a common phenomenon; he is a man who is perfectly aware of the selfish tendencies of those around him and blissfully unaware of his own. His is a dream world in which he posits the theory that the circumstances which govern the lives of other individuals are not applicable when he is involved. The mother who with her children emigrates to America to rejoin her husband is on a "wild-goose venture" (249), but it never occurs to him that the same might be said of his own voyage. Bevan's warnings about dishonest land speculators go unheeded because Martin has unbounded confidence in his own judgment. His egoism clouds this judgment; and so, in spite of Mark's apprehensions, he purchases a plot of land from the Eden Land Corporation.

Eden itself is symbolic on two levels. Situated at the geographic heart of the continent, it is the physical manifestation of the corruption of American society. As Mark observes, "It's a reg'lar little United States in itself" (517). Like Dickens' America, it is a land of promise unfulfilled, a "realm of Hope" which upon closer inspection becomes "the grim domains of Giant Despair" (377), a wasteland built by "smartness" and self-interest. Everything has been half-built and then abandoned to its fate. The crumbling National Credit Office is quite literally bankrupt, as is the integrity of American society. Yet the wasteland of self-interest is also the purgatory of selfishness. It is the place in which Martin is finally made to face reality—the reality of the world and the reality of his own nature.

Eden is a test of moral fiber, a seasoning, "and we must all be seasoned, one way or another. That's religion, that is, you know" (383). Martin has no one but himself to blame for his situation. This realization, and the blow which it gives to his egoism, is the first part of his reformation. One cannot agree with Barbara Hardy in feeling that this change takes place too suddenly to be thoroughly convincing. The toppling of Martin's air-built castle by the reality of Eden is certainly a blow to his selfishness, but it is not the final cure. His egoism still asserts itself even in disaster. His first impulse upon reaching shore is to surrender himself to a special destiny. To Mark's kindly remonstrance not to give in, he replies, "I am destined to die in this place. I felt it the instant I set foot upon the shore" (383). Once again we discover that he feels himself possessed of a special, personal providence; and the monumental egoism involved in such a conception graphically demonstrates that a full cure has not yet been achieved.

To recover fully, he must be willing to perform an act of total unselfishness—and this he does by his attendance on Mark during the latter's illness. The kindly fellow feeling which he has always possessed is finally aroused and displays itself in action. The remainder of his reformation is a natural consequence of this deed. Eden is what may be termed the "school of hard knocks," and Martin learns his lesson only after considerable buffeting. No longer certain of his judgment and required by circumstances to attend to another person's needs, he is able for the first time to view himself from an objective position: "In the hideous solitude of that most hideous place, with Hope so far removed, Ambition quenched, and Death beside him rattling at the very door, reflection came, as in a plague-beleaguered town; and so he felt and knew the failing of his life, and saw distinctly what an ugly spot it was" (525). Martin has undergone the archetypal, and (to Dickens) the classical Christian reformation: he has lost himself in order to be saved. The illusions which he possessed as to the nature of the world have been destroyed by the harsh reality of America. Yet the very harshness of this reality has provided him with the opportunity of achieving a *modus vivendi* with which he may reenter society without becoming immersed in the self.

Mark Tapley's peculiar kind of selfishness is also cured by his American experiences. Endowed with a "jolly" disposition, he feels he must find "credit" in being jolly. The acquisition of "credit" becomes a kind of religious virtue analogous to the acquisition of grace. Mark's selfishness is, therefore, based upon a kind of spiritual egoism, upon a desire to "come out strong" in the face of adversity. Like Martin, America is for him also a land of hope, but of a perverse hope. It is a land whose very selfishness will provide him with more than enough credit to last him the rest of his life. His greatest hope lies with Martin. Yet in all he is deluded. America is selfish enough, yet Martin is reformed by it. Moreover, Mark's jollity under adverse circumstances is merely an appearance. His grin is mechanical, and his thoughts are far from pleasant. His reformation lies in the discovery that the only true credit to be got by being jolly rests in the attempt to be cheerful and courageous when only the self is affected by a certain set of adverse circumstances; and this is the discovery he makes in Eden, the symbol of selfish pursuits. One cannot forebear a smile at the emaciated figure of Mark raising himself upon an elbow to write "jolly" upon a slate, and one can imagine the toothsome grin upon his face when he admits to Tom Pinch that "Human Natur' is in a conspiracy again' me; I can't get on" (733). He too is ready to reenter society. America is a bit too jolly for his tastes, and he returns to marry the buxom landlady of the Blue Dragon Inn—and, no doubt, to find credit in bouncing a hoard of boisterous offspring on his aching knees. Like Martin, his reformation involves a certain loss of innocence precipitated by the harsh realities of American society.

There remains to be considered, finally, the relationship of the American and British episodes of *Martin Chuzzlewit*. In general, it may be said that this relationship is one of theme and motif. As J. Hillis Miller suggests, perhaps it is possible to connect the various episodes only "when the novel is complete and all the relationships between the hermetically sealed milieus of the novel can be seen in a single, retrospective, panoramic glance." [9] The self pervades the novel and is manifested in some form in each of the major characters presented. Martin's egoism is at least equaled by his grandfather's egocentric belief that everyone with whom he comes into contact desires his favor because of its monetary value. Again, the pursuit of wealth is another link between England and America. A brief analysis of the force which motivates the actions of a majority of the Chuzzlewit family indicates that the self-centered pursuit of material wealth is as important a factor here as in America. Moreover, the dichotomy which exists between appearance and reality in American society is also reflected in English social life. The apparent solidity of the Anglo-Bengalee Life Assurance Company is as illusory as the map of Eden townsite which decorates the wall of Zephaniah Scadder's Land Corporation. Like many Americans, Pecksniff conceals his hypocrisy behind a smoke screen of language and, to many (including Tom Pinch), he actually becomes what his words purport him to be. The ubiquitous Mrs. Gamp and her illusive friend Mrs. Harris are themselves striking examples of the manner in which words may be used either to create or to obliterate reality. The violence of American society is not nearly as graphically portrayed as the violent methods used by Jonas Chuzzlewit to assure his own security. Mercy Pecksniff's decision to marry Jonas also demonstrates the difficulty of attaining meaningful moral standards in a hypocritical society. Her brutal treatment at the hands of her husband illustrates a form of slavery at least as vicious as that practiced across the Atlantic. Add to this the fact that she has almost literally been sold to Jonas and the comparison is complete. Lastly, the theme of reformation is common to both sections of the book, and in both it involves a descent into an underworld that effects a loss of innocence, the destruction of an illusion. Tom Pinch is as deluded in his personal representation of Pecksniff as Martin in his confident desire to make his fortune in America. Although *Martin Chuzzlewit* remains essentially a picaresque novel, retaining the loosely knit, episodic structure common to Dickens' early work and to the genre itself, there does exist a certain parallelism in the plots involving Martin and his grandfather. One notes, for example, that the chapter in which young Martin sets foot upon the soil of Eden and thereby begins his reformation is immediately followed by the chapter in which Old Martin sets foot across Pecksniff's threshold, thereby initiating his own reformation in the very heart of the English wasteland of self-interest.

In *Martin Chuzzlewit,* then, Dickens deals with "the number and variety of humours and vices that have their root in selfishness" from two different perspectives. England is the center of the individual selfishness which finds its supreme expression in the figure of Pecksniff. Self-righteous, hypocritical, possessed of a low cunning, he is the individual embodiment of the extremes to which the pursuit of selfish ends may drive a man. America, on the other hand, is the representation of a whole society which has dedicated itself to selfishness, and, as a result, it is a kind of moral exemplum of the extremes to which the pursuit of self-interest may drive mankind in general, an exemplum promised by the novel's almost allegorical introductory chapter. Yet an even more complex relationship exists between the countries; for in both, social and individual selfishness exist side by side. This is, perhaps, the real "message" that Dickens was attempting to convey to his countrymen. A continuation of the visibly present trends of English society might one day convert that society into his American utopia of self.

Comedy is the dominant mood of *Martin Chuzzlewit,* yet it must be admitted that this comedy takes on a darker and more vindictive aspect in the American sections of the novel. Harry Stone attributes this to

Dickens' inability to separate his autobiographical impressions of America from a consideration of its society. This, he feels, leads to a loss of artistic control which makes the American sections of the novel tonally inappropriate to the remainder of the work.[10] Of course, we must admit, with Dickens, that the representation of America presented here is an extremely exaggerated one. It must also be conceded that, occasionally, he does lose control in the recollection of his disappointment and in the moral indignation these memories arouse. Yet the relationship between an author's experiences and his work is a complex one; and, clearly, Dickens drew upon these experiences for his novel—but he also reshaped them for artistic purposes. *Martin Chuzzlewit* is an examination of the role of the self in human society; and as such, the American episodes can no more be seen as "unaccountable excrescences" upon the meaning of the novel than is the figure of Pecksniff himself.

Christopher Mulvey

DAVID COPPERFIELD

The Folk-Story Structure

DAVID COPPERFIELD has problems. "Whether," he begins, "I shall turn out to be the hero of my life, or whether that station will be held by anybody else, these pages must show." Is he the most important person in his own story? Has he been a respected man in his days? Both questions puzzle David; the wordplay based on *hero* and *life* continues in the next sentence of the novel: "To begin my life with the beginning of my life." Within the space created by these ambiguities, we can watch the play of Dickens' astute mind. The intentional circularity here suggests the mirrorlike quality of autobiography, the self observing self—something central to the structure of the novel that Dickens wrote between 1849 and 1850 and that he called *The Personal History of David Copperfield.* The comedy makes obvious the distance between the selves: the personality who writes "I record" and the creature who "was born (as I have been informed and believe) on a Friday, at twelve o'clock at night. It was remarked that the clock began to strike, and I began to cry, simultaneously."

The mock-heroic vein firmly establishes the separation of narrator and child. Dickens uses irony to introduce certain themes and motifs which are to be important in David's life. His birth is like the birth of heroes: it is accompanied by strange signs and wonders.

> In consideration of the day and hour of [my] birth, it was declared by the nurse, and by some sage women in the neighbourhood who had taken a lively interest in [me] several months before there was any possibility of [our] becoming personally acquainted, first, that I was destined to be unlucky in life; and secondly, that I was privileged to see ghosts and spirits; both these gifts inevitably attaching, as they believed, to all unlucky infants of either gender, born towards the small hours on a Friday night.

There are other than natural reasons why David should so be born. Taken together with the lesser wonders, this caul creates conditions which are less suitable perhaps for an autobiography than for a folk tale, the kind of story typified by "The Devil with the Three Golden Hairs" whose opening line is, "There was once a poor woman who gave birth to a little son; and he came into the world with a caul on." [1]

The hero of the tale is born of humble parents, more humble than the Copperfields, for the heroes reflect the social ranks of their audiences: the folk story is no less peasant than the novel is middle-class. At first only the mother of the luck-child is mentioned; his father is insignificant. David, we are told, is a posthumous son; his father is given only a brief paragraph. The cauls of both heroes are taken as a sign of luck, if not of unusual abilities.

Superstition had it that possession of a caul protects the owner from death by drowning. Nonetheless, sailors will not buy David's: "Whether sea-going people were short of money about that time, or were short of faith and preferred cork jackets, I don't know." The old lady who eventually wins the caul at the country raffle is noted to have escaped drowning all her life and to have died "triumphantly in bed at ninety-two." It is also pointed out that in ninety-two years she had never been on the water. The fate from which David is granted immunity threatens at once in the folk story. The hero is cast into a river. He survives and his luck holds to the end. In David's case, the birth auguries are mixed. If it is lucky to be born with a caul, it is nonetheless unlucky, we are told, to be born at midnight on a Friday.

The novel suggests folk stories and these folk stories invoke myths. Attempts to make a rigorous distinction between folk story and myth deny the continuity of forms that extends from the humblest fireside tales and jokes to the loftiest myths of the higher religions. Folk stories deal at a local and peasant level with the motifs and themes with which myths deal at a universal and exalted level. In structural terms, the folk story stands between the novel and the myth in a pattern that includes the dream. In the dream, the hero is the dreamer himself, working through the nightmares and fantasies of the sleep adventure; in the novel, the hero is a character shaped by the writer to work through the trials and triumphs of the imaginative action. In the folk story and in myth, the idiosyncratic dreamer and the individual character give way to the everyman and the universal hero who work through the suffering and aspiration of a group or of humanity. All novels then, it may be argued, owe something to myth and to search out an inevitable mythic structure is a sterile exercise. But there are special cases and Charles Dickens is a special case among novelists and *David Copperfield* a particularly interesting case among Dickens' novels. Here the correspondences between myth and novel seem to be as explicit as possible within the conventions of the nineteenth century form—conventions Dickens was keen to observe, as his prefaces demonstrate. Nonetheless he goes further than any novelist before Joyce in the elaboration of a mythic structure. (Yet there is no evidence in Dickens of the conscious endeavors to this end that influence Joyce's concept of the novel and are one of the causes for his abandonment of the conventional forms.) For both writers the mythological dimension provides a technique for making the ordinary extraordinary—equally the purpose of *David Copperfield* and *Ulysses*—just because myth holds in focus the individual perspective and the universal vision.

Myths are made about the childhood of mankind, but these myths express the universal experiences of childhood. Every man's childhood is mythological. It is outlandish, remote, and filled in memory with wondrous fears and strange joys. For the purposes of his novel, Dickens reinforces these tendencies of the adult memory so that Copperfield's childhood becomes myth indeed. Dickens is able to fill his account of this period of David's life with what are strongly felt, but in actual fact unindividualized, impressions and emotions: "My mother with her pretty hair and youthful shape, and Peggotty, with no shape at all; . . . a quantity of fowls that look terribly tall to me, walking about in a menacing and ferocious manner; . . . a long passage—what an enormous perspective I make of it!" (13–14). These are reactions that any child might have; as a result, these details are peculiarly effective in suggesting the childhood of the specific boy, Master Davy. From this point by decomposition, by reduplication, and by splitting, by the techniques of myth, Master Davy is steadily surrounded by a series of doubles and beyond them a ring of colorless copies. David's life is the paradigm; their lives are variations. In this way, his growing up continues to be, like his childhood, at once individual and universal.

David has no father; neither has Steerforth, Traddles, nor Heep. David is sent to Salem House to become a member of Mr. Creakle's School because in the absence of his real father he bit his second father; Steerforth is sent to Salem House because in the absence of his real father, he needs a second father; Traddles is sent to Salem House because in the absence of his real father, no one cares what is done with him. Heep is the only one among them who knew his father. But if Steerforth might seek to excuse himself because he lacked a father, "It would have been well for me (and for more than me) if I had had a steadfast and judicious father!" (322) Uriah Heep is discovered to have learned his most loathsome trait from the figure whose absence Steerforth so laments: " 'People like to be above you,' says father, 'keep yourself down.' I am very umble to the present moment, Master Copperfield, but I've got a little power!" (575).

When these boys grow to be young men, all of them are out of place in the society in which they find themselves. They have no bearings and they are all seeking a position. David and Traddles eventually find virtuous roles to play; Steerforth and Heep find villainous parts. Different as they may be—one corrupted through luxury, the other corrupted through poverty—they are alike in that they take ways David might have taken. They represent two shameful directions that the "personal history of David Copperfield" might have pursued. Heep and Steerforth are the antitypes of the crime-free David. Against the pattern of their lives, ending in transportation and violent death, respectively, the life of David can be seen to be one of prudence and success. Had Steerforth or Heep emerged as the *hero* of the novel, it would indeed have been an autobiography "never . . . to be published on any account."

Here we can see how Dickens uses a mechanism of myth, a mode of characterization common to all story forms, for his own individual purposes. The doubles of David Copperfield are obviously far more than simply that, since the characters who emerge have an authenticity and meaning of their own. The stories of their lives provide parallels with David's own so that each, in his own way, may suggest what "the personal history and adventures of David Copperfield" would have been, had that history not followed the particular evolution of character begun at Blunderstone one Friday at midnight. This is why Master Davy appears with such separate vitality in the opening chapters of the novel. Davy holds the provisional station of *hero* of his own *life*, but he is surrounded from the beginning by rivals for that position.

A fascinating detail of this particular instance of decomposition is that we are able to watch the process take place. Dickens has left an intriguing record in the series of tentative titles which he first proposed for his novel. They suggest a number of different characters who never in fact become the hero and also a number of different forms for the novel never fully realized. Thomas Mag, David Mag, Charles Copperfield, Trotfield, Spankle, Stonebury, Flower, Magbury, Copperby, and Copperstone appear before Dickens finally settles on David Copperfield the Younger of Blunderstone. The book itself is variously described as a Disclosure, a Record, a Confession, a Survey, a Last Will and Testament, and a Legacy.[2]

In its evolution lies the clue to the structure of the novel. Dickens makes his story all these different things. None of the shadowy claimants to the station of hero is rejected utterly. Instead, David Copperfield takes his place as the central figure amidst a band of sons, and his mother and father provide the pattern for all the men and women of the novel. The basic drama in which these three engage is rehearsed, rerun, and repeated in what threatens at times to become an endless series. The folk story relies upon a steady rhythm of repetition to cast its spell and display its truths. In a similar but more elaborate rhythm, *David Copperfield* contains its power and meaning.

Like the luck-child, David takes a large number of journeys. Like the luck-child, at the end of each journey, David finds a new home. The first and the greatest journey brings him caul-wrapped "from the land of dreams and shadows." He finds himself in an idyllic world. These are the days "when my mother and I and Peggotty" were "all in all to one another." The very phrasing of this, "my mother and I and Peggotty," nicely presents David's universe and its focal point. Appropriately for the creation of a myth of David's golden age, Dickens relies on the garden.

> Now I am in the garden at the back, beyond the yard where the empty pigeon-house and dog-kennel are—a very preserve of butterflies, as I remember it, with a high fence, and a gate and padlock; where the fruit clusters on the trees, riper and richer than fruit has ever been since, in any other garden, and where my mother gathers some in a basket, while I stand by, bolting furtive gooseberries, and trying to look unmoved. (15–16)

The present tense is used because the garden has an existence only as long as David remembers it and only in the manner he remembers it. Its fruit is "riper and richer than fruit has ever been since, in any other garden" because this garden has passed beyond the tyranny of reality and is re-created in a prelapsarian vision of beauty, love, and trust. The topography of this Blunderstone is a projection of the infant imagination. It is allegorical. Everything is in place. Everything has a controllable size and location, not least the view of "the quiet churchyard out of the bedroom window. . . . There is nothing half so green . . . anywhere, as the grass of that churchyard; nothing half so shady as its trees; nothing half so quiet as its tombstones." Everything about Blunderstone murmurs reassurance and love. The village church is part of this picture: a warm, summertime, drowsy church. The only fearful specter in this world is that of a risen dead man: "One Sunday night my mother reads to Peggotty and me, . . . how Lazarus was raised up from the dead. . . . I am so frightened" (14).

David has an uncomplicated view of the two women who divide between them the role of mother for him. Of Peggotty, who like Mrs. Copperfield is christened "Clara," he writes: "I propped my eyelids open with my two forefingers, and looked perseveringly . . . at herself, whom I thought lovely. . . . I thought her in a different style from my mother, certainly; but of another school of beauty, I considered her a perfect example" (16–17). David's love for Peggotty goes back to the earliest memories of his childhood, and from that period he dates the earliest sense of the difference between his love for her and that for his mother: "The first objects that assume a distinct presence before me, as

I look far back, into the blank of my infancy, are my mother with her pretty hair and youthful shape, and Peggotty, with no shape at all" (13). No subtler distinction could be expected of infant memory, but no subtler distinction is necessary. In his baby way, David is making his first discrimination between woman the beautiful and woman the useful.

David's actual mother is Clara Copperfield. Her position in David's infant world is in contrast to the mother role presented through Peggotty. Clara is made the archetype of the beautiful and sexually attractive woman. Clara, much weaker than Peggotty, is yet the more powerful influence on David. She constitutes for him the first love possession—a possession which he has won through his deserving, not through his simply being. She gives rise to his first agonies of jealousy and rejection, and to his first experience of loneliness. In the bright-eyed girl, who sits combing her hair, a distant fairy-tale creature may be observed: fragile, fractious, and, except on her own terms, unapproachable. "I watch her winding her bright curls round her fingers, and straightening her waist, and nobody knows better than I do that she likes to look so well, and is proud of being so pretty" (16). David as much as Mr. Murdstone is attracted by the beauty of her hair.

Up to this point, we might feel that the drama has been incomplete. Although we have the hero and his mother, we might ask, as does David himself, Where is the father? The answer is that he is not far away although he could not be further, for he is in the churchyard. From the beginning, David Copperfield senior has evoked an ambiguous response in his son.

> There is something strange to me, even now, in the reflection that he never saw me; and something stranger yet in the shadowy remembrance that I have of my first childish associations with his white gravestone in the churchyard, and of the indefinable compassion I used to feel for it lying out alone there in the dark night, when our little parlour was warm and bright with fire and candle, and the doors of our house were—almost cruelly, it seemed to me sometimes—bolted and locked against it. (2)

There is an uneasy balance in this paragraph between warmth and brightness—"fire and candle," the home and compassion, on the one hand, and gravestones, churchyards, bolts, locks, death, and cruelty, on the other. Dickens' superb control of the material is shown in the delicate shift in the direction of emotion produced by having David slip so naturally from talking about his father to talking about the gravestone. "He" gives way to "it," and the child's compassion is felt not for a human being but for a piece of stone. This reflects perfectly the imaginative animism of the child, and, at the same time, enables David to forget his father and avoid the realities of his parentage.

David Copperfield senior continues to be treated in this ambiguous manner throughout the first two chapters. His son insinuates a sense of sympathy for his father's "delicate constitution" and early death, but qualifies this by a sense of resentment that his mother was left so helpless, young, and unready to take upon herself the duties of self-dependence. David's father exists as a figure to be loved and to be feared, to be respected and to be despised. He has a place, but it is not of this earth. He dwells "for ever in the land of dreams and shadows, the tremendous region whence I had so lately travelled" (12). In this powerful and powerless fashion Copperfield senior enters the myth patterns of his son's life, imagination, and story. He is both good and evil. He remains so throughout the novel, entering and reentering its action in the guise of many characters, who are judged his good and evil manifestations insofar as David likes or dislikes them. The first resurrections of this Lazarus-like "Pa" are Edward Murdstone and Daniel Peggotty.

The distinguishing feature of the men who represent the hateful manifestation of the father is their gruff masculinity. They are all deep-voiced, hairy creatures. Murdstone sets the style: "His hair and whiskers were blacker and thicker . . . than even I had given them credit for being. A squareness about the lower part of his face, and the dotted indication of the strong black beard he shaved close every day, reminded me of the waxwork that had travelled into our neighbourhood some half-a-year before" (22). The coarse and domineering masculinity that David encounters first in Murdstone is found in varying degrees in all the characters created in the negative image of David Copperfield senior: from the extreme brutality of Creakle and his one-legged assistant through the "respectable" and malicious Littimer to its appearance in weakened and vulnerable form in the ostentatious Spenlow.

The idyl of Blunderstone is shattered point by point in Chapters iii and iv. When David returns from his journey to Yarmouth the empty kennel becomes filled with a great dog—"deep-mouthed and black-haired like Him—and he was very angry at the sight of me, and sprang out to get at me." The garden has become desolate; "I turned to the window and looked out there at some shrubs that were drooping their heads in the cold." The church has been darkened by "the taint of the Murdstone religion, which was austere and wrathful." The quiet grave-yard has given rise to "something" which "seemed to strike . . . like an unwholesome wind." The rookless Rookery is now invested with human birds of prey, and in place of the vaguely benevolent dust of David Copperfield senior is the obviously malevolent flesh and blood of

Mr. Murdstone. The topography of Eden is replaced by a landscape more immediate and cruel.

But David's father appears as a kindly man as well as a cruel one. Under this aspect, his first resurrection is as Daniel Peggotty, one who presides over and protects the orphaned and the helpless. He makes little of himself and defies anyone to express gratitude to him: "The only subject . . . on which he ever showed a violent temper or swore an oath, was this generosity of his; and if it were ever referred to, by any one of them, he struck the table a heavy blow with his right hand (had split it on one such occasion), and swore a dreadful oath that he would be 'Gormed' if he didn't cut and run for good, if it was ever mentioned again" (33). Patriarchal and biblical associations are made apparent in the "common coloured pictures, framed and glazed, of scriptural subjects" which decorate the walls of Peggotty's home. The identification of the gentle and generous fisherman with Noah is made explicit when David asks, "Did you give your son the name of Ham, because you lived in a sort of ark?" (32).

Daniel Peggotty's boat is a source of security, happiness, and childish delight to David. Like Wemmick's castle in *Great Expectations,* Mr. Tartar's chambers in *Edwin Drood,* or Riah's rooftop in *Our Mutual Friend,* it provides a retreat or escape from everyday realities, offers a world in which fantasy and truth merge, and permits a new ordering of human relationships. To those who come to them, these retreats offer "cosiness," a condition of felicity that Dickens would seem to value over rapture. The womblike associations of these places are obvious, particularly evidenced in the roundness, warmth, ease, and smallness of Peggotty's boat.

Just as Mr. Wemmick's castle can reorganize the relationships between man and man, so that Wemmick becomes the friendliest of men once his drawbridge is raised and he is freed of the Law and Little Britain, so Dan Peggotty's boat has the power of negating, nullifying, or denying the reality of sex. Perhaps the greatest anomaly of the Peggotty household is the fact that the four people who constitute it appear so much to be an actual family, but the only blood ties are those of uncle to nephew, uncle to niece. Dickens encourages the reader to see Daniel Peggotty's home as a fantasy place freed from sex and its problems. The "family" represents an extension of the childish delights of the home itself, which David sees as something out of a fairy tale: "If it had been Aladdin's palace, roc's egg and all, I suppose I could not have been more charmed with the romantic idea of living in it" (30). The reorganization of human relationships brings them into line with a child's wishes.

In his benevolence, warmth, and selflessness Daniel Peggotty is an antithesis to Murdstone. There is about Peggotty nothing of Murdstone's aggressive sexuality that so frightens and angers David as a child. In the fantasy world of the Yarmouth boat, David finds a father made to prescription. Peggotty's "family" permits David to escape from the terrors of his home. Daniel Peggotty himself maintains an aura of sexual innocence throughout the novel, and when he sets out "through the wureld" to seek Emily, like a patriarch who has lost his people, he is engaged in a quest to find "the pure light . . . of childhood."

Sexual innocence is a characteristic of most of those men, few in number, whom David likes or loves: Mr. Peggotty himself, the "bacheldore"; Mr. Barkis, more interested in Peggotty's cooking than in her person; Mr. Dick, a kite-flying boy; Dr. Strong, interested more as a father than a husband in his young wife, Annie. These characters are mild men, beginning with Mr. Chillip, "the meekest of his sex, the mildest of little men." Mr. Mell's initial appearance forebodes ill. He is "a gaunt, sallow young man, with hollow cheeks and a chin almost as black as Mr. Murdstone's," but he proves to be a gentle and merciful man who, David says, "was never harsh to me." Mr. Wickfield seems at first a hard lawyer seeking out every man's "motive," but he proves a generous guardian of David, the devoted father of Agnes, and the easy victim of Heep. Where David Copperfield senior emerges in mildness and weakness, David can find it in him to love his father.

Mr. Micawber remains unfettered by this organization of the novel. He is too volatile a character to remain long identified with either Peggotty or Murdstone. He is one of the very few characters for whom David is shown to have truly ambiguous feelings. David's reactions toward him are as mixed as those he has toward David Copperfield senior, and this fact explains the splendid anomaly of Micawber. He represents neither half of Copperfield senior but both halves together. He is a farcical manifestation of the melodramatic archetype. While the senior Copperfield is an inhabitant of the "land of dreams and shadows," evoking fear and compassion, Wilkins Micawber is very much of this earth, evoking contempt and affection. Paradoxically, Micawber, the most comical of the figures in the novel, is the most fully representative of the father figures. The hyperboles with which he is characterized give him a centrality which results from his erring equally in opposite directions.

Mrs. Micawber shares this hyperbolic centrality. She is young, pretty, and silly like Clara Copperfield, but she can be as motherly as Peggotty. In the early portion of the novel she is like some fertility goddess, always nursing a child: "Mrs. Micawber . . . was sitting in the parlour . . . with a baby at her breast. This baby was one of twins; and I may remark here that I hardly ever, in all my experience of the family, saw both the twins detached from Mrs. Micawber at the same time. One of them was always taking refreshment" (157). But when the mood is on her, Mrs. Micawber can become as morose as Miss Murdstone.

It is the conjunction of these disparate forces in the Micawbers that gives them their vitality. At work in Mr. Micawber are the ambiguities of David Copperfield senior, and it is the duality of this figure that shapes the manic-depressive oscillations of Micawber's life. It is the pressure of these equal and opposite forces within him which gives the self-explosive quality to Micawber's speeches.

> "Under the impression . . . that your peregrinations in this metropolis have not as yet been extensive, and that you might have some difficulty in penetrating the arcana of the Modern Babylon in the direction of the City Road—in short . . . that you might lose yourself." (156)

> "The blossom is blighted, the leaf is withered, the God of day goes down upon the dreary scene, and—and in short you are for ever floored." (175)

> "The twins no longer derive their sustenance from Nature's founts—in short . . . they are weaned." (257)

Micawber's trick of language is a syntactical demonstration of his inner conflicts. The world of fantasy—Yarmouth—begins to flower in his speech, only to be exploded by the sudden intrusion of the world of actuality—Murdstone and Grinby's.

When Mr. Micawber is swallowed up in the King's Bench Prison, David is again abandoned in this world. He is once again orphaned, once again deserted by his father. The prison itself is a kind of grave (a concept more fully developed in *A Tale of Two Cities*). It is at best a life-in-death. At this point, it is as if David's father has once more returned to "the land of dreams and shadows" after a most feeble attempt to take part in the struggle of life. David never again looks to the Micawbers for any serious help with the business of living. The methods of this extraordinary novel work superbly here to present and interpret the emotion and situation of the hero at this juncture of his life. A major change must take place if David is to grow up: new sufferings must be endured in order to pass the next rite of passage. David must now enter adolescence and naturally he must set out upon a new journey. What he proves most to be in need of is a new home and a mother unlike any of the three women of Blunderstone: Clara Copperfield, Miss Murdstone, and Peggotty. Up to this point, they have represented the range of motherhood for David.

The only one of them to whom David might turn is his old nurse—the figure of unselfish maternal devotion, for Peggotty has remained a single fixed point in David's universe; her love for him never changes, and his trust in her never fails but in Chapter xii when he forms his "great resolution" to fly from London, there is no thought of going to her. It is not because he has forgotten that she has promised him: "Young or old, Davy dear, as long as I am alive and have this house over my head . . . you shall find [the bedroom] as if I expected you here directly minute. I shall keep it every day, as I used to keep your old little room, my darling; and if you was to go to China, you might think of it being kept just the same, all the time you were away" (148). When David has to leave London, he will not, can not, return to this. What he goes in search of on the Dover Road is the promise of the fairy tale: fame, fortune, the princess. His maturation would be brought to a pathetic stop if he were to return to the alpha and omega of mother love.

In one of those touches in which the novel abounds, David (and the reader) has been taught a lesson which clearly indicates why David should not return to Peggotty. A digression from the first journey to Salem House brings David in the company of Mr. Mell to the London almshouse inhabited by Mrs. Mell, the schoolmaster's mother. Mrs. Mell is a woman who adores her son and who is rewarded by his attention and his flute-playing. In the almshouse, David is half asleep by the fire, watching this mother and son.

> I dreamed, I thought, that once while he was blowing into this dismal flute, the old woman of the house, who had gone nearer and nearer to him in her ecstatic admiration, leaned over the back of his chair and gave him an affectionate squeeze round the neck, which stopped his playing for a moment. I was in the middle state between sleeping and waking, either then or immediately afterwards; for, as he resumed—it was a real fact that he had stopped playing—I saw and heard the same old woman ask Mrs. Fibbitson if it wasn't delicious (meaning the flute), to which Mrs. Fibbitson replied, "Ay, ay! yes!" and nodded at the fire: to which, I am persuaded, she gave the credit of the whole performance. (76)

David's experience in Mrs. Mell's room may be described as a psychic allegory, in which the role of Mr. Mell, the dismal flute player or failed artist, figures as importantly as that of Mrs. Mell, the loving mother. The description of the whole sequence occupies little more than a page and a half, and it counts as a minor interruption of David's journey to his school. The house is never revisited, and the old woman is only referred to once again—when Mr. Mell is dismissed from Salem House. But the scene is as relevant and as necessary as a minor scene in Shakespeare. What David witnesses in his half-sleep is a picture of mother love. David has no idea that the two are mother and son, nor does he fully understand what such love means, but two things strike him most forcibly: the love itself, and the discrepancy between the flute-playing and the "ecstatic admiration" that the old woman shows.

Another figure appears in this scene: Mrs. Fibbitson. She is drawn rapidly but completely and shown to be a malevolent, deeply selfish, and miserably possessive creature. "Although it was a warm day, she seemed to think of nothing but the fire. I fancied she was jealous even of the saucepan on it. . . . I saw her, with my own discomfited eyes, shake her fist at me once. . . . The sun streamed in at the little window, but she sat with her own back and the back of the large chair towards it, screening the fire as if she were sedulously keeping *it* warm" (75). She begrudges Mrs. Mell's joy in her son and attributes any credit for his performance to something other than himself—in fact, to the fire which she guards so carefully and which is the whole of her life. "If the fire was to go out, through any accident, I verily believe she'd go out too, and never come to life again." If, in Mrs. Mell, David has met the second of the many Peggottys in his life, in Mrs. Fibbitson, he meets the second Miss Murdstone.

Mr. Mell is a good son, but a miserable musician. It is worth remembering at this point that *The Personal History of David Copperfield* is a portrait of the artist as a young man. Like Charles Dickens and James Joyce, David grows up to be a novelist. The fatal effects of the suffocating influence of the mother's "estatic admiration" are further reinforced by the careers of Steerforth and Heep, both of whom are the sons of doting mothers. David's "great resolution" therefore is to go in search of a new (though as we shall see not entirely new) kind of mother: Miss Betsey Trotwood.

Between her and London lies a long and horrendous journey and not only because it must be made on foot. David is set upon by a multitude of Murdstones from the very outset. There is a young man who steals his box, a tinker who steals his handkerchief, and (most horrible of all) a clothing man who tries to steal his jacket. This monster rushes from his "den" with "trembling hands which were like the claws of a great bird," crying all the while, "Oh, what do you want? . . . Oh, my eyes and limbs, what do you want? Oh, my lungs and liver, what do you want? Oh goroo, goroo!" (184). As Harry Stone has commented, "Dickens unites the clothing dealer with a . . . sinister childhood objectification of evil . . . ogreism, cannibalism, and ghoulism" [3]—particularly, when we think of Copperfield senior, ghoulism.

Betsey Trotwood is a strange person and much that is strange about her is explained by the suggestion that she is a fairy godmother. This is a commonplace of Dickens criticism, for a number of obvious clues establish Betsey's fairy identity. The most plain occurs when

David says, at the end of the first chapter, "She vanished like a discontented fairy; or like one of those supernatural beings whom it was popularly supposed I was entitled to see: and never came back any more" (12). She is irascible, eccentric, and filled with an ominous power. "She gave my mother such a turn, that I have always been convinced I am indebted to Miss Betsey for having been born on a Friday" (4). It is not so much that she is not invited to the birth as that she brings the birth about. She is no "ordinary Christian."

Fairies, good or bad, embody qualities, spiritual and psychological, which shape individual character and direct human relationships. The wicked fairy appears, suddenly and dramatically in a story, to wish ill fortune on the newborn child and to foretell a grim destiny usually ending in unpleasant death. This fairy is representative, on a material plane, of that aspect of life which is nasty, brutish, and short; on a spiritual plane, of the forces of evil; and on a psychological plane, of the hostility which is present toward the family intruder. The hostility is toward, if there is a sibling, this rival for parental affection; toward, if there is a father, this coveter of the womanly love. The King and Queen may forget to invite the wicked fairy to Princess Aurora's christening, but they cannot and do not dispute the fairy's right to be there once she has arrived. Discontent asserts itself and demands recognition.

The bearing of this on *Copperfield* is made intricate and effective because of the initial complications of its use. There are not two fairies, a good and a bad at the birth, but only Betsey Trotwood. She is both good and bad fairy at once. Her behavior, ominous and irascible, and her conduct unlike that of any ordinary Christian are suggestive of the role of bad fairy, doom-speaker, Death. Her malevolent appearance is based upon a misunderstanding of Betsey's eccentricity; her later conduct proves her to be the good and protecting fairy in the life of her charge. Why, then, does Dickens mislead the reader at the start of the book? The reason, clearly, is more than that Betsey is a good fairy who is merely mistaken for a bad one. Her negative role must be taken seriously. She must be seen for what she is in the first chapter, however later developments may modify the reader's idea of her.

The Betsey Trotwood of the first chapter is one of Dickens' great caricatures. She is to be compared with Quilp, Mrs. Gamp, or even Krook, but most of all, she is to be compared with the eccentric Miss Havisham of *Great Expectations*. Both are aging women, both disappointed in love, both autocratic, irascible, determined. Both offer, or seem to offer, their protégés great expectations. More important than any of these qualities, both share an underlying sexual bitterness. Both use this as a source of strength, motivation, and consolation. It is because Betsey Trotwood has this is common with Miss Havisham that Betsey (as essentially different from Miss Havisham as comedy is from tragedy) can properly play the role of wicked fairy at the opening of a novel in which she is later to prove to be the most generous of women. The link with the corrupting evil of Miss Havisham's soul is made clear in Chapter xiii when Betsey is reintroduced into the story. David says of her maid, Janet: "Though I made no further observation of her at the moment, I may mention here what I did not discover until afterwards, namely, that she was one of a series of protégées whom my aunt had taken into her service expressly to educate in a renouncement of mankind, and who had generally completed their abjuration by marrying the baker." (194). Dickens here gives comic expression to the motivation that in his later novel makes for the sad perversion of Estella's life. Betsey Trotwood might have made an Estella out of Betsey Trotwood Copperfield, if she had been born on that Friday night. Betsey is denied the opportunity to play wicked godmother to a daughter so that she may eventually take upon herself the role of true mother to the son who comes homeless from the Dover road, "Taking," he tells us "very little more out of the world, towards the retreat of my aunt, Miss Betsey, than I had brought into it, on the night when my arrival gave her so much umbrage" (179).

As David finds the right kind of mother in Miss Betsey, he also finds the right kind of father in Mr. Dick. He, like Mr. Peggotty, is one of those gentle, innocent, and docile men who play the role of benevolent father to David. " 'I shall be delighted,' said Mr. Dick, 'to be the guardian of David's son' " (214). It is a subtle autobiographical touch and a reminder of Charles Dickens' own relationship with his father that Mr. Dick is preoccupied with writing a Memorial about himself but which somehow gets confused with King Charles the First. He had been "upwards of ten years endeavouring to keep King Charles the First out of the Memorial; but he had been constantly getting into it, and was there now" (205). This king of England and the creator of Mr. Dick are both christened "Charles," and Mr. Dick's name is cut short from "Dickens" as King Charles' head was cut short from his shoulders. Some vaguely formed ideas about castration seem to float in poor Mr. Dick's head, while Mr. Dickens may feel that the story of the original Charles may be "getting into" this memorial of David Copperfield.

Betsey Trotwood gives to David a "new life, in a new name, and with everything new." This new scenario for the drama of the three actors, she gives in a form which the young boy can accept and can allow to supplant earlier and terrifying family patterns. Her acceptance of David is her own psychic and spiritual salvation. By it, she overcomes her own obsessions. Betsey Trotwood's hysteria is most frequently provoked by donkeys and boys who invade her "immaculate spot." Hence her initial animosity toward David when he arrives at Dover and walks across this lawn in front of her cottage. Her most powerful outbreak of the donkey-mania is caused when Miss Murdstone rides with abandon and impudence over the piece of lawn. The reason for Betsey Trotwood's huge indignation is not far to seek. The cruel and malignant Miss Murdstone is the very person that Betsey would have become had David not saved her. What are, in effect, the death throes of her mania's controlling hold vent themselves upon this person, albeit a woman, who so blatantly invades the "immaculate spot." What are seen in Miss Murdstone and Aunt Betsey are the developments of the ambiguous aspects of Betsey Trotwood, the eccentric visitor to the Rookery. Miss Murdstone is an incarnation of the malevolent fairy; Aunt Betsey of the good. Their coming together necessarily produces conflict, and it is part of the optimistic scheme of the book that Miss Murdstone, along with her brother, is routed. David's wanderings are over for a time and in the peaceful Dover home he is able to grow up.

The first significant act that he makes when he is grown up, or put another way the indication that he has grown up, is that he takes a journey. This time he returns in triumph along the London-Dover road on his way back to Yarmouth. This trip marks the end of his boyhood as he erases the defeat and retreat of his childhood: "It was curious and interesting . . . to be sitting up there, behind four horses: well educated, well dressed, and with plenty of money in my pocket; and to look out for the places where I had slept on my weary journey" (284). David's initial journeys are all provoked by Murdstone as those of the good-luck child in the fairy story are all provoked by the wicked King. Each stage not only acknowledges Murdstone's power, but it also registers a diminution of that power. As the luck-child gradually gains the ascendancy over the wicked King, so David gradually grows in strength against Murdstone. From this perspective, Murdstone, like the wicked King, is not merely the measure of the hero's growing manhood but equally the goad or incentive to the hero, driving him from the pillar of childhood to the post of manhood.

But it is no easy business. Though David is making his return journey along the Dover road at his own behest, neither being driven by nor fleeing from Murdstone, the trip is a humiliating one. Nobody is prepared to recognize David for the man he now thinks he may take himself to be. Throughout, David is embarrassed and mortified at being treated as a child—by the coachman, by the horse dealer who takes his place on the box seat, and by the waiter at the Golden Cross, who gives him the lees of the sherry and a poor bedroom. These gruff, forceful, very masculine men will not grant David a place among their ranks; like so many Murdstones, though less terrible than those who had beset him when he fled from London to Dover, they deny him his rightful position. He says of the loss of the box seat: "I have always considered this as the first fall I had in life." His humiliation centers upon his high-pitched voice and his thinness of beard. He affects to be grown up by trying "to speak extremely gruff." When Littimer or the maid at the Golden Cross bring him his shaving water, it seems to be done in a spirit of mockery and reproach. Littimer further offends the prickly adolescent by seeming always to be on the point of saying to David, "You are very young, sir; you are very young."

David's arrival in London is the starting point for the most complicated and lengthy regrouping of the "promiscuous array" of characters into the drama of the three actors. Gradually Dickens reassembles the cast of the Blunderstone home so that the whole opening sequence from David's birth to his acceptance in the Dover Cottage is rehearsed. This time David is in a role of greater power and control corresponding to his growth in years and maturity. This action gains full momentum when David meets Dora Spenlow. The intervening chapters between his arrival in London in Chapter xix and this meeting in Chapter xxvi see the parallel developments of Steerforth's attraction for Little Emily, Heep's desire for Agnes Wickfield, and Traddles' love for his Sophy.

In the Spenlow household David finds Miss Murdstone acting at once as guardian and tyrant of Dora. Mr. Spenlow, a possessive and selfish father, has what David wants, just as Edward Murdstone took what David had. Thus we are led to make the crucial identification of Dora Spenlow with Clara Copperfield, an identification reinforced by Dora's appearance and behavior. As a further reminder, Mr. Murdstone himself reappears in Chapter xxxiii when he comes to Doctors' Commons to obtain of all things a marriage license, to wed "a new wife . . . just of age . . . so lately, that I should think they have been waiting for that," says Mr. Spenlow. In this same chapter, Peggotty is once again brought into close contact with David. Her husband has died, the flight of Emily has broken up the home provided by Dan Peggotty, and so the old nurse has come to London to be near David. This regrouping of the Blunderstone characters coincides with the collapse of Betsey Trotwood's fortune and her own arrival in London, no longer offering security to David but seeking it from him.

In this situation David is given the opportunity of becoming a hero under the very same circumstances that led to his defeat when he was faced with them as an infant. The forces that he himself could not overcome then had to be overcome by Betsey Trotwood. She, his fairy godmother, defeated the Murdstones in the confrontation at the Dover cottage. But the victory was Pyrrhic. David alone was saved; everything else was lost. In the second confrontation, David faces the specters of his infant terror with an ease equal to his success. The dragons and ogres disappear before him. The stature and the power of the Murdstones crumble. Miss Murdstone has become a lady's maid, a Miss

Murdstone no less bitter or vindictive but a Miss Murdstone who no longer terrifies; Mr. Murdstone can be seen, at last, as a despicable and cheap marriage opportunist, a confidence trickster of the domestic emotions. David is not to be resisted now. His very wishes hold sway: Spenlow drops dead at the height of his opposition to the marriage with Dora.

The death of Spenlow sweeps Miss Murdstone away to be replaced by the Spenlow aunts. Like Betsey Trotwood, they become friendly guardians to a ward who had disappointed them at birth. "Having been, on the occasion of Dora's christening, invited to tea, when they considered themselves privileged to be invited to dinner, they had expressed their opinion in writing, that it was 'better for the happiness of all parties' that they should stay away. Since which they had gone their road, and their brother had gone his" (559). By this gesture alone, they align themselves with the fairy-tale elements in the story. Without more ado, David comes into the possession of his desire: he has won the princess and he marries the child-wife. But they do not live happily ever after. Why?

The image of Clara Copperfield has haunted David. Taken from him dead in his childhood, she takes something of himself with her. Her death is a source of pain to him not only because it deprives him of her presence, but because it prevents him from ever refinding the self who exists so fully and so unconsciously happy in pre-Murdstone Blunderstone: "The mother who lay in the grave, was the mother of my infancy; the little creature in her arms, was myself, as I had once been, hushed forever on her bosom" (133). His sense of loss is never more painful than when he comes closest to repossessing it by his marriage to Dora.

> The old unhappy feeling pervaded my life. It was deepened, if it were changed at all; but it was as undefined as ever, and addressed me like a strain of sorrowful music faintly heard in the night. I loved my wife dearly, and I was happy; but the happiness I had vaguely anticipated, once, was not the happiness I enjoyed, and there was always something wanting. . . .
> What I missed, I still regarded—I always regarded—as something that had been a dream of my youthful fancy; that was incapable of realisation; that I was now discovering to be so, with some natural pain, as all men did. (697)

The name that Dora asks David to use in this disappointing marriage is one that might be equally well applied to Clara.

> "Will you call me a name I want you to call me?" inquired Dora, without moving.

"What is it?" I asked with a smile.

"It's a stupid name," she said, shaking her curls for a moment. "Child-wife." (643)

Clara wants the same kind of clemency from Murdstone that Dora seeks from David through this name.

David cannot repossess Clara except in the unfulfilling form of Dora. Dora is not in reality what she is in desire, and David attempts to remedy this by changing Dora: "What other course was left to take? To 'form her mind?' This was a common phrase of words which had a fair and promising sound, and I resolved to form Dora's mind" (694). The attempt is, as it must be, unsuccessful: "Finding at last, however, that, although I had been all this time a very porcupine or hedgehog, bristling all over with determination, I had effected nothing, it began to occur to me that perhaps Dora's mind was already formed" (695). Later in this chapter, the first suggestions of Dora's death emerge: " 'Good night, Little Blossom,' I sat down at my desk alone, and cried to think, Oh what a fatal name it was, and how the blossom withered in its bloom upon the tree!" (700). Dora endures David's program of reform as Clara endured Murdstone's policy of "firmness." It is this last which killed Clara, as Betsey Trotwood points out to Murdstone: "Through the best part of her weakness you gave her the wounds she died of" (213). Clara is killed by deliberate cruelties, where Dora is killed by kindly neglect.

David must once more engage in the bitter drama of the three actors for he has not yet become King. The final, slightly weary, reenactment begins again with a journey. David leaves England altogether and does not return until he is unconsciously ready to do battle again. The roles of the three actors are distributed this time among David, Agnes, Peggotty, Betsey Trotwood, and Mr. Dick—the most favorable grouping that David can expect. There is perhaps a difficulty which Dickens seems not to have fully resolved. While Agnes is well suited to fill the part vacated by Dora and Clara, she is for that reason not altogether promising as a person with whom David can live happily ever after.

For David, she too is conceived in the image of his mother and can therefore take the place of Dora. From the beginning David holds an image of Agnes as the angel in the stained-glass window, just as he holds in his memory the picture of his dead mother with "the little creature in her arms." More important, Agnes is incorporated into David's sense of family, so that in the course of his life he directs his love to his actual mother (Clara), his fantasy daughter (Dora), and his fantasy sister (Agnes). "But Agnes, if I have indeed any new-born hope that I may ever call you something more than Sister, widely different from Sister!" (862). It is because Agnes has been his sister that she can now be his wife. Dora has brought Agnes to David: " 'She told me that she made a last request to me, and left me a last charge . . . that only I would occupy this vacant place.' And Agnes laid her head upon my breast" (865). Just so, Clara had brought David to Dora.

Balanced against this trio of beautiful and chaste women—Clara, Dora, Agnes—is a trio of beautiful but fallen women—Little Emily, Martha Endell, and Rosa Dartle. Emily provides David with his first romance after that with his mother. She is in the same petite, babylike, pettish school of beauty; she too has curls. As a child he is attracted to Emily for the same reasons and to as high a degree, if not higher, as he is, when a man, attracted to Dora: "I am sure that I loved that baby quite as truly, quite as tenderly, with greater purity and more disinterestedness, than can enter into the best love of a later time of life, high and ennobling as it is" (37). This love is for David the more exalted because the more pure.

The romance with Little Emily is concluded by James Steerforth and not by David Copperfield. From the beginning, Steerforth, unlike David, is presented as a sexually strong, attractive personality. Indeed, initially, the attraction of Steerforth for David has a distinctly homosexual overtone.

> "You haven't got a sister, have you?" said Steerforth yawning.
> "No," I answered.
> "That's a pity," said Steerforth, "If you had had one, I should think she would have been a pretty, timid, little, bright-eyed sort of girl. I should have liked to know her. Good-night, young Copperfield." (87)

This, by way of a dramatic irony, is a reference to Little Emily, who is just that "sort of girl," but it is nonetheless a strong indication of the attraction which exists between the boys. The conversation is immediately followed by David's first glimpse and description of Steerforth asleep: "I thought of him very much after I went to bed, and raised myself, I recollect, to look at him where he lay in the moonlight, with his handsome face turned up, and his head reclining easily on his arm. He was a person of great power in my eyes; that was, of course, the reason of my mind running on him" (87–88).

When they meet later in London, Steerforth treats David as if he were a girl: "A dashing way he had of treating me like a plaything, was more agreeable to me than any behaviour he could have adopted" (301). Steerforth sums up the careless ambience of the friendship when he takes to calling David by the feminine name of "Daisy." " 'My dear young Davy,' he said, clapping me on the shoulder again, 'you are a very Daisy. The daisy of the field, at sunrise, is not fresher than you are'" (288). This name is partially suggested by David's naïveté and unsophisticated ignorance of London fashion, but like Mrs. Crupp's calling him "Mr. Copperfull," it suggests more than one aspect of the relationship between the namer and the named. Only Miss Dartle, Steerforth's discarded mistress, makes any comment on it. She does so in her elliptical and obscure fashion, implying that there is something beyond youth and innocence in the name's suggestions.

> "But really, Mr. Copperfield," she asked, "is it a nickname? And why does he give it you? Is it—eh?—because he thinks you young and innocent? I am so stupid in these things."
> I coloured in replying that I believe it was.
> "Oh!" said Miss Dartle. "Now I am glad to know that! I ask for information, and I am glad to know it. He thinks you young and innocent; and so you are his friend? Well, that's quite delightful!" (297)

The strongly sexual aura which surrounds Steerforth and which is the basis for David's admiration of his hero culminates in the part they both play in the seduction of Little Emily, "the pretty, timid, little, bright-eyed sort of girl." There are many links which associate David with Steerforth's seduction of Emily. The introduction to Peggotty's boat-home for which David is responsible is but one, and David summarizes his behavior as "my own unconscious part in [Steerforth's] pollution of an honest home."

Steerforth's arrival in the "honest home" coincides with the announcement of Emily and Ham's engagement. The suggestions of the love between brother and sister (repeated later in David's wooing of Agnes), the childlike affection of Ham, and Emily's refusal to give any of the usual signs of love and affection to him combine to suggest the difficulty that the recognition of sex entails in the boat-retreat. To this innocent and pure home Steerforth is drawn, in his own words, "by instinct."

The sea has made the home what it is. It has taken off the fathers and husband and united this unlikely group. The sea has provided the home itself, in the form of a disused, or reused, boat. The sea represents an ever-present danger to the boat, which is in an anomalous, not to say an unnatural, position "high and dry on the ground," just as the realities of sex suggest an anomalous, not to say unnatural, condition in the family.

Steerforth's instinct is that of the sea, and it is the sea which controls the whole of Steerforth's action. The lure of the sea brings Steerforth to Yarmouth; it gives him an entrée to the lives and business of the Peggottys; it provides him with the means of seducing Little Emily from her own people on the boat he has named for her; and, the seduction complete, the sea allows Steerforth to take his mistress abroad, beyond the retrieval of those who love her. The sea finally brings him back to Yarmouth and to death in the "tempest" which destroys the boat-home.

The power of the sea and the power of Steerforth's sexual instinct become identified and it is this force which necessarily brings destruction within the once magic circle of Peggotty's boat where the realities of sexuality have been denied. The strength of this natural power overwhelms the unnaturally placed boat "high and dry on the ground." It brings death by drowning to the innocent Ham as well as to the guilty Steerforth. It is not a moral force, simply a natural force neither to be played with nor denied. This seems to be the lesson in the fate of the two men drowned at Yarmouth. Now the significance of David's caul becomes again apparent. The immunity from drowning which the hero is granted on the first page of the book is a promise that he has immunity from the destructive forces of sexual impulse; it is a token that he will not be destroyed in the turbulent waters of sexual contact, nor overwhelmed in the series of family dramas which occupy the pages of his personal history.

David experiences an agony when Emily, a woman like Dora and Agnes conceived for him in the undying image of his mother, makes overt her sexual nature and is as a consequence reduced to the contaminated and outcast condition of Martha Endell and Rosa Dartle. Protected as he is from drowning, David is not, like Steerforth, destroyed by his encounters with the sexual woman; he is chastened, however, and the reader is warned of the dangers that the hero runs as he makes his way from the forbidden love of his mother through the unfulfilling love of Dora to the "love founded on a rock" in Agnes. Here, Dickens asserts, David finds happiness.

The question put by David at the beginning of his story—"whether I shall be the hero of my life, or whether that station will be held by anybody else"—is then answered by the energy he displays in his encounters with the manifold reappearances of his father and the endless struggle to establish a family he might call his own. The meaning of heroism in *David Copperfield* is contained in this: a child despite all odds becomes a man and himself the father of children. And the odds though great are not extraordinary because every one of us, like the luck-child, is threatened from the beginning by destruction. *The Personal History of David Copperfield* is not only autobiographical in the sense that Dickens created it out of his own childhood experiences; it is also David's autobiography. In our dreams, we are all heroes and so in this autobiographical novel the ordinary process of growing up becomes, through mythological projection, extraordinary, universal, and heroic. David does turn out, after all, to be the hero of his life.

Nina Auerbach

DICKENS AND DOMBEY

A Daughter After All

DICKENS' DAUGHTER'S indictment—"my father did not understand women" [1]—continues to gain momentum, until for some readers, it has threatened to obliterate his entire achievement.[2] His heroines are regularly dismissed as "so many pale-pink blancmanges, in the same dutiful mold"; [3] he is placed historically as "not so much the recorder of Victorian womanhood as the dupe or the exploiter of its ideal." [4]

But if Dickens dreamed the Victorian dream of "wooman, lovely wooman" diffusing rarified conjugal salvation to man in his besotted worldliness, his life and his novels quietly dramatize its component human loss. The "two nations" into which his England was divided defined the worlds of the sexes as well as those of Disraeli's rich and poor. Men and women were allotted different boundaries, different dreams, different vices and virtues; the ideal woman revolved alone in her unique "sphere," suggesting a cosmic dimension to the home she created and purified as an intermittent refuge for men from the machinery of their lives. Despite the wedding bells that clang manically through Dickens' novels, there is a note of sexual sadness and loss at the heart of all his work that suggests the isolation inherent in this sexual division, looking forward to such formulated feminist complaints as that of Elizabeth Wolstenholme: "Of the saddest results of the separate education and life of the sexes, it is impossible here to speak; as a slighter, but still mischievous result, it is sufficient to notice the profound ignorance of each other's real nature and ways of thinking common to both men and women. . . . Many a life has been wrecked upon mistakes arising out of this ignorance." [5]

As *Great Expectations* is Dickens' most definitive indictment of his own earlier dream of miraculous metamorphosis from waif into gentleman, so *Dombey and Son* seems to me his most thorough exploration of his own and his contemporaries' doctrine of the "two spheres," with each sex moving in a solitary orbit inaccessible to the other one. The distance between the icy merchant, Paul Dombey Sr., and his boundlessly loving daughter Florence, and the incessant need of each for the other, disclose more intimately one reality behind Victorian sexual relationships than does the transfiguration of Dickens' forgettable lovers when the plot forces them together. Unable to sit easily together in the same room, father and daughter illuminate a cultural abyss which is reflected in the stereotyped gestures toward bliss of Dickens' husbands and wives.

Throughout his novels, Dickens' dream of love is inseparable from his dream of kinship. Even Pip's obsession with Estella, which is usually considered the most sustained and adult passion in the canon, is revealed at the end to be effectively the love of brother for sister. After his own separation from his wife, Dickens tried to stave off rumors about his affair with Ellen Ternan in conventional language with ambiguous overtones: "I know her to be innocent and pure, and as good as my own dear daughters." [6] As in Freud's Victorian paradigm of emotional development, the language of love is at one with the language of family. But among the novels, *Dombey and Son* alone stays within the family walls and reveals the emotional waste beneath its institutional pieties. In most of Dickens' novels, "home" is "an intimate and emotion-laden word," [7] a vague haven of love and light waiting to embrace the wandering protagonists. But in *Dombey,* Dickens writes: "Oh for a good spirit who would take the house-tops off, with a more potent and benignant hand than the lame demon in the tale, and show a Christian people what dark shapes issue from amidst their homes, to swell the retinue of the Destroying Angel as he moves forth among them!" (648). The novel's narrator, who is himself the "good spirit" hovering over the action and exposing it, reveals the pestilence hidden in "home," rather than reassuring us at the end with its glow.

The rift of home in *Dombey and Son* is defined by the rift between Mr. Dombey and Florence, who spend much of the novel haunting their solitary rooms in the great dark house and brooding about each other. They are the polar deities of this polarized novel, and the tension between them generates the tension of the book. They exist as absolutes, memorable less for their individual psychologies than for their magnitude as embodiments of masculinity and femininity as these were conventionally perceived. According to Sylvia Manning: "In his work Dickens reveals a certain consciousness, though never articulated, of a polarity between the male and female that is both physiological and psychological and of this duality of the sexes as a reflection of metaphysical realities." [8] Dombey and his daughter are scarcely plausible as physiological and psychological beings alone; in the novel's scheme, they seem less to reflect than to embody the "metaphysical realities" Manning defines, as the iron force of Dombey's masculine will gives way before Florence's quietly irresistible magnetic field. In Victorian terminology, the power of the man who controls the world gives way before the influence of the woman who controls the mind. A popular conduct book of the day demarcates the spheres in which power and influence, respectively, exert their sway:

> [Man's] power is principally exerted in the shape of authority, and is limited in its sphere of action. [Woman's] influence has its source in human sympathies, and is as boundless in its operation. . . . We see that power, while it regulates men's actions, cannot reach their opinions. It cannot modify dispositions nor implant sentiments, nor alter character. All these things are the work of influence. Men frequently resist power, while they yield to influence an unconscious acquiescence.[9]

Men and women possess the world and the self, respectively, and their holdings do not touch. Seen in the light of these radically separate spheres, *Dombey and Son* tells the story of male and female principles who can neither evade nor understand each other, whose tragedy and whose force come from their mutual exclusiveness.

— 2 —

In the first chapter of the novel, the postures and the rhythms of the central characters introduce us to the warring worlds they embody. Stiff and erect as always, Dombey jingles his "heavy gold watch-chain" over his newborn son and heir. Meanwhile Florence clings to her dying mother, her hair spreading over the pillow as Mrs. Dombey's consciousness ebbs away on "the dark and unknown sea that rolls round all the world" (10). The ticking of Dombey's watch fights the silence of birth and death, seeming to speed up incessantly in a senseless race with that of Dr. Peps, until, in Florence's embrace, his wife cuts herself loose from time.

The loud watch which is so inseparable a part of Dombey is the voice of the civilization which gives him his power. The implacable, arbitrary dominance of clock-time counterpoints his wife's equally implacable diffusion into death and space; time here is masculine; space, feminine. The tendency of his watch to accelerate is an emblem of his own attempt to force natural processes to march to the imperious rhythm of his manufactured ticking: "Therefore he was impatient to advance into the future, and to hurry over the intervening passages of [Paul's] history" (91). "Dear me, six will be changed to sixteen, before we have time to look about us" (138), he insists as he sends Paul to Dr. Blimber's "great hothouse" in which "all the boys blew before their time" and "Nature was of no consequence at all" (141). Captain Cuttle, who lives near the sea's cycle, has a ritual formula to prevent his own treasured silver watch from outrunning nature—"Put it back half an hour every morning, and about another quarter towards the arternoon, and it's a watch that'll do you credit" (269)—but Dombey, with his network of power, seems to have no reason to check the time he carries with him in his pocket.

The new reliance on watches, with their arbitrary and manufactured measurement of arbitrary and manufactured time-units, was a reality in the 1840s and 1850s: England was in the process of attuning itself to the railroad and its schedule. Later in the novel, the loud ticking of Mr. Dombey's watch will swell into the railroad's prefabricated roar, in a manner which is anticipated beforehand:

> Wonderful Members of Parliament, who, little more than twenty years before, had made themselves merry with the wild railroad theories of engineers, and given them the liveliest rubs in cross-examination, *went down into the north with their watches in their hands,* and sent on messages before by the electric telegraph, to say that they were coming. Night and day the conquering engines rumbled at their distant work, or, advancing smoothly to their journey's end, and gliding like tame dragons into the allotted corners grooved out to the inch for their reception, stood bubbling and trembling there, making the walls quake, as if they were dilating with the secret knowledge of great powers yet unsuspected in them, and strong purposes not yet achieved. (218–19, my italics)

As the railroad and the watch came to demarcate the day, the agricultural calendar, with its seasons and ceremonies of growth and harvest, receded into a picturesque anachronism: natural rural time was out of joint with most men's lives.[10] But its organic and cyclical rhythms are still a powerful reality in *Dombey and Son:* in the sea that "rolls round all the world" which Dombey tries to wind up like his watch; in the "odd weedy little flowers" in the bonnets and caps of Miss Tox, and the "strange grasses" that are "sometime perceived in her hair"; and in the agricultural immortality with which Polly Toodles comforts Florence for the loss of her mother:

> "Died, never to be seen again by any one on earth, and was buried in the ground where the trees grow."
> "The cold ground?" said the child, shuddering again.
> "No! The warm ground . . . where the ugly little seeds turn into beautiful flowers, and into grass, and corn, and I don't know what all besides. Where good people turn into bright angels and fly away to Heaven!" (24)

To Dombey, who lives by progression, events are completed by the ceremonies which define them: funerals, christenings, and weddings. At the same time, the females are the custodians of the natural cycle of eternal return, guarding its unwilled comings and goings with their somewhat ominous ability to wait.

To Dombey, this other, revolving world is invisible: he "intimated his opinion that Nature was, no doubt, a very respectable institution" (289). He is as single-minded an artifact of civilization as his watch is. Early in the novel, we see him "turning round in his easy chair, as one piece, and not as a man with limbs and joints" (15). His identification of himself with the machinery of his civilization is at one with his emphatic masculinity. Throughout the book, he is referred to in terms of his stiffness, rigidity, unbendingness, which at times seem to make him less a phallic symbol than the thing itself: "The stiff and stark fire-irons appeared to claim a nearer relationship than anything else there to Mr. Dombey, with his buttoned coat, his white cravat, his heavy gold watch-chain, and his creaking boots" (52). "He is not 'brought down,' these observers think, by sorrow and distress of mind. His walk is as erect, his bearing as stiff as ever it has been" (240). Toward the end of the novel, Mrs. Brown reduces his perpetual erectness to one unconquerable attribute: "Oh, hard, hard, hard!" (725). This almost incantatory insistence upon a single set of traits makes Mr. Dombey seem the appropriate male divinity of an iron world.

His ethos is at one with his inveterate phallicism. Though he is supposed to be the Victorian businessman par excellence, reducing everything to financial terms, his outlook is more fundamentally sexual than it is monetary; he is more aware of his firm's thoroughgoing maleness than of its profits. His vision is cosmic and complete. He will not bring the flowing Polly Toodles into contact with his son until he has masculinized her by forcing on her the name of "Richards." His firm is the masculine axis at the turning of the world: "The earth was made for Dombey and Son to trade in, and the sun and moon were made to give them light. Rivers and seas were formed to float their ships; rainbows gave them promise of fair weather; winds blew for or against their enterprises; stars and planets circled in their orbits, to preserve inviolate a system of which they were the centre. Common abbreviations took new meanings in his eyes, and had sole reference to them. A. D. had no concern with anno Domini, but stood for anno Dombei—and Son" (2). Unlike other overweening institutions in Dickens' novels—Chancery in *Bleak House,* or the Circumlocution Office in *Little Dorrit*—Dombey and Son is defined in terms that are sexual and metaphysical rather than social. It exists as a gigantic end, the source and destination of all motion, all order, the center not so much of its society as of its universe.

Implicit in this religion is its sense of the female as defective because she is out of tune with the basic masculine rhythm of the cosmos. "But what was a girl to Dombey and Son! In the capital of the House's name and dignity, such a child was merely a piece of base coin that couldn't be invested—a bad Boy—nothing more" (3). Dombey's devaluation of the lovely Florence is the first hint of his lack of business skill, his obsession with gender rather than profits, for in fact a girl is an excellent investment if she is equipped to marry well: Mrs. Skewton knows this as she hawks her accomplished and exquisitely-groomed Edith, Mrs. Brown as she sells her Alice. Dombey's inability to see beyond his inviolate masculine "system" into the female business of love is the flaw that will bring down his House. His vision of a girl as nothing more than "a bad Boy" recalls the sick spleen of Tennyson's narrator in *Locksley Hall,* published four years before *Dombey:*

Weakness to be wroth with weakness! · woman's pleasure, woman's
  pain—
Nature made them blinder motions bounded in a shallower brain:

Woman is the lesser man, and all thy passions, matched with mine,
Are as moonlight unto sunlight, and as water unto wine—

$$(149-52)$$

Like Dombey, Tennyson's speaker judges woman by himself, refusing to recognize her as unique and discrete. The lesson of *The Princess* will correct him: "For woman is not undevelopt man, But diverse" (VII, 259–60). From the recognition of incompatibility comes conversion into love. This vision of love predicated on divergence is inherent in the titles of the two lectures that form John Ruskin's *Sesame and Lilies,* "Of Kings' Treasuries" and "Of Queens' Gardens." His strictures in the latter admonish many Dombeys: "We are foolish, and without excuse foolish, in speaking of the 'superiority' of one sex to the other, as if they could be compared in similar things. Each has what the other has not: each completes the other, and is completed by the other: they are in nothing alike [.]" [11] But this sweet ideal of mutual completion scarcely takes place in the torn *Dombey* world. As Dombey becomes increasingly aware of Florence as something more potent than "a bad Boy," he is also increasingly—and, it seems, justly—aware of her as his antagonist, exposing rather than completing him by her unlikeness: "Who was it whose least word did what his utmost means could not! . . . She was leagued against him now. Her very beauty softened natures that were obdurate to him, and insulted him with an unnatural triumph" (561). As Sarah Lewis writes in her conduct book: "Men frequently resist power, while they yield to influence an unconscious acquiescence."

Dombey himself, who is all power, seems at first impervious to any influence whatever: "it seemed as if its icy current, instead of being released by this influence [of his schemes for his son], and running clear and free, had thawed for but an instant to admit its burden, and then frozen with it into one unyielding block" (47). But the influence equipped to thaw this unyielding block of power is expressed prophetically in Polly Toodles' first words about Florence: "I never saw such a melting thing in all my life!" (23). Florence herself is literally melting in that she weeps incessantly, but she is most important as an almost disembodied influence that causes the melting of others around her. Unlike her father's power, her influence is unwilled: she will never "make an effort," as her aunt Louisa bemoans. Its operation is unconscious, almost psychic: "[Mr. Dombey] almost felt as if she watched and distrusted him. As if she held the clue to something secret in his breast, of the nature of which he was hardly informed himself. As if she had an innate knowledge of one jarring and discordant string within him, and her very breath could sound it" (29). In contrast to her father's rigidity, Florence is, like George Eliot's Dorothea Brooke, "incalculably diffusive," almost shapeless, seeming to seep into the recesses of the mind. Her genius for presiding over sickbeds has seemed ghoulish to some readers; [12] the avidity with which she nurses her dying brother, and seems almost to leap at her father whenever he is sleeping, injured, or ill, reminds us that to many Victorians, woman's true sphere was neither the kitchen nor the bedroom, but the sickroom.[13] Yet a sickroom needs a patient, and Florence's melting influence needs her father supine; she can touch him only at the end, when she can nurse him. As Moynahan puts it, "Florence wants to get Dombey's head down on the pillow where she can drown him in a dissolving love."[14] Her "woman's mission" is to make the stiff and erect spreading and diffuse in a manner ungraspable by definition: women's influences "act by a sort of moral contagion, and are imbibed by the receiver as they flow from their source, without consciousness on either side."[15] If Dombey is so rigid that he seems to lack joints, Florence, the novel's undiluted woman, seems to have liquidity as her essence: she, too, is less a body with limbs and joints than purely a "melting thing."

The kinship between Dombey and Florence lies in the single-minded obsessiveness of their approaches to life. If "the one idea of Mr. Dombey's life" is the House, an inviolate masculine system of regulated enterprise, "nothing wandered in [Florence's] thoughts but love—a wandering love, indeed, and cast away—but turning always to her father. There was nothing . . . that shook this one thought, or diminished its interest" (254–55). As these absolute ideas cannot coexist in a single universe, father and daughter can only try to obliterate each other. After his son's death, Dombey hands to the statuary his inscription for the monument:

"Will you be so good as read it over again? I think there's a mistake."

"Where?"

The statuary gives him back the paper, and points out, with his pocket rule, the words, "beloved and only child."

"It should be 'son,' I think, Sir?"

"You are right. Of course. Make the correction." (241)

And when Florence is struck by her father: "She only knew that she had no Father upon earth, and she said so, many times, with her suppliant head hidden from all, but her Father who was in Heaven" (681). This radical denial is in part a result of the distance between "Kings' Treasuries" and "Queens' Gardens"—that "profound ignorance of each other's real nature and ways of thinking" that Elizabeth Wolstenholme was to see as one of the tragedies of the age, and which in *Dombey and Son* is the blight of the family.

For despite their distance from each other, Dombey's power and Florence's influence are alike in their potentially murderous seeds: "[Mr. Dombey] stood in his library to receive the company, as hard and cold as the weather; and when he looked out through the glass room, at the trees in the little garden, their brown and yellow leaves came fluttering down, as if he blighted them" (52). Florence seems at times an equally blighting force: "As the image of her father whom she loved had insensibly become a mere abstraction, so Edith, following the fate of all the rest about whom her affections had entwined themselves, was fleeting, fading, growing paler in the distance, every day" (652). The language of this passage implies that, like that of the vampire, Florence's love drains its objects into ghosts. In this she resembles the child described by Paul's lugubrious nurse, Mrs. Wickam: "She took fancies to people; whimsical fancies, some of them; others, affections that one might expect to see—only stronger than common. They all died" (106). Florence's love seems as secretly lethal as Dombey's ambition is overtly life-withering. Their very isolation in their own absoluteness, whereby they contain nothing of each other, is the only bond between father and daughter, and, it seems, between the sexes in general. In part, they kill because "they are in nothing alike."

— *3* —

This schism between masculine and feminine spheres seems more fundamental to the novel's world than the usual division critics make between the "money world" of the firm and the "water world" of the Wooden Midshipman group. Gender links these inviolate male systems together against the depredations of the Mrs. MacStingers of the earth. In *Dombey and Son* and throughout Dickens' other novels, money is ultimately fluid and plentiful, and class lines are illusory and easily crossed. The real, and absolute, barrier is sexual, and it separates not merely individuals, but the landscape of the novel itself.

The two main symbols that dominate *Dombey and Son* can be divided equally into male and female poles which exclude each other. We have seen the link between Dombey's accelerating watch and the new rhythms of the railroad, between the incessant flow of Florence's tears and that of the sea. Each can generate life, but, untempered by the other, each becomes the reaper of its own kind of death.[16]

Like Mr. Dombey, the railroad is an artifact of civilization, the sphere of the mechanical and masculine rather than the organic and feminine. It too is part of a closed and regulated system, without flowing and diffusing beyond one. Like Dombey on a grand scale, the railroad embodies phallic force; and like clock-time's, its progress is implacably linear. Dombey is always wishing for time to end in the apocalypse of Paul's development from self into Son: a boy has "a destiny" as the train has a preordained destination, to which terminus its violent movement is directed. The train, like the man again, has no private language; its voice is deafeningly public; its speech is "a shriek, and a roar, and a rattle," "a shrill yell of exultation." Dombey's careful periodic eloquence is meant only to be heard by all ears. In Chapter i, he can scarcely lower his voice to say "my dear," and later he forces Carker to intervene between himself and Edith, so repugnant is private conversation to him. The railroad pulls together all the values of his masculine sphere.[17] Its shrieking linear progress makes us turn with relief to the secret, private sphere of feminine dissolution.

Florence's realm, the sea, exists independent of the mechanized products of civilization. It is natural and eternal: Paul's dying vision relates it both to Brighton and to the River of Life, flowing through Paradise. Like the ebb and flow of the female cycle, its cyclical ebbs and flows bear no relation to the human will; its rhythms are involuntary and unconscious, related to the flow of emotion and dream; lacking a destination to shape its movements, it has all the interminable attraction of a world without end. Unlike the railroad's shriek, its voice is quiet and its language is private: only Paul can hear "what the waves are always saying," and that only when he is on the edge of death. The mindlessness of its repeated motions reminds us of Florence's incessant returns to the unyielding breast of her father until it melts for her. Her persistence seems more plausible in geological than in psychological terms: throughout most of the novel, her movements are as involuntary and unwilled as the sea's are. Her kinship with the sea is appropriate to her role as vessel of woman's influence, which is "imbibed by the receiver as [it] flows from [its] source, without consciousness on either side."

Opposed as they are in every way, the railroad and the sea have similar effects: both are simultaneously fertile and murderous. Our first awareness is of the lively, generative power of the railroad: it brings prosperity to the good and prolific Toodleses, and gives birth to the bursting community of Stagg's Gardens. But on Dombey's long journey to Leamington, it snakes into an engine of death, plowing through a wasteland, its iron will the final blind extension of the Dombey creed of "making an effort": "The power that forced itself upon its iron way—its own—defiant of all paths and roads, piercing through the heart of every obstacle, and dragging living creatures of all classes, ages, and degrees behind it, was a type of the triumphant monster, Death" (280). The waste and sterility with which its power is finally associated erupt symbolically in Carker's "mutilated fragments"; retributive though his death is, the explosion of his body and Dombey's swoon suggest the train's unnatural, annihilating arrival at its final destination. The last words in the chapter describe "some dogs" "[sniffing] upon the road, and [men soaking] his blood up, with a train of ashes" (779). The "conquering engines" have become "a train of ashes," whose accelerating progress, like Dombey's, destroys more life than it conceives.

The sea, too, seems full of vitality at first. Its power underlies the thriving firm of Dombey and Son itself, as well as its raucous and kindly analogue, the Wooden Midshipman's, with its chanteys and sea-tales and toasts. Yet Mrs. Dombey and Paul ebb away on the sea, which, like the railroad, becomes a type of "the old, old fashion—Death!" Florence's loving influence is itself a sweet drowning and dissolution. In its boundless sweep toward eternity, the sea carries the danger of loss of contour, of sanity, of life itself, until the living and the dead reach to interpenetrate:

> "As I hear the sea," says Florence, "and sit watching it, it brings so many days into my mind. It makes me think so much—"
> "Of Paul, my love. I know it does."
> Of Paul and Walter. And the voices in the waves are always whispering to Florence, in their ceaseless murmuring, of love—of love, eternal and illimitable, not bounded by the confines of this world, or by the end of time, but ranging still, beyond the sea, beyond the sky, to the invisible country far away! (811)

As Florence seems to preside over the sea, traditional mysticism comes together with a ravenous hunger for death. This sense of life "not bounded by the confines of this world," but spilling over to touch death, gives the tone to Dombey's cathartic rebirth at the end of the novel, as Florence succeeds at last in encircling his prone head in her oceanic arms. Moynahan is right to see a loss of will, of contour, of intelligence and strength, in Dombey's final conversion into a weeping old man dripping love at the seashore: "Ambitious projects trouble him no more. His only pride is in his daughter and her husband" (873). Carker's iron death was an abrupt explosion into an ending; Dombey's baptismal death is more of an interminable ebb. But the shrieking "train of ashes" and the "ceaseless murmuring" of the waves both produce the vitality of loss, not of growth. The masculine and the feminine, the mechanical and the vital, the temporal and the spatial, untempered by each other's qualities, become destroyers. The separation between railroad and sea metaphysically extends the separation between Mr. Dombey and Florence at the heart of the novel's split world.

— *4* —

Many of the secondary characters in the novel play variations on the idea of the two spheres. The separation between the sexes that prevails in *Dombey and Son* reminds us over and over that "they are in nothing alike"; but certain bizarre and equivocal mutations lead to a suggestion of what we now call an androgynous vision, or to Emily Davies' stubborn insistence in Dickens' own time that "there is a deep and broad basis of likeness between the sexes." Perhaps the likeness that glimmers sometimes in *Dombey and Son* will lead to a reconciliation that the central movement of the book does not provide.

Like Dombey, Major Bagstock lives in a sphere inhabited exclusively by men and manliness: the "systems" at the center of his world are the army and his club, although he does peer vindictively through his telescope at his faded neighbor Miss Tox, as Dombey peers under his handkerchief at Florence. His explosive wheezes that he is "tough, sir, tough" seem an inflammatory variant of Dombey's icily self-sustaining pride; and despite his toadyism and treachery, his sponsorship of Dombey is a more compatible relationship than either of Dombey's marriages. Indeed, at his second wedding, Dombey seems to be marrying the Major rather than Edith, so firmly are the two knit together at that point. The Game Chicken, whose life consists of eating and hitting, is a similar parody of manliness rampant. He glues himself to Toots as Bagstock does to Dombey, in a sad alliance of sportsmanlike celibacy against the depredations Florence has made in Toots' heart and wardrobe.

In a sense, the novel's hell and heaven are found in communities of men. Dr. Blimber's Academy is an inviolate male system like the Dombey firm, although it admits the unfeminine Cornelia, who has been classically educated like a boy, and tolerates as chorus the effusions of her mother. With its remorselessly-ticking clock and its pale reading boys, the "forcing apparatus" of Blimber's establishment is made to bear responsibility for the loss of Toots' wits and Paul's life. The blighting male "system" Dombey worships finds its most potent incarnation at Blimber's.

But at the blessed masculine unit of the Wooden Midshipman, Toots and Paul—in the form of the resurrected Walter, Florence's sturdy brother-lover—are to some degree restored. The domestic habits and rituals of Sol Gills, Captain Cuttle, and Walter Gay are dwelt upon at great length, being in fact the only domesticity we are allowed to see in the novel. As a result, we are inundated with their curiosities of housekeeping and the logistics of cooking with a hook. Captain Cuttle's early injunction to Walter seems one of the novel's few genuine sacraments: " 'Wal'r!' he said, arranging his hair (which was thin) with his hook, and then pointing it at the Instrument-Maker, 'Look at him! Love! Honour! And Obey! Overhaul your catechism till you find that passage, and when found turn the leaf down. Success, my boy!' " (41).

The "marriage" between the three of them, and their consecrated home, are given purpose and solidarity by absent women: by the dreadful vision of Mrs. MacStinger, drowning the men in her washing-day and snatching the Captain in wedlock, and by their collective aspiration to Florence, who offers a less overtly coercive baptism. The dependence of this home on the sea, and the tears that are shed so copiously there, link it with Florence's "melting" world. When she escapes to it from her father's house, there is a subtle, involuted suggestion that there, at least, the sexes may be in something alike: "Unlike as they were externally—and there could scarcely be a more decided contrast than between Florence in her delicate youth and beauty, and Captain Cuttle with his knobby face, his great broad weather-beaten person, and his gruff voice—in simple innocence of the world's ways and the world's perplexities and dangers, they were nearly on a level. . . . A wandering princess and a good monster in a story-book might have sat by the fireside, and talked as Captain Cuttle and poor Florence thought—and not have looked very much unlike them" (684–85). The mutual housekeeping Cuttle and Florence perform for each other in Chapters xlviii and xlix, where each outdoes the other in dexterity, is the novel's only sustained description of the sexes working and thinking in a single sphere; and as the language above demonstrates, the Wooden Midshipman is a fairy-tale world and these similarities may be fairy-tale transformations. Gills and Cuttle are sanctified, in a somewhat saccharine manner, by their exemption from manhood. Cuttle is literally maimed, and Gills is saved from bankruptcy only by Dombey's icy magnanimity; like a woman's, their sphere is self-possessed in being dispossessed. As the hero, Walter must conventionally "succeed" in a nebulous way and leave the Wooden Midshipman once he grows up; but as character actors, Gills and Cuttle exchange loss of power for female selfhood. Their all-male system becomes a domestic idyll whose table can at the end accommodate both Dombey and Daughter.

Failure and poverty can create a childlike haven where men are free to melt toward womanhood, but little Paul Dombey, forced into power, is not so lucky. His life begins when his father jingles a watch-chain at him, and it ends in Florence's arms, rushing from the river to the sea which is Death. Since Paul *is* the child of which Captain Cuttle is the facsimile, one might hope that his presence would reconcile the antinomies of Dombey and Florence. But though he does his best, even suggesting to his father's horror that Florence be allowed into the firm, he is finally wrenched between the two worlds and destroyed in his passage from one to the other. His postures in the first scene in which we see him foreshadow the rhythm of his short life. At five, he is his father's eerie parody:

> They were the strangest pair at such a time that ever firelight shone upon. Mr. Dombey so erect and solemn, gazing at the blaze; his little image, with an old, old, face, peering into the red perspective with the fixed and rapt attention of a sage. Mr. Dombey entertaining complicated worldly schemes and plans; the little image entertaining Heaven knows what wild fancies, half-formed thoughts, and wandering speculations. Mr. Dombey stiff with starch and arrogance; the little image by inheritance, and in unconscious imitation. The two so very much alike, and yet so monstrously contrasted. (91–92)

As in the tableau of Florence and Captain Cuttle above, union springs out of "monstrous" differences. Though Paul's participation in the stiff, erect posture of his father's sphere is inherited and instinctive, it is unnatural as well: his inheritance withers him, giving the child "an old, old, face." When Florence comes, he melts back into nature, with "a countenance so much brighter, so much younger, and so much more child-like altogether," but in his passage to his sister's sphere he sinks back toward a state of pre-birth. When she takes him in her arms, he seems almost to dissolve: "She was toiling up the great, wide, vacant staircase, with him in her arms; his head was *lying* on her shoulder, one of his arms *thrown negligently* round her neck. So they went, toiling up; she singing all the way, and Paul sometimes crooning out a *feeble* accompaniment" (95, my italics). Dombey's stiff Paul and Florence's boneless one look almost like two different boys. The moral of his transition might be, "damn braces, bless relaxes"; but from another perspective, Paul moves from unnatural alertness to tender debility: enervated by his father's world, he drowns in his sister's. Little Paul Dombey passes in the book from a harbinger of a new, androgynous whole to a victim of his House's unhealed division.

So far, it seems as though only children and childlike men can incorporate the feminine into their natures; the Wooden Midshipman thrives because of it, and Paul dies in part because of it. But Carker, the villain of the novel, is in one sense farthest of all from Dombey's stiff and erect masculinity, despite the fact that, unlike Gills and Cuttle, he never weeps, never loves, and seems never to have been innocent. This "sleek, hushed, crouched" man works on those around him, not with the direct authority of Dombey's male power, but with the indirect insinuation of female influence.

Carker seems at first an exaggerated shadow of the stiffness and rigidity of his master. But we soon learn that he is quite the opposite of that upright public man: he is infinitely flexible and secret, and he is *acting* Mr. Dombey for his own private amusement. Like Florence's, his medium is silence. He does not make his power felt directly through language, but telegraphs sympathy in his "voiceless manner of assent" that makes his statements rather felt than heard. He communicates with Florence in a manner eerily close to telepathy: "Confused, frightened, shrinking from him, and not even sure that he had said those words, for he seemed to have shown them to her in some extraordinary manner through his smile, instead of uttering them, Florence faintly said that she was obliged to him, but she would not write; she had nothing to say" (352). Carker's occultly revealed words and the "nothing" that Florence has "to say" to her father seem to rise out of the same quasi-magical source. In their conjunction, the silence of Cordelia meets that of the Cheshire Cat.

According to Sarah Lewis, indirection is one of the defining characteristics of female influence: it is never asserted, but diffuses unconsciously into the breast of the other. Dombey's fear that Florence is in uncanny possession of "something secret in his breast" is repeated in Edith's fear of Carker's equally wordless knowledge: "But, does Edith feel still, as on the night when she knew that Mr. Dombey would return to offer his alliance, that Carker knows her thoroughly, and reads her right, and that she is more degraded by his knowledge of her, than by aught else? Is it for this reason that her haughtiness shrinks beneath his smile, like snow within the hand that grasps it firmly, and that her imperious glance droops in meeting his, and seeks the ground?" (444). Like Florence's, Carker's influence causes its object to melt and droop. But the possession of such influence seems to make of a woman a heroine, a man a villain.

Florence creeps stealthily through the house at night to crouch before her father's rooms; alone in his office, Carker plays secret games that bring the House down. Mr. Dombey can play no games and has no affinities with these silent, secret characters, though ironically, he might have been a better businessman if he had: "feminine" flexibility and love of play may be part of the remunerative virtue Florence would have brought into the firm had Paul been permitted to include her. Instead, Carker's feminine indirection destroys firm and family. Their fall is Florence's ascension, but Carker, who is so much like her, seems to be destroyed by all the vengeful masculine power of the universe (liv, lv). Edith stands before him with a knife [18]; the enraged Dombey is at the door, and suddenly, Carker is swept into a frenzy of linear motion. Night and day flash past each other on his stagecoach journeys, repeating the inhuman acceleration of Dombey's watch in Chapter i. His flight recapitulates the furious noisy plunge of Dombey's railroad journey to Leamington until the final explosion of death, a giant eruption of the maleness he had tried to soften with his wiles. Carker's death inverts little Paul's, who had reached toward the feminine and disappeared into it: the recreant Carker is destroyed in a phallic roar. The good Toodles speaks what could be his epitaph in the voice of the train: "You see, my boys and gals . . . , wotever you're up to in a honest way, it's my opinion you can't do better than be open. If you find yourselves in cuttings or in tunnels, don't you play no secret games. Keep your whistles going, and let's know where you are" (534). Feminine tears may flow, but feminine secrecy and silence cannot temper the "shriek, and the roar, and the rattle" of the book's iron masculinity.

Like the men in the novel, the women range from being elaborate embodiments of their sexual essence to incorporating traits of the other sex that strengthen and doom them. Miss Tox, who is repeatedly described as being about to evaporate, follows Dombey around with a shadowy submissiveness that parallels Florence's. When we see "poor excommunicated Miss Tox water[ing] her plants with her tears" (419), we are taken back to Florence's liquid essence and her solitary alliance with the natural cycle. But neither Florence nor Miss Tox is infected by the vituperation that expels them from Dombey's system. They transmit a "moral contagion," but they receive none: "[T]here was no such thing as anger in Miss Tox's composition" (532).

The moral contagion transmitted by Mrs. Skewton is the degenerate parody of the "womanly influence" celebrated in Florence's eventual triumph. Mrs. Skewton is "wooman, lovely wooman" in all her tendency to decay. Her arch romanticism, her invocation of "nature" and "heart," and even her tendency to dissolve—she literally comes apart every night, in a corrupt female foreshadowing of Carker's "mutilated fragments"—suggest the cloying underside of the "melting thing" and the values attached to it. "New Voices in the Waves," the chapter in which her hideous death is described, adds an ugly sound to the "ceaseless murmuring" of Florence's liquid sphere. In repudiating her mother's values, Edith repudiates more than the humiliation of the marriage market: she seems to rebel against the novel's entire notion of a womanhood in which "heart" and "nature" melt together with "no such thing as anger" in its composition.

Opposed to the lachrymose and decomposing elements in Mrs. Skewton and Miss Tox are a forbidding bevy of "anti-women," in Sylvia Manning's phrase: Louisa Chick, Cornelia Blimber, Mrs. Brown, and Mrs. Pipchin. Louisa's martial creed of "making an effort," Cornelia's spectacles and books and worship of precision, make them the unnurturing opposite of Florence's crooning love. Mrs. Brown, chewing on her pipe as she forces Florence into her own daughter's rags, is the visionary ogre of a mother Florence may be lucky to have lost, of whom Polly Toodles is the endlessly bountiful and one-dimensional inversion. Mrs. Pipchin, too, is an "ogress and child-queller," monstrous in part because she has relinquished wetness and grafted on to herself the hardness and dryness of the novel's male sphere: she has a "hard grey eye, that looked as if it might have been hammered at on an anvil without sustaining any injury"; "one was tempted to believe . . . that all her waters of gladness and milk of human kindness had been pumped out dry, instead of the mines" (99). Mrs. Pipchin has some kinship with the mutilated Captain Cuttle, in that both suggest the hybrid that may be the other side of the triumphantly reconciling androgyne. But the dangerously self-aware Edith Grainger gives us an anti-heroine who blurs together the two extremes of decomposing "wooman" and arid anti-woman.

As Carker insinuated "feminine" privacy and fluidity into the masculine sphere of Dombey and Son, so Edith brings "masculine" pride and professionalism to the female sphere of home. From the beginning, Edith preempts Dombey's masculine language. She is "handsome," rather than "beautiful" or "pretty," and in her pride, she is equally "hard, hard, hard": "So obdurate, so unapproachable, so unrelenting, one would have thought that nothing could soften such a woman's nature, and that everything in life had hardened it" (624). But her basic affinity with Dombey lies in the fact that she, too, is a merchant, and she knows it. The insistent connection between Edith and her "shadow," the fallen woman Alice Marwood, points to the anomalous position of the Victorian woman on the marriage market, displaying her accomplishments like a merchant hawking his wares. Society, economics, nature and God combined to define the real business of a woman's sphere as Esther Summerson's quest in *Bleak House:* "to win some love to myself if I could." In practice, the purposeful pursuit of love was a woman's "trade," a word which is the meeting-place of "profession" and "barter." Thus, sentiment combines with ironic plausibility in Florence's early dream of her new mother: "And now Florence began to hope that she would learn, from her new and beautiful

Mama, how to gain her father's love; and in her sleep that night, in her lost old home, her own Mama smiled radiantly upon the hope, and blessed it. Dreaming Florence!" (407). Motherless as she is, Florence's education in enticing accomplishments has been neglected, and Edith might plausibly teach her the tricks of the trade of winning some love. The professionalization of femininity by "a world of mothers" created an uneasy liaison between lady and whore which is dramatized in *Dombey and Son* and fully exposed in Eliza Lynn Linton's notorious article, "The Girl of the Period," written over twenty years later.[19] Eliza Lynn Linton brought to her readers' conscious awareness Dickens' insight that respectable young women were neither shunning nor saving their fallen sisters, but emulating their style in order to catch men. Lady and whore were one, not by virtue of a sanctified bond of sisterhood— which Dickens burlesques as a "freemasonry in fainting" in Chapter xxix—but by virtue of their similar trades.

Sisterhood is a tenuous thing in *Dombey and Son*, easily snapped because it is not institutionalized as male fellowship is, and exalted only between such remotely connected beings as Alice and the chaste Harriet Carker, or Edith and the innocent Florence. The genuine kinship between Edith and Alice is in no way elevated by the narrator, because of its masculine, professional nature: "[Alice] caught her arm, and drawing it before her own eyes, hid them against it, and wept. Not like a woman, but like a stern man surprised into that weakness; with a violent heaving of her breast, and struggle for recovery, that showed how unusual the emotion was with her" (482). "[Edith] had changed her attitude before he arrived at these words, and now sat—still looking at him fixedly—turning a bracelet round and round her arm; not winding it about with a light, womanly touch, but pressing and dragging it over the smooth skin, until the white limb showed a bar of red" (565).

In a series of pantomimic gestures, Edith and Alice reveal their essential masculinity. Like Dombey, whose stiffness is his soul, their bodies reveal their essences. But the ultimate masculine trespass of both women—the analogue of Carker's "secret games"—is the rage which removes them irrevocably from Miss Tox, who waters her plants with her tears, her lachrymose nourishment containing "no such thing as anger." "*I* am angry. I have been so, many years," says Alice to Dombey (725). Edith almost repeats her words to Carker: "My anger rose almost to distraction against both [Dombey and Carker]. I do not know against which it rose higher—the master or the man!" (761).

At one important point, this rage seems even to scar Florence, the book's paradigm of femininity. After her flight, she finds her inheritance written on her breast as a sort of brand of a female Cain: "Then she knew—in a moment, for she shunned it instantly—that on her breast there was the darkening mark of an angry hand." But her response to this masculine stain is characteristically Tox-like, looking forward to the baptismal rhythm of the end: "Her tears burst forth afresh at the sight; she was ashamed and afraid of it; *but it moved her to no anger against him.* Homeless and fatherless, she forgave him everything; hardly thought that she had need to forgive him, or that she did; but she fled from the idea of him as she had fled from the reality, and he was utterly gone and lost. There was no such Being in the world" (680–81, my italics).

Love washes the angry mark of masculinity out of the universe. The death of Alice, a fallen woman who is more erect than the heroine, seems the death of a personified metaphysical principle in the novel's world: "Scorn, rage, defiance, recklessness, look here! This is the end" (823). And so it is. Before she is banished to Italy, Edith seems to melt under Florence's forgiveness: "Edith, as if she fell beneath her touch, sunk down on her knees, and caught her round the neck" (868). As Carker must be dismembered, the angry women must dissolve so that an increasingly ghostly Florence can preside: " 'No, [I am] nothing, Walter. Nothing but your wife.' The light hand stole about his neck, and the voice came nearer—nearer. 'I am nothing any more, that is not you' " (789). Drained of her anger and aggression, she seems as close to evaporating as Miss Tox was at the beginning. Having become "a light hand," "a voice," and nothing more, she is ready to mount her throne as the womanly woman triumphant.

"Dombey and Son is a daughter after all." Miss Tox and the indefatigably maternal Polly Toodles return to close the great house that had banished them both. The entire world seems to melt into the feminine sphere, which is now "Chiefly Matrimonial." Susan Nipper, whose defiant fury was a comic analogue of Edith's and Alice's, follows her mistress into bustling marriage to a transformed Toots who has begun to talk like a more reverent Mr. Dombey. Miss Tox's suddenly potent influence redeems Rob the Grinder, the victim of Dombey's charitable system, into penitent respectability. The chapter concludes as Mrs. MacStinger drags Bunsby to the altar, leaving Captain Cuttle prey to horrible matriarchal visions of an eternal proliferation of daughters in a world without men: "One of the most frightful circumstances of the ceremony to the Captain, was the deadly interest exhibited therein by Juliana MacStinger; and the fatal concentration of her faculties, with which that promising child, already an image of her parent, observed the whole proceedings. The Captain saw in this a succession of man-traps stretching out infinitely; a series of ages of oppression and coercion, through which the seafaring line was doomed" (857).

Dombey himself seems less to succumb to Florence than to become her; by the end of the novel, he *is*, literally, "a daughter after all." Louisa Chick accuses him of the same sin of which she had accused

Florence at the beginning: "If my brother will not make an effort, Mrs. Pipchin, what is to become of him? I am sure I should have thought he had seen enough of the consequences of *not* making an effort, by this time, to be warned against that fatal error" (834). When Florence finds him, he is drifting through the empty house in a dream, just as she herself had done after his departure for Leamington. In their union, that part of civilization represented by Mr. Dombey seems to devolve back into her waiting sea, which destroys as much as it nourishes. The last chapter finds Dombey as faded as Miss Tox and as enfeebled as the dying Paul, weeping on his granddaughter at the seashore. The great system of which he was the center is replaced by a relationship remarkable for its privacy and secrecy. "He hoards her in his heart," having moved from total exteriority to total interiority. The end is something like that of *Idylls of the King*, with the sea waiting to swallow the last relics of a burnt-out civilization; in both, the ocean and the women that belong to it are placidly antagonistic to the efforts of a masculine civilization which excludes them. The ocean watches the fall of empires with a dead face. If we read *Dombey and Son* carefully, we can feel the rage that underlies its quiet rhythms.

— 5 —

I do not think that Dickens ever moved beyond the polarized vision delineated in *Dombey and Son*, and never afterward does he explore so thoroughly the schism between masculinity and femininity as his age defined them. Despite those forced happy marriages that look so much like deaths in his novels, his treatment of sexuality is infused with a troubled, tragic awareness of the gulf between the sexes. Its veneer may be complacency, but its essence is loss, as a famous letter expresses: "Why is it, that as with poor David, a sense comes always crushing on me now, when I fall into low spirits, as of one happiness I have missed in life, and one friend and companion I have never made?" [20] Life never produced the dream of love he willed so hard to believe, and his best writing is true to this sense of deprivation. It seems callow to denounce Dickens as a patriarch when his exploration of a patriarchy can produce the sexual laceration of a *Dombey and Son*, and I think it is misleading to overemphasize the change in his books that resulted from the furtive, apparently unhappy liaison with Ellen Ternan. His later heroines are still strangers, of a different species from the male characters, insulated in a sphere so much their own that they can never reach over to become "friends and companions." Born in the same year as his daughter Katey, Ellen seems to have remained a stranger to Dickens as well: " 'I had it,' said Canon Benham, 'from her own lips, that she loathed the very thought of the intimacy.' " [21]

Though "Nelly" was so much like the ingenue daughter he wrote about, who saves the wicked old man from his sins by loving him at the last minute, she denied Dickens after his death. But he had real daughters as well, who eerily resembled the daughter he created in *Dombey and Son* when they were children. Mamie apparently remained as true as Florence to the memory of her father stage-managing Christmas: "My love for my father has never been touched or approached by any other love. I hold him in my heart of hearts as a man apart from all other men, as one apart from all other beings." [22] Writing on her deathbed, Mamie preserved her father in the remote and solitary sphere which on her own deathbed Katey punctured in the name of their mother: "I loved my father better than any man in the world—in a different way of course. . . . My father was a wicked man—a very wicked man. . . . Ah! We were *all* very wicked, not to take her part[.]" [23] Kate Perugini's posthumous corroboration of the gossip about Dickens and Ellen may finally have broken through the silence between father and daughter. Like Florence, she used her indirect influence to redeem her mother by wearing away the armor of her father's reputation. In so doing, she gave us our present Dickens, the haunted man, and took away the memory of Christmas.[24]

Joseph Butwin

THE PARADOX OF THE CLOWN
IN DICKENS

IN THE novels of Charles Dickens there are few more complete images of familial esprit de corps, social cooperation, and good humor than Sleary's Horse-Riding in *Hard Times*. Critics generally agree that Dickens saw in Sleary's brief apologia the common denominator of his own comic art: "People mutht be amuthed, Thquire, thomehow." In addition to amusement, the circus offers an admirable, if somewhat unrealistic, alternative to the cutthroat competition that characterizes industrial Coketown. Acrobatics allows people to be flexible, agile, and eccentric even while they are bound by the form and cooperation represented, say, by the human pyramid.

> The father of one of the families was in the habit of balancing the father of another of the families on the top of a great pole; the father of a third family often made a pyramid of both those fathers, with Master Kidderminster for the apex, and himself for the base; all the fathers could dance upon rolling casks, stand upon bottles, catch knives and balls, twirl hand-basins, ride upon anything, jump over everything, and stick at nothing. All the mothers could (and did) dance, upon the slack wire and the tight-rope, and perform rapid acts on barebacked steeds.[1]

And yet Dickens chooses to mar this image of a saving remnant by eventually placing at its center the most disgusting of creatures, Tom Gradgrind done up as a blackface clown.

> In a preposterous coat, like a beadle's, with cuffs and flaps exaggerated to an unspeakable extent; in an immense waistcoat, knee-breeches, buckled shoes, and a mad cocked hat; with nothing fitting him, and everything of coarse material, moth-eaten and full of holes; with seams in his black face, where fear and heat had started through the greasy composition daubed

[115

all over it; anything so grimly, detestably, ridiculously shameful as the whelp in his comic livery, Mr. Gradgrind never could by any other means have believed in, weighable and measurable fact though it was. And one of his model children had come to this! (283)

The clownish costume becomes a brickbat used to punish "the whelp." If people must be amused, who is responsible for this amusement?—a grim, detestable, shameful creature done up in rags. Another clown, Signor Jupe, drinks heavily, beats his dog, abandons his daughter, and weeps after every unsuccessful attempt to make people laugh. Given the choice, his daughter, Sissy, leaves the circus and makes her way in a more conventional if corrupt outer world. Why does the seemingly congenial image go sour? A look backward may help to clarify the paradox of the clown in Dickens.

In Dickens' time the clown was a recent invention in England. When Shakespeare used the term he generally meant country bumpkins and fools rather than performers in a comic entertainment. After Shakespeare, the Italian *Commedia dell'arte* which brought Harlequin, Pantaloon, and Columbine to France in the seventeenth and eighteenth centuries also sent its representatives to England. The character actually known as "Clown" was developed *in* England by Joseph Grimaldi, son of an Italian performer. Grimaldi's Clown was a robust, boastful, grown child, a brightly decorated creature of the Mother Goose pantomimes, grinning from ear to ear, proclaiming himself John Bull, hooting threats at the French enemy, perpetually stuffing himself with stolen sausages. Grimaldi dominated the stage at Sadler's Wells and Covent Garden during the Napoleonic Wars, and though his career was effectively ended by the failure of his health in the 1820s, the "joey"—his name became generic—survived as the primary image of the English clown throughout the century.[2]

Clown and his French cousin Pierrot became first a curiosity and then a preoccupation of European poets and painters in the nineteenth and twentieth centuries. We see his image in the work of Mallarmé and Laforgue, Picasso and Rouault, to name a few. Literary and artistic use of the clown which has been so notable on the Continent (and, incidentally, so well observed by scholars) has been neither so notable nor so well observed in England.[3]

The first English writer to absorb the image of the clown was Charles Dickens. Although he could have only seen Grimaldi himself perform, if at all, when he was very young, Dickens edited the memoirs of the great clown in 1838.[4] George Cruikshank, who had already illustrated the *Sketches by Boz* and was working on *Oliver Twist,* provided engravings for the Grimaldi book, and they remain the best part of it.

Dickens' own brief introduction to the book is a sentimental celebration of stage illusion recollected from early childhood: "It is some years now since we first conceived a strong veneration for Clowns." For his present task he says that he had edited the text "altering its form throughout and making such other alterations as he conceived would improve the narration of facts, without departure from the facts themselves." Dickens worked from a text that had already been doctored by one Thomas Wilks, and the result betrays very little of the master's style, probably very little of the clown's.

The original manuscript does not exist. Wilks turned it into a third person narration and, according to the modern editor, cut some parts and added others from his recollection of Grimaldi's talk. Dickens did his job in a hurry taking little more than a month at the end of 1837, and much of what remains is a financial rather than theatrical history of the clown's life. We learn the receipts of every benefit in and out of London but very little of what was done to earn them. And yet the book makes good reading. All England is there with special emphasis given to its periphery. Byron attends the benefits (and leaves five pounds); the Duke of York comes around after the show; and later still highwaymen wait on the road to Finchley. In Grimaldi himself we have an amiable and somewhat gullible, honest, generous, and thoroughly competent actor who may put us in mind of the benevolent Mr. Sleary. But that is not the whole story of the clown. For the rest we would have to look to his less-successful friends, to his morbid father, to his insane son and to Grimaldi himself at the end of his career, stricken with premature age and mirthless sorrow.

Dickens' clowns are not simple people. Sooner or later, like Grimaldi, they are made to suffer. A life given to playing the clown left him thoroughly debilitated in his early forties, and in his last performances he must endure the dreadful paradox of the clown—he suffers while an unwitting audience laughs. "The spectators, who were convulsed with laughter while he was on stage, little thought that while their applause was resounding through the house he was suffering the most excruciating and horrible pains" (258). And when doctors told him that he could no longer act, "he covered his face with his hands and wept like a child" (258). Though Grimaldi was to live longer, Dickens says that he will "lay no unnecessary stress upon this cheerless portion of his existence" (261).

Dickens was not so squeamish in his fiction. The fact that there could be at least two sides to the clown's life haunted him from the time of the *Sketches* and the *Pickwick Papers* which precede the Grimaldi book. The *Sketches* include visits to booths at the Greenwich Fair and Astley's Circus. Clowns in "Greenwich Fair" promenade outside "in all the dignity of wigs, spangles, red-ochre, and whitening. . . . They look so noble in those Roman dresses, with their yellow legs and arms, long black curly heads, bushy eyebrows, and scowl expressive of assassination, and vengeance, and everything else that is grand and solemn" (115). Certain words in the description bear no relation to each other. There is no way to explain the "dignity of wigs and spangles." "Noble," "Roman," "grand," and "solemn" have nothing to do with yellow legs and arms. The reader's faith that these contradictory words can even be used together depends on an established understanding that clownship is devilishly incongruous; the words assort themselves as a linguistic equivalent to this incongruity.[5]

The ladies on stage are somewhat shabbier than genteel. Their "blue satin shoes and sandals (a *leetle* the worse for wear) are the admiration of all beholders; and the playful manner in which they check the advances of the clown, is perfectly enchanting." In reality the behavior that he describes is no more "enchanting" than wigs and spangles are "dignified." What enchants us is Dickens' way of saying what he does not mean, his ability to convert incongruity into amusement. In effect, Dickens steals the show.

Where in this cheerful observation does one find an ancestor of "the whelp in comic livery"? Judgment, if one can use so sober a term, is not explicit. What is explicit is praise, but the praise is inappropriate, and as readers we correct it. If as a result of our corrections we quietly decide that clowns are undignified, ignoble, neither grand nor solemn, we would nonetheless hesitate to label them frauds. They are simply creatures of contrast, and these contrasts can, as in the case of the whelp, be exploited to expose serious fraudulence.

What Dickens describes at Greenwich Fair is the "enchanting" mask of the clown; what we infer is the disenchanting reality. This persistent interest in the difference between what the clown is and what he pretends to be is never absent from Dickens' treatment of the theme. The clown becomes an appropriate vehicle for the exposure of corruption. Finally, when Dickens' eye penetrates the clownish mask it penetrates life itself and reveals the ultimate corruption, death. The penchant for exposure is basically morbid; what seems so very much alive, especially in the case of the bright, robust English clown, is not.

The clearest case for the basic morbidity in Dickens' observation of the clown is "The Stroller's Tale" narrated by Dismal Jemmy in *The Pickwick Papers* (iii). Jemmy, whose sobriquet suggests a certain debility of his own, describes the decline and fall of the most melancholy of clowns. Dickens allows Jemmy a certain air of condescension which he may or may not deserve when he describes the career of the clown.

> The man of whom I speak was a low pantomime actor; and, like many people of his class, an habitual drunkard. In his bet-

ter days, before he had become enfeebled by dissipation and emaciated by disease, he had been in the receipt of a good salary, which, if he had been careful and prudent, he might have continued to receive for some years—not many; because these men either die early, or, by unnaturally taxing their bodily energies, lose, prematurely, those physical powers on which alone they can depend for subsistence. (35)

Certain details recur in nearly all contemporary reports of clowns. Grimaldi himself suffered a severe and premature depletion of energy and though he was no famous drinker, many were. In dealing with this character Jemmy betrays a snobbery that is only slightly undercut by his own dismal condition. Otherwise the allusion to "*low* pantomime," to "people of his class," and the general priggishness—"if he had been careful and prudent"—enforces our sense of a distance between the author-narrator and the subject. The difference between the narrator and the clown is the difference between respectable employment and shabby beggardom. A step back from the inserted tale tends to reduce the distance between the arrogant narrator and his subject. Even as Dismal Jemmy begins his description of the "habitual drunkard" he has accepted another glass of brandy and water, half of which he consumes before speaking. His own appearance leaves little to distinguish him from his "emaciated" friend: "It was a care-worn looking man, whose sallow face, and deeply sunken eyes, were rendered still more striking than nature had made them, by the straight black hair which hung in matted disorder." His story, which begins with a backstage meeting of the two, recalls better days: "Here I saw this man whom I had lost sight of for some time; for I had been travelling in the provinces, and he had been skulking in the lanes and alleys of London." "Travelling" and "skulking" summarize the difference. "I was dressed to leave the house" and he was dressed in quite another way.

Never shall I forget the repulsive sight that met my eye when I turned round. He was dressed for the pantomine, in all the absurdity of a clown's costume. The spectral figures in the Dance of Death, the most frightful shapes that the ablest painter ever portrayed on canvas, never presented an appearance half so ghastly. His bloated body and shrunken legs—their deformity enhanced a hundred fold by the fantastic dress—the glassy eyes, contrasting fearfully with the thick white paint with which the face was besmeared; the grotesquely ornamented head, trembling with paralysis, and the long, skinny hands, rubbed with white chalk—all gave him a hideous and unnatural appearance, of which no description could convey an adequate idea, and which, to this day, I shudder to think of. His voice

was hollow and tremulous, as he took me aside, and in broken
words recounted a long catalogue of sickness and privations,
terminating as usual with an urgent request for the loan of a
trifling sum of money. I put a few shillings in his hand, and as I
turned away I heard the roar of laughter which followed his
first tumble on to the stage. (36)

This creature is so explicitly grotesque that at first it is not evident that
he is even meant to amuse. By conjuring a specific and familiar iconography, Dickens connects the clown with the zanies who participated in
the medieval dance of death.

The commonplace association of death and comic folly is one that
Dickens could have easily imbibed from literary sources. In his essay on
"The Praise of Folly" William Empson cites the familiar lines from
Richard II.

> for within the hollow crown
> That rounds the mortal temples of a king
> Keeps Death his court, and there the Antic sits
> Scoffing his state, and grinning at his pomp.

Here the antic in the role of jester plays the sage and unpunishable
critic of the king. His wisdom is his certain knowledge of mortality. The
king is the fool. Folly, as one of Empson's "complex words," can thus be
made to subsume its opposite.[6]

In one sense the fool denies God; in another his ignorance of this
world prepares him for the next. *Sub specie aeternitatis* the fool is wise.
Similarly his ignorance of mortality is foolish, but his idiotic conduct in
the face of death propels him beyond death's sting, makes him simultaneously a figure of foolish mortality and sage immortality. In either
case the medieval figure of the fool—clown and jester—is closely associated with death.

Hans Holbein, who illustrated Erasmus' *Praise of Folly,* also produced more than fifty woodcuts for a series called *The Dance of Death.*[7]
In each the figure of death invades the lives of his victims who, from
the Pope to the common drunkard, are equally unprepared. Only the
fool, balancing a bladder, one finger in his mouth and his left foot already lifted to the tune of Death's bagpipe, seems to join the dance
willingly, to look upon Death with convivial intimacy. Only a fool, we
might say, would accept such an invitation, but on reflection it is the
others, vainly resisting, who are the fools.

Dickens leaves no doubt about the morbidity of his clowns. Presumably a medieval audience was prepared to see the deadly fool for
what he was, a visible image of invisible calamity, pestilence, famine,

and death. In the Pickwickian instance the frightful deadliness of the clown is the backstage knowledge of the observant narrator. On the other side of the footlights the crowd roars with laughter demonstrating what Empson calls the "mutuality" of folly: "Everyman displays by contrast the folly of the wise, and the clown jeers at his betters; the contradictions that appear in the doctrine were felt to be a gain, not an obstruction, because they brought out this feeling of mutuality: 'I call you a fool of one sort speaking as myself a fool of another sort.' " In "The Stroller's Tale" it is the narrator and by extension the reader who enjoy the revenge that might be given to the clown. We see the folly of an audience that laughs when it should weep or at least "shudder."

Whatever pathos might be evoked by the suffering clown is not turned to sympathy in Dickens' text. Even in his last death scene we are told that he fears the justifiable revenge of his frequently beaten wife and starved child. In effect, his death is another of his performances, and we witness it from the same distance that we witnessed his tumble on to the stage.

> I saw the wasted limbs, which a few hours before had been distorted for the amusement of a boisterous gallery, writhing under the tortures of a burning fever—I heard the clown's shrill laugh, blending with the low murmurings of the dying man. . . . A short pause, and he shouted out a few doggerel rhymes—the last he had ever learnt. He rose in bed, drew up his withered limbs, and rolled about in uncouth positions; he was acting—he was at the theater. . . . He grasped my shoulder convulsively, and, striking his breast with the other hand, made a desperate attempt to articulate. It was unavailing—he extended his arm towards them, and made another violent effort. There was a rattling noise in the throat—a glare of the eye—a short stifled groan—he fell back—dead! (39–40)

This final convulsion reveals the terrible paradox in the life of the clown—his supreme vitality is no more than a death rattle.[8] His art is a desperate imitation of life, and Dickens is bound to expose him. What he exposes first is the economic vulnerability of the clown, and poverty is a clear manifestation of mortality.

Dickens himself knew the real hardship of stage life. His own early assault on the stage had come to nothing, and it was only his success as a journalist that drew him away from that world and the popularity of the *Sketches* and *Pickwick* that kept him away. And yet when he describes aspiring performers in these early works he maintains a cool distance and spices his descriptions with more mockery than pity. His exposure of the clowns at Greenwich Fair is a model for his treatment of actors in any of the small theaters of London. "Look at the dirty white Berlin gloves, and the cheap silk handkerchief stuck in the bosom of his threadbare coat" (108). And the actor who is "envied and flattered as the favoured lover of a rich heiress" on stage is forced to remember "all the while that the ex-dancer at home is in a family way, and out of an engagement" (109).

Dickens himself was a vigilant critic and, some would say, an egregious example of both the clown and the dandy.[9] In fact, the two types are similar, and Dickens describes them side by side in the *Sketches.* Both emanate from the theater which gives them the required mask and audience. The dandy of the *Sketches* is the young actor who thinks that he can adopt gentility with the manners and costumes that he puts on for the stage. It is his failure that puts him in contact with the clown.

Nonetheless the relentless exposure of stage dandies ceases to be funny; coupled with the biographical detail of his own fruitless theatrical ambitions we begin to see a kind of personal purgation that would never be absent from Dickens' fiction. Twenty years after the writing of the *Sketches,* he placed his spiritual counterpart, Pip, in the midst of a theatrical scene in a low London theater where a comic interlude turns to anxious self-appraisal. When Wopsle-Waldengarver plays Hamlet, his folly becomes Pip's: after the play Pip dreams that his "expectations were all cancelled" and that he had to "play Hamlet to Miss Havisham's Ghost, before twenty thousand people, without knowing twenty words of it" (244). Through this nightmare shift of perspective—Empson's mutuality—Pip loses his privileged status as spectator and becomes an absurd actor on an expanded stage which he is forced to share with that living image of mortality, Miss Havisham.

Pip is reduced by the implicit comparison with Wopsle. He goes to the theater for comic relief, but he is unable to maintain the distance and superiority that would allow him to laugh afterward. Even the ludicrous description of the "Danish nobility" backfires: "On our arrival in Denmark, we found the king and queen of that country elevated in two arm-chairs on a kitchen-table, holding a court. The whole Danish nobility were in attendance; consisting of a noble boy in the wash-leather boots of a gigantic ancestor, a venerable Peer with a dirty face who seemed to have risen from the people late in life, and the Danish chivalry with a comb in its hair and a pair of white silk legs." We recognize the comic tone of the theatrical *Sketches,* but in the middle of *Great Expectations* we may reflect that Pip and his sponsor, Magwitch, share more than they might wish to acknowledge with the "venerable peer . . . risen from the people late in life," and that Wopsle's ambitions are not unlike Pip's "expectations." Pip's nightmare confirms the mutuality of Wopsle's folly.

Pip is also victimized by what the nineteenth century would recognize as the reversibility of Hamlet's tragedy. The hero is also a clown, and the greater the morbidity of the play, the greater may be its comedy. Like Sterne, Dickens would recognize Yorick as a type of comic genius and the graveyard as his special domain. In the Grimaldi book he records the antics of a certain "Jew" Davis (famous for his stage Jews) who was fond of turning Hamlet's gravedigger into a clown by means of grins and grimaces which inevitably diverted the audience in the way that a serious Hamlet could not approve. When Kemble, as Hamlet, put his foot down very hard on the stage, Davis leapt into the open grave in mock terror, and incidentally gave Cruikshank the occasion for one of his splendid illustrations of the text (112–19). Elsewhere in the *Memoirs* we learn that the father of the clown, himself a mime, was addicted to churchyards.

> He was a most morbidly sensitive and melancholy being, and entertained a horror of death almost indescribable. He was in the habit of wandering about churchyards and burying-places for hours together, and would speculate on the diseases of which the persons had died; figure their death-beds, and wonder how many of them had been buried alive in a fit or a trance; a possibility which he shuddered to think of, and which haunted him both through life and at its close. Such an effect had this fear upon his mind, that he left express directions in his will that, before his coffin should be fastened down, his head should be severed from his body, and the operation was actually performed in the presence of several persons. It is a curious circumstance that death, which always filled the older Grimaldi's mind with the most gloomy and horrible reflections, and which in his unoccupied moments can hardly be said to have been ever absent from his thoughts, should have been chosen by him as the subject of one of his most popular scenes in the pantomimes of the time. Among many others of the same nature, he invented the well-known skeleton scene for the clown, which was very popular in those days, and is still occasionally represented. (31–32)

Certainly the preoccupation of Grimaldi senior is exaggerated, but it is not uncommon. Barnum and Bailey still show a clown butted around the ring by the skeleton of a goat thus acknowledging durable association of death and the clown.

In *The Old Curiosity Shop* Dickens fixes the twin image in the wooden character of a stage Punch. In one of the several visits to churchyards that punctuate Little Nell's long apprenticeship for the grave, she meets the puppeteers, Codlin and Short. The graveyard, according to Short, is sufficiently removed from the eyes of their regular audience so as not to "destroy the delusion, and take away all the inter-

est." The illusion of the stage comedian is basically a *de*lusion, and
every detail of our backstage experience tells us that death is the mystery hidden from the deluded audience. While the men repair a small
stage gallows, their Punch dangles "loose and limp and shapeless" on a
tombstone "pointing with the tip of his cap to a most flourishing epitaph, and . . . chuckling over it with all his heart." The clown laughs
last. His deluded audience is the fool.

The dour Codlin is another Dismal Jemmy reminding us that the
stage joy of Punch is temporary, only an illusion. Standing beside the
curtain he makes "a dismal feint of being [Punch's] most intimate private friend, of believing in him to the fullest and most unlimited extent, of knowing that he enjoyed day and night a merry and glorious
existence in that temple, and that he was at all times and under every
circumstance the same intelligent and joyful person that the spectator
then beheld him." The next day on the road he labors under the heavy
burden of the temple, now a casket for "that beaming Punch utterly
devoid of spine, all slack and drooping in a dark box, with his legs
doubled up around his neck, and not one of his social qualities remaining." [10]

Codlin's wooden puppet is no more conscious of the contrasts that
he embodies than Dismal Jemmy's clown, rapt as he is with delirium
tremens. The consciousness that what is seen is only an imitation of life
is transferred to the reader through the mediation of a slightly detached observer. Put this way, sad dandies and sorrowful clowns might
be seen as a common device of the novelistic imagination which, since
Cervantes, has always been pleased to assume that what seems to be is
not. In that case, what could the cheerful performer be but melancholy? But the model, so firmly established in Dickens' fiction in the
1830s and 1840s, is also evident in a contemporary as dedicated to
recorded truth as Henry Mayhew. For Mayhew, as for Dickens, the
precariousness of clownish joy begins as a fact of *economic* life. It is as a
journalist exposing poverty rather than as a novelist reflecting on fiction that Mayhew comes to us.

The large part of any section in *London Labour and the London Poor*
is taken up with the subject's personal and presumably true narration;
in any case it would not appear to be Mayhew's contrivance. His inter-
views reveal the personal histories, the general motivation, the wages
and the way of life of the otherwise anonymous "street-folk" of the metropolis. They are "street-folk" in every sense—streetwalkers, street
sweepers, finders and sellers of anything they might collect off the
streets, street animals, entertainers, and, among these last, a street
clown. And this clown's story follows the pattern established by Dickens
in the previous decade and that recurs in *Hard Times*. [11]

London Labour and the London Poor reveals a population living in misery. Of course, in such company the clown is bound to be miserable. Sometimes he earns as little as one or two shillings a week and never more than fifteen when, according to contemporary accounts, the poorest agricultural workers were earning six or seven. But the misery of the clown is a special case. Others among the poor are not expected to be cheerful; it is the clown, pretending gaiety, whose misery leads him thus into a double life: "Many times I have to play the clown, and indulge in all kinds of buffoonery, with a terrible heavy heart." Neither Dickens nor Mayhew ever describe a clown who is melancholy in his performance. For both, the clown remains a jolly, spry fellow, brightly decorated. But the man in Mayhew's interview "was a melancholy-looking man, with the sunken eyes and other characteristics of semi-starvation, whilst his face was scored with lines and wrinkles, telling of paint and premature age." The conventional sausage-stuffing gluttony of the joey becomes the "semi-starvation" of the clown in his private life.

It is, of course, Mayhew's job to reveal the private lives of his subjects, and his angle into this story is the difference between the private and public lives, rather crudely put: "His story was more pathetic than comic, and proved that the life of the street clown is, perhaps, the most wretched of all existence. Jest as he may in the street, his life is literally no joke at home." And Mayhew, like Dickens, follows the clown home. But what he finds in the account of the private life is something that, according to the clown, is worse than poverty: shame. He has been a street clown for sixteen years and only the grimmest necessity keeps him there. He entered the line as a result of other failures, and since then he has tried other jobs—even the police—with no luck. The difference is not the money. "I'd pull trucks at one shilling a-day, rather than get twelve shillings a week at my business." There is something shameful in playing the buffoon. The job is "a curse . . . with its insults and starvations." It is a curse that he hides from his neighbors and even from his children. He dons his bright costume away from home in a pub (where clowns are drawn for more than lavatory facilities) so that no one he knows will see him make the change. When he speaks of his thirteen-year-old daughter his sense of shame and sorrow anticipates the relation of Signor Jupe and Sissy that we will see in *Hard Times:* "She has seen me dressed at Stepney fair, where she brought me my tea. . . . She laughs when she sees me in my clown's dress, and wants to stay with me: but I would rather see her lay dead before me (and I had two dead in my place at one time, last Whitsun Monday was a twelve month) than she should ever belong to my profession. I could see the tears start from the man's eyes as he said this." The tears are startling here. Mayhew was a serious and sympathetic observer, but, by Victorian standards, seldom sentimental. If we are to accept the tears as a fact, then we have touched a spring of clownesque sorrow. Were the "profession" that he speaks of prostitution, he could not be more ashamed.

Why is the clown ashamed? For one thing he gains not the slightest gratification from his job beyond the few shillings he might get. He joylessly recites his jokes and says that he has never known a clown who has made up his own. The older the better. He has tried reading *Punch* for something new, but he knows the jokes there are "too high" for his audience—"indeed, I can't say I think very much of them myself." The pub does more than *Punch* can. Clowns, he admits, "like a little drop of spirits, and occasionally a great deal." No pride of creation here. He cannot imagine being funny without drink, and he has never known a clown who was a teetotaler. Sooner than later clowns die wretched in the workhouse. Thus far, without Dismal Jemmy's superciliousness, the facts accord with "The Stoller's Tale." And so does the vignette with which Mayhew frames his report: "A few minutes afterwards I saw this man dressed as Jim Crow with his face blackened, dancing and singing in the streets as if he was the lightest-hearted fellow in all London."

Before his ignominious end, the clown's life is a series of "insults" received in payment for his joyless imitation of mirth. A man would be driven to this only by the direst economic need. Thus in donning the clown's costume he is announcing himself to be a loser in a society that understands economic life to be competitive. Only a fool or a desperate failure could be induced to expose himself in this way. In pursuit of his livelihood, Mayhew's clown transgresses standards of respectability that he himself accepts. Thus he is ashamed of what he is doing, and his shame is his sorrow. The greater the sorrow, the greater the gap between the joy that he performs and the melancholy that he feels. He is just acting. The difference between his performance and his feeling is a source of new shame. He is, in effect, ashamed of art.

In *Hard Times* Dickens traces to its source the shame of the clown. It begins in the Stone Lodge, that fortress of middle-class opinion belonging to Mr. Thomas Gradgrind of Coketown. There we hear the daughter of the clown identifying her family for the daughter of the house:

> "[Mother] was;" Sissy made the terrible communication nervously; "she was a dancer. . . ."
> "Father's a;" Sissy whispered the awful word, "a clown. . . ."
> "Merrylegs;" she whispered the awful fact; "is his performing dog." (58–60)

Of course Dickens does not consider the facts "awful." He simply acknowledges but does not endorse the prejudices that account for Sissy's shame.

And yet in the course of the novel Sissy is abandoned by a father who wallows in shame and sorrow, and she is not allowed to remain with the saving remnant of circus folk. Tom's appearance as a blackface clown is made to demonstrate disgrace. The whole approach to the circus cannot be summarized by Sleary's defense nor by Gradgrind's disdain. It lies with Charles Dickens, somewhere between the two.

Our first exposure to Sleary's establishment is on Gradgrind's walk through the middle ground between Coketown and his Stone Lodge. The terrain "was neither town nor country yet was either spoiled" (11). The circus on the outskirts of town is a variation of the French *fête foraine,* the demipastoral, demirespectable diversion shunted to the suburbs. The result is a debased pastoral, tainted like the very suburbs by the waste of the town. This would be the landscape of Picasso's sad saltimbanques wandering through the same wasteland sixty years later. Beyond the town and beyond the law the clowns carry on their extraordinary version of pastoral. Just as their turf is not quite city and not quite country, the performers themselves are barely human and barely animal, or in the case of Sleary himself, "never sober and never drunk." E. W. B. Childers with his legs too short and his back too broad is "a remarkable sort of Centaur, compounded of the stable and the playhouse." Kidderminster is a cupid with a rough voice. And altogether their language bears uncertain relation to standard English. "Nine oils, Merrylegs, missing tips, garters, banners, and ponging"—Bounderby's list could go on.

Although it is with Gradgrind that we first encounter Sleary's Horse-Riding, the fact that he is unresponsive to "the sound of music" leaves the task of introduction to Dickens himself. Gradgrind "took no heed" of what follows, and what follows sounds very much like the gently satirical portraits of theatrical life that can be found in the early *Sketches* of Astley's and Greenwich Fair. The music that Gradgrind unconsciously censors is described as "a clashing and banging band . . . in full bray," and if we accept the narrative voice, Gradgrind's insensitivity is an act of reasonable self-defense. The circus tent itself is a curious mingling of Gothic architecture and modern advertisement which suggests a whimsical version of Ruskin's critique of the age: "A flag, floating from the summit of the temple" bears the name of Sleary's Horse-Riding and claims the "suffrages" of the people. "Sleary himself, a stout modern statue with a money-box at its elbow, in an ecclesiastical niche of early Gothic architecture, took the money." The repetition of "money . . . money" turns the God of this particular church into Mammon for a new saint whose attribute is his coffer, an anticipation of Ruskin's Britannia of the Market Place.

The strictly commercial aspect of the establishment continues in the descriptive voice that is borrowed from the circus barker and the playbill: "Miss Josephine Sleary, as some very long and very narrow strips of printed bill announced, was then inaugurating the entertainments with her graceful equestrian Tyrolean flower-act. Among other pleasing but always strictly moral wonders which must be seen to be believed, Signor Jupe was that afternoon to 'elucidate the diverting accomplishments of his highly trained performing dog Merrylegs.' " As in the description of the clowns out front at Greenwich Fair, the stilted Latinized language is just the kind of misleading puffery that reveals its opposite, low comedy. The same Jupe flings fountains of iron into the air—"a feat never before attempted in this or any other country," performs in a "hippo-comedietta," and punctuates the performance "with his chaste Shakspearean quips and retorts." The circus is a mixed bag of absurdity wrapped in the inevitably false dignity of modern publicity. The foreign diversions ("Tyrolean," "signor") offer the enticement of exoticism with the promise of respectable restraint ("strictly moral" and "chaste"). That mingling of the exotic, the Gothic, and the moral could be seen on any contemporary patent medicine bottle as well.

Read in the vein of the *Sketches,* the passage satirizes the commercial side of circuses, advertisers, and the society that is willing to receive them. But in the context of the early pages of *Hard Times* the circus serves as another kind of critique of society, that is, of the society already represented within the novel by Gradgrind in the schoolroom. Next to that stifling prison, the noise, variety, inconsistency, and comedy of the Horse-Riding is a valuable refreshment. A moment later, when Gradgrind drags his children away, we are left with the sense that they are missing what would be the better half of their education. "I would sooner catch them reading poetry," their father complains. And the novel is among other things the story of how poetry or the circus might have been made to serve and correct the "starved imagination." Anyone who cannot imagine a man in the moon or a great bear in the stars will also reject the unlikely promises of the Tyrolean flower-act. Thus in this context, to receive (if not exactly believe) the claims of the circus is a mark not of corrigible folly (as it might be in the *Sketches*) but is itself a correction of the greater folly of hyperrational factualism. In this case the circus—also "poetry"—is a vital, even natural, alternative to the school and the Stone Lodge to which the "metallurgical Louisa" and little Tom are taken home "like a machine" (11–12).

The clown himself, in spite of a life infused with the spirit of the circus, is sad. Signor Jupe has a private life. It is described to us, and, as we would expect, it is the contrary of his advertised public life. Only his daughter knows. Even the other members of the troupe "never knew how he felt" and would make him the butt of their jokes backstage. "He was far timider than they thought," Sissy explains to Louisa. Like Mayhew's street clown, Jupe can only wish his daughter out of the circus. And as self-esteem declines, his wishes for Sissy rise. It was "because he felt himself to be a poor, weak, ignorant, helpless man . . . that he wanted me so much to know to know a great deal, and be different from him" (59).

He drinks and he weeps. Only when Sissy reads to him from what at the Stone Lodge would be forbidden books is he distracted from his sorrows, "wondering whether the sultan would let the lady go on with the story, or would have her head cut off before it was finished." Scheherezade's art, like his own, is a matter of life and death, and life depends on approval of the audience. "But they wouldn't laugh sometimes, and then father cried." His audience laughs less and less, and he comes home drunk, beats the dog and falls to the floor, weeping. On the day that he left Sissy behind he came home in tears from another dismal performance. "At last poor father said that he had given no satisfaction again, and never did give any satisfaction now, and that he was a shame and disgrace, and I should have done better without him all along." Shame, disgrace, and tears seem to be the lot of the clown.

The novel runs its course between the first and last appearances of Sleary's Horse-Riding. When the circus returns, shame and disgrace have devolved upon Thomas Gradgrind and his son. It is then that we see them as sad clowns wearing the mark of their fall. The misguided "whelp" has embezzled money from Bounderby's bank and is being helped to escape through Sleary's good offices. Gradgrind Sr. comes with Louisa and Sissy to meet Tom at the Horse-Riding where he has been incorporated into the act in the disguise of a blackface clown. The children thus return to the circus from which they once had been dragged. When the show is over, "Mr. Gradgrind sat down forlorn, on the Clown's performing chair in the middle of the ring." On one of the benches beyond the otherwise empty ring his son appears, "ridiculously shameful . . . in his comic livery" (283). Seeing both in the guise of clowns, we are reminded of the father's misguidance and the son's sloth. Gradgrind's model family has failed, and when we look at the whelp as a clown we see that a certain kind of art—or artifice—has also failed. The disgrace of some clowns becomes the shame of all, and in *Hard Times* these exemplars of an art that appears to be comic and socially regenerative are made to suffer, and, what is worse, made to appear worthy of their punishment.

For one thing, they are not funny.[12] Both Dickens and Mayhew allude to an audience that laughs, but neither is willing to leave his reader with an impression that what the clown does actually deserves laughter. In the sketch of Astley's we are given this little dialogue between the clown and the ringmaster at a pause in Miss Woolford's riding act. The clown begins—

"I say, sir!" —"Well, sir?" (it's always conducted in the politest manner). —"Did you ever happen to hear I was in the army, sir?" —"No, sir." —"Oh, yes, sir—I can go through my exercise, sir." —"Indeed, sir!" —"Shall I do it now, sir?" —"If you please, sir; come, sir—make haste" (a cut with the long whip, and "Ha' done now—I don't like it," from the clown). Here the clown throws himself on the ground, and goes through a variety of gymnastic convulsions, doubling himself up, and untying himself again, and making himself look very like a man in the most hopeless extreme of human agony, to the vociferous delight of the gallery, until he is interrupted by a second cut from the long whip. (107–8)

Dickens goes on to recite "similar witticisms" and to record "the delight of every member of the audience," but we are left with a sense that the act itself is vacuous and that the laughter, following convulsions and whippings, is somewhat sinister. Mayhew's judgment of the street clown's comedy is untouched with irony: "He told me several of his jests; they were all of the most venerable kind, as for instance: —'A horse has ten legs: he has two forelegs and two hind ones. Two fores are eight, and two others are ten.' The other jokes were equally puerile."

At the end of *Hard Times,* before Sissy and Louisa recognize the whelp hidden in the act at Sleary's, they are detained if not diverted by a clown show. The personages of the Astley's act—ringmaster, bareback rider, and clown—rehearse a similarly inane joke which serves to draw out the tension of the larger scene.

Mr. Sleary had only made one cut at the Clown with his long whip-lash, and the Clown had only said, "If you do it again, I'll throw the horse at you!" when Sissy was recognised both by father and daughter. But they got through the Act with great self-possession; and Mr. Sleary, saving for the first instant, conveyed no more expression into his locomotive eye than into his fixed one. The performance seemed a little long to Sissy and Louisa, particularly when it stopped to afford the Clown an opportunity of telling Mr. Sleary (who said, "Indeed, sir!" to all his observations in the calmest way, and with his eye on the house) about two legs sitting on three legs looking at one leg, when in came four legs, and laid hold of one leg, and up got two legs, caught hold of three legs, and threw 'em at four legs, who ran away with one leg. For, although an ingenious Allegory relating to a butcher, a three-legged stool, a dog, and a leg of mutton, this narrative consumed time; and they were in great suspense. (279–80)

Sorrowful off stage and inane on. How then do we take the apology of the "philosophical" Sleary that punctuates the novel at beginning and end? "Don't be croth with uth poor vagabondth. People mutht be amuthed. They can't be alwayth a learning, nor yet they can't be alwayth a working, they an't made for it. You *mutht* have uth, Thquire. Do the withe thing and the kind thing too, and make the betht of uth; not the wurtht!" (293). If this defense of comic art is based on what we know of clowns in *Hard Times* and elsewhere in Dickens, it is fairly desperate. "You *mutht* have uth," becomes a kind of warning: make the best of us. In Gradgrind's world this would mean—we are useless paupers but we do serve to amuse people; we neither advance work nor instruction; we are, in fact, a burden but one that *must* be borne. Or a necessary evil appealing to the baser and duller side of man, a side that cannot be ignored, like original sin. Or a corrective element, a dose of which is necessary to make the working world work.

Dickens is speaking to himself. His sense of the clownish element includes his own doubts. (By saying "clownish" instead of "comic" I acknowledge the negative charge, the side of the clown that does not amuse and is not amused.) Dickens would seem to throw a bit of himself into the admonitory reproof of the ringmaster. For amusement's sake he can turn the tawdry clown into comedy through his playful treatment of the subject. Otherwise the clown is a vehicle for his sense of the shallowness of mere amusement. People must be amused but only after "working" and "learning," and even then a glance backstage reveals something much more grim. In *Hard Times* the clown wrests a concession from Gradgrind and from Dickens himself.

But only a concession. Sissy could not remain in Sleary's menagerie any more than Nicholas Nickleby could remain with the Crummles troupe in Portsmouth. Both are bidden to another world. The circus in *Hard Times* is an alien place, not quite urban, not quite English, and its inhabitants are not quite human. It may be instructive and exemplary, but it is impossible. Even when their father leaves, Sissy still could choose this world. Sleary offers her one kind of family where the bonds are all the stronger for its acrobatic and professional precariousness; Gradgrind offers her another. Sleary offers apprenticeship to the circus art; Gradgrind offers "a sound practical education" which Sissy knows to have been her father's interest. Gradgrind's condition is that she break all ties with the circus, that, as he says later, she even *forget* her past connection. "From this time you begin your history. . . . You will be reclaimed and formed" (47). The rigidity of this separation is mistaken and, luckily, also impossible. Sissy cannot be wholly reformed to match his own lost children. But when she is removed from the circus world, she is in a sense reclaimed for the other world which is, after all, Gradgrind's world.

Gradgrind's world is, of course, a "muddle." That is Stephen Blackpool's word but it would be equally appropriate to Mayhew's London or to the uncertain identity that most social critics at midcentury applied to the age. In Baudelaire's analysis of "modern life" the time was ripe for the arrival of the dandy: "Dandyism appears especially in those periods of transition when democracy has not yet become all-powerful, and when aristocracy is only partially weakened and discredited." [13] Not only the dandy but a host of new characters step into the void that Matthew Arnold describes, "between two worlds/One dead and the other powerless to be born." The unsettling of political leadership in the 1840s makes room for a dandified Disraeli. Elsewhere the industrial proletariat, in the act of being defined by Marx and Engels, offers itself up to new popular leaders. At the same time Carlyle prescribes the equally novel Captain of Industry as a contemporary equivalent of traditional leadership.

In *Hard Times* Dickens tests a variety of new men—the industrialist (Bounderby) and his political economist (Gradgrind), the industrial worker (Blackpool) curiously separated from the proletarian leader (Slackbridge). Drawn in from the fringe are the dandy (Mr. James Harthouse) and a host of clowns. Perhaps few of his contemporaries would take the last of these seriously, but these are Dickens' own people, personal versions of the comic artist as a self-made man. The clown, like the dandy, labor leader and industrialist, defies the inherited class system at a time when it is beginning to dissolve into the morass of urban industrialism. The dandy pretends to rise above class; the clown inevitably sinks below.

If the clown is the creation of urban industrialism, he is also its victim. We see him desolate, forlorn on city streets in the prints and paintings of Daumier and the prose poems of Baudelaire where he pops up as the self-advertising huckster in front of his booth, competing for attention. He explodes in a riot of emotion and then dissolves. He is the ultimate capitalist who flings himself on the market, falls, and lies sprawling on the pavement, only to be released by the laughter of his audience—if he has one. And yet his failure is his success or at least it is his identity. His ragged costume is a badge announcing him to be the prince of flops and failures. When the competition is brutal enough, there is a certain distinction attached to the one who comes in last.

Christianity promises that the last shall be first, but before that comes about, the clownish loser is a kind of spiritual advisor and critical alter ego of the winner. To the king the jester says, "You too are mortal, you too are a fool." The clown is no less a scourge to the capitalist. In *Hard Times* the last clown that we meet is a failed bank clerk, a grotesque reflection of his father's principles. He exaggerates and then reverses all that his society values; economic self-interest becomes theft. He is the clown stripped of comedy, the unaccommodated man who lurks behind the scenes, looks over the shoulder of the comic performer and finally silences the audience. Even his creator looks away.

Stanley Tick

TOWARD JAGGERS

"IN ALL writers," Graham Greene points out, "there occurs a moment of crystallization when the dominant theme is plainly expressed, when the private universe becomes visible even to the least sensitive reader." [1] In the writing of Charles Dickens, that moment comes quite close to the end of *Great Expectations:* Pip not only takes his place, publicly, at Magwitch's side, but puts into the official record details of his relationship with the accused ex-felon: "I began that night to write out a petition to the Home Secretary of State, setting forth my knowledge of [Magwitch], and how it was that he had come back for my sake. I wrote it as fervently and pathetically as I could, and when I had finished it and sent it in, I wrote out other petitions to such men in authority as I hoped were the most merciful, and drew up one to the Crown itself" (434–35). For a decade, from its first appearance in *David Copperfield,* a metaphor expressing secrecy and hinting at guilt had been forcing its presence onto Dickens' pages. At first unable to dramatize this metaphor, Dickens sought a means in Tulkinghorn of *Bleak House* and in Jarvis Lorry of *A Tale of Two Cites* to come to artistic terms with what had become his "dominant theme." Jaggers-Wemmick represents part of Dickens' supreme effort at expressing this theme—one through which the novelist tried to explain and excuse himself for thirty years of an uneasy, then guilty silence about his early years.

Though Pip's significance is generally agreed upon, the characterization of Jaggers-Wemmick is sufficiently ambivalent to have led commentators along varying and even divergent paths of interpretation. For some, the peculiar arrogance and detachment of the "dark, burly" lawyer indicate a God-like figure: some abstract divinity or its earthly correlative, the artist. Other, less extreme, views find Jaggers to be one of several father surrogates and teachers for Pip. These readings are opposed by many that interpret Jaggers as an instance or indictment of urbanized, bourgeois society which corrupts those involved in its processes. [2] Certainly, there are enough ironic impulses in the title, *Great*

Expectations, to sustain these different interpretations, each of which illuminates some area of this disturbingly complex figure. But if I am correct in understanding Jaggers-Wemmick as the metaphor that Dickens had been compulsively fashioning for a decade, then its full meaning must be sought first in the missing part of its context, the preceding novels, and ultimately in the private universe of Charles Dickens.

The thematic impulse which crystallized in Jaggers revealed itself for the first time in 1846, at the moment when Dickens broke off writing his autobiography almost as suddenly as he had begun. Heretofore silent, even evasive, about his unfortunate early years, Dickens had unaccountably started to write out his story for the world to know. But for reasons we can only guess at, the novelist stopped work on the autobiography after a fragmentary outline was set down. And no one, save John Forster, the novelist's confidant and adviser, was ever permitted to read those few pages. Doubtless, Dickens feared that his revelation might jeopardize a now flattering reputation and highly gratifying social status. It may be, too, that the craftsman in Dickens was dissatisfied with the few pages of autobiography that he wrote (every great artist re-creates himself most truly only in creating himself anew). But for whatever reason, Dickens decided that he could not relate his story directly, and so the autobiographical confession was abandoned.

The secreted past, the biographical matrix out of which Dickens' major metaphor was to spring, is traceable to the blacking factory experience dating back to 1824. Now, in 1846, the novelist had twenty years of silence to acknowledge and, if possible, redeem. It is worth emphasizing that it was his adult silence, not the adolescent humiliation, that caused Dickens his deep sense of guilt. Though the imprisonment of his father for debt and his own consequent employment at Lamert's blacking factory were indescribably distressing for the sensitive twelve-year-old who aspired to become a gentleman, these events in themselves could cast no long shadow of guilt. The incomprehensible forces of circumstance which compose the "given" of every child's life are accepted as fate's doing. Though they may well shape one's future, such fated events do not affect the conscience; the child, though he may regard himself as the victim of such circumstances, knows himself to be innocent of their cause. What elicited Dickens' powerful guilt feelings, then, was not his experience in Lamert's factory but his rigorous suppression of the episode, a concealment he as an adult very consciously maintained for the rest of his life. It was an adequate metaphor for this guilt that Dickens was driven to seek, in novel after novel, from *Bleak House* to *Great Expectations*—where the metaphor is finally composed.

In the earlier novels, we cannot detect much of what was to become Dickens' dominant theme. For a long time, we must assume, his secret was not so burdensome or fearful that its urging had to be appeased. Time and conscience are not always quick to punish the young. One day, however, during a casual conversation with Forster in 1846, Dickens listened in shocked wonder to a story about a certain Mr. Dilke who thought he remembered seeing the young Charles Dickens working in a blacking warehouse off the Strand.[3] It was at this moment, we might say, that Jaggers was conceived.

Dickens' first attempt to come to terms with his now troubled conscience was, as I already noted, by means of direct confession in the form of a published autobiography. But the novelist's courage apparently failed before more than a fragment got done, and only Forster (who might already have guessed near to the truth) was to see these few pages. Unable to publish the facts, Dickens turned uncertainly back to fiction. Some of the passages in *David Copperfield,* Dickens' next novel, are copied directly from the now discarded autobiography. But Forster, who was the first to point this out, also observed that Dickens' "weaving of fact and fiction" was managed in such a way that "the language of the fiction reflects only faintly the narrative of the actual fact" (601). That is to say, the novelist entirely disguised the truth of his experience even as he revealed some of its salient details. No reader had the least idea that the "little labouring hind" of Murdstone and Grinby's factory was, in truth, a re-created Charles Dickens; no one was supposed to know or even encouraged to guess. It is surely arguable that Dickens would have liked nothing more than to be found out, so that the secret suddenly grown shameful to him would be uncovered and its weight loosed. But the psychic vectors of pride, vanity, and fear were evidently such that Dickens resorted to impenetrable disguise in *David Copperfield.* As a result, his own past remained secret, and his guilt became heavier. Previously unable to complete an autobiography, Dickens now fails to show himself even through the guise of "autobiographical" fiction.[4]

We should observe that as David Copperfield matures, he grows less and less honest with himself and with us. How much did Dickens know and fear, one wonders, when he penned the opening sentence of that novel: "Whether I shall turn out to be the hero of my own life, or whether that station will be held by anybody else, these pages must show"? The most opportune dramatic situation in the novel for Dickens to have explored the ramifications of secrecy and guilt is in the story involving Steerforth and Emily: they are the ones who deceive and who share a shameful secret. But Dickens takes great care to keep his hero well outside that action (what if Steerforth had confided in David?). When the elopement is announced, David is as astonished as the most provincial fisherman. And at no time afterward can David reconcile his erstwhile friend's charm to his treachery. Insofar as David *is* the hero of his own story, this clandestine drama remains external to his life: he is not, so far as we can see, influenced by its meaning—though the heart of its lesson bears more closely than any other event on the problem of Dickens' own life.

As the narration goes on and David approaches maturity, he disappoints us more and more in his limited introspection; his truth-telling seems partial and minor. As a lad, he could freely confess that when news of his mother's death is brought to him, his first reaction was the thought that he would now gain status in the eyes of his fellow pupils. And when, somewhat older now, he meets Mr. Micawber again in Canterbury, he admits to us that he is less than delighted to discover this reminder of his past (a past which he never discusses or alludes to, for his paramount desire now is to be thought a gentleman). When in Chapter xvii Micawber does remind David of the London days ("still in the wine trade?"), the hero immediately changes the topic of conversation and then pulls Micawber away so that Uriah and Mrs. Heep should not fathom the truth. Who can doubt that David is relieved when the Micawbers sail off to Australia? Thenceforth, no one is about who might reveal his secret past. (But by so saving this autobiographical hero from facing up to his past, Charles Dickens was unknowingly preparing the way for that far more painful moment of Pip's confession; by then the guilt of repression had become so strong that a happy ending could no longer even be fantasized.)

By the time David comes of age, even partial truth-telling is, at important moments, stopped. It is as much his immature pride and cowardice, for example, as it is gallantry that seals David's lips about the truth of his life with Dora. We glimpse enough of her infantile petulance and incapacity to infer that for a man like David such a marriage must have been a rude disillusionment and a dreary waste of days. Were he at any point honest with himself, David would acknowledge at least that much and perhaps lament his unhappy fate. (The author not only promulgates such silences on his hero's part but rewards them by killing off Dora and preserving Agnes intact.) Because a fantasy of wish fulfillment directs the concluding section of *David Copperfield,* Dickens' private anxiety about his secrecy and cowardice continued and deepened.

There is an odd and easily overlooked moment in the novel when Dickens seems to be recasting his dilemma in the unlikely personage of Micawber. Near to the end, that likeable but hapless gentleman finds his conscience (and his prose) greatly troubled by his involvement with Uriah Heep. Certain that his employer is a scoundrel, yet quite considerably in financial debt to Heep, Micawber must weigh the needs of his family against the potential harm of Heep (lii). Given the circumstances of the novel, we are confident that Micawber will, as he does, make the right, "brave" choice; the episode is therefore of small dramatic meaning. Yet Dickens takes considerable time and space to record the bizarre antics expressing Micawber's inner turmoil as he contemplates his decision. I cannot help thinking that it was the author's displaced anxiety that caused such emphasis—if not the incident itself—to be recorded.

Dickens' guilty secrecy, signaled by the extraordinary move toward autobiography, is less a theme than an awareness informing *David Copperfield:* there is no consistent metaphoric marker for secrecy that we can point to in this novel. The hero strikes us as naïvely honest for the most part, particularly as he is led to observe the guilty or furtive ways of others. It may be that Dickens, having copied out passages from his autobiography for the early parts of the novel, hoped that his guilt was now laid, and so composed an idyllic ending. If that was the case, the novelist was mistaken. No sooner did he begin his next novel, *Bleak House,* than a metaphor for secrecy intruded itself directly into his pages.

Mr. Tulkinghorn, as virtually all commentators agree, is enigmatic; even the shrewd Inspector Bucket admits that he cannot comprehend the solicitor's behavior. A reader of *Bleak House* can reasonably well discern what Tulkinghorn does in the story, less surely how he does it, and not at all why: his motivation is finally incomprehensible. What we are quite properly saying here is that in analyzing *Bleak House* we discover no theme that makes sense of Tulkinghorn's life or death; his ominous silences and his securing of family secrets illuminate little of the novel. It is not fancy which leads me to think that Dickens himself knew this, and that he placed the allegorical Roman on Tulkinghorn's ceiling in order to point not at any subject we can find in the novel but rather to himself, the guilty novelist.

Dickens makes us deeply suspicious of Tulkinghorn by repeatedly describing the elderly lawyer as a "silent depository" of family confidences, and as a man who hides all he knows, and who never converses "when not professionally consulted." We are led to interpret his pile of strongboxes as a metaphor for the man, and his black clothing as an omen of his effect. Yet he plays almost no part in the developing story of *Bleak House.* He is simply someone who gathers and preserves secrets, let the innocent and guilty alike look to him as they will. Tulkinghorn is a grim, inert conscience: all doors, we note, are always open to him. The point which so confounds us about this character is that he does nothing with the secrets he possesses. (It is not Tulkinghorn but the easily understood young Guppy who is ready to blackmail Lady Dedlock, or even marry Esther, as a means of gaining from the secret.) When Tulkinghorn confronts Lady Dedlock about her shameful past, he insists that they must do nothing whatever that might reveal the secret; his single-minded aim is to keep the story hushed up. Lady Dedlock, tortured but not threatened by Tulkinghorn (she *is* threatened by Guppy), goes to her death, confession being out of the question given the nature of her guilt. When Tulkinghorn is murdered, we scarcely feel much sympathy, though he has committed no great crime that we know of. He has been a skulking, silent, solitary presence, almost always making people uncomfortable, his power and authority based on the possession of secrets.

Twice now Dickens tried and failed to do the necessary but unbearable thing and tell his secret to the world. First, he could not bring himself to write more than a handful of pages of an autobiography; then, in *David Copperfield,* he turned the confessional, first-person opportunity for truth-telling into a means for coy evasiveness. Now, in *Bleak House,* he finds himself composing private symbols and allowing major characters to seem motiveless and perplexing.[5] Dickens could invent no drama in the story to explain Tulkinghorn's role, and no reason either to require his death. The character is apparently damned and assuredly doomed for making a profession of maintaining people's guilty secrets. We are moving toward Jaggers.

The novelist takes slight but painful revenge on himself in the person of Bounderby, the hypocritical boor of *Hard Times.* When the truth about his unheroic past is exposed, there is universal laughter but scarcely more contempt than we had already felt. Bounderby is, in part, a blunt self-mockery by which Dickens punished himself without allaying his guilt. In the grim, grey allegory of *Little Dorrit,*the recurring images are of prisons and prisoners; we are forced to observe that most of the principal characters are depicted as victims of some secret shame or guilt. The Clenham house, for example, is rotten with dark secrets of past crimes, and in its collapse we discern another version of the death of Tulkinghorn and the exposé of Bounderby—that is to say, another expression of the now dominant theme of Charles Dickens. Unable to confess *in propria persona,* the novelist is driven to re-create his private universe and thereby offer his disguised confession in novel after novel.

We know that Dickens was never to make his secret public; we know further that when Forster published his *Life of Dickens* and revealed the unlikely facts of Dickens' boyhood, the millions of interested readers were neither dismayed nor titillated. But if Dickens' vanity can therefore be judged as misguided, his artistic intuition is redeemed by our realization that the recurring theme of secrecy impelled Dickens to achieve his finest work.

The phrase "the theme of secrecy" requires some elaboration at this point. In the early novels, such characters as Carker, the dissembling villain of *Dombey and Son,* and Nadgett, the inquiry agent in

Martin Chuzzlewit, act in secret or furtive ways much of the time. Both are conventional characters, however, one a blackguard, the other a cryptoprivate detective; both act out conventional roles in that they make a means not an end of their secrecy. Mr. Tulkinghorn, on the other hand, is mystifying because he guards not his own secrets but others'. His need to gather and preserve these secrets is explicable only in clinical terms. In Tulkinghorn, Dickens has given us a metaphor expressive of secrecy not a character who is dramatically (or even rationally) motivated by it. The same shall be true to some extent about Jaggers. In the novels after *David Copperfield,* the author's psychological guilt initiates and to some extent directs the dramatic guilt embodied in the narrative.

A Tale of Two Cities is, among other things, Dickens' half-accepted rationalization and self-apology for his now inescapable guilt over the keeping of secrets. With its "buried alive" concept, the novel abounds in allusions to ghosts and spirits from the past, to open graves, and to the accumulated guilt in France of ancient outrage. Dickens' private theme is enacted principally by two characters, one a parodic comment on the other. Jarvis Lorry is a good and respectable man—an idealization of the legitimate keeper of secrets. Jerry Cruncher is a rough, indeed criminal, type whose secret is the revolting one of body-snatching. The two form a paradigm of Dickens' inner theme.

Tellson's Bank, a venerable and dignified institution, is known far and wide for its old-fashioned ways and its integrity. A good part of Tellson's trade, it seems, is supplied by people wealthy enough to require strongboxes and confidentiality, and Mr. Jarvis Lorry is pretty much in charge of both. This trusted "true-hearted old gentleman" is so far above reproach that we have no occasion to question his motives. He is the bank's most faithful servant: "No better man living to hold fast by what Tellson's had in keeping, and to hold his peace" (294). Like Tulkinghorn, Lorry is elderly and old-fashioned; like Tulkinghorn, Lorry has in his trust innumerable family secrets which are preserved in strongboxes. But unlike Tulkinghorn, Lorry does not confuse the means of his livelihood with its ends. Though he pretends to be "a speaking machine" and "a mere man of business" without any sentiment, he shows himself to be a person of ready affection and deep sympathy.

Dickens is evidently trying to ameliorate his own anxiety in two ways now: by asserting that the keeping of secrets in the case of professional need is ethically sound (this angle is never made clear in Tulkinghorn's case); and to show that the necessarily detached keeper of secrets can yet be warmly human and thus gain the good man's reward of a loving, adoptive family. (A tentative but incomplete contrast is posed by Sydney Carton, the man who despises his profession and leads an empty, loveless existence.) By and large, Lorry keeps his professional and what we might term "human" lives separate, which in part accounts for the superficiality of his characterization. When his dear friend, Dr. Manette, suffers a relapse, the seventy-five-year-old Lorry, we are told, absents himself from Tellson's "for the first time in his life." And when, in Paris, Lucie's presence could endanger the bank's precarious neutrality, Lorry sees to it that she finds another place to stay: "One of the first considerations which arose in the business mind of Mr. Lorry when business hours came round, was this:— that he had no right to imperil Tellson's by sheltering the wife of an emigrant prisoner under the Bank roof. His own possessions, safety, life, he would have hazarded for Lucie and her child, without a moment's demur; but the great trust he held was not his own, and as to that business charge he was a strict man of business" (250).

The thinness of Lorry and the insubstantial quality of the Manettes suggest how limited a truth that portion of *A Tale of Two Cities* is communicating. It is as if Dickens knew that his manipulation of metaphor was here at best only plausible. As an apparent means of reminding himself that one cannot succeed by such dodges, Dickens is artistically honest enough to parody Lorry (and the excruciating piety of Sydney Carton, as well) by means of the low-life character Cruncher. The joke, such as it is, has to do with Cruncher being a grave robber. This otherwise gruesome sideline is lightened for us by the comic reflection it provides at the expense of the respectable Lorry. Cruncher repeatedly refers to himself as "the honest tradesman," by which he means not the work he does for Tellson's (where he is pictured as being almost as loyal and competent as Lorry himself, though in a lower capacity) but his criminal activities of the night. The confidences *he* keeps are not those of the bank. He and Lorry have a mildly amusing exchange early in the novel when the latter sends the message "Recalled to Life," a notion Cruncher finds perplexing and irritating.

Even more grotesque is Cruncher's parodic lead-in for Carton's Christian self-sacrifice. Cruncher's nefarious "trade" makes him, in the idiom of the day, a Resurrection-Man; and when his son learns the secret of Cruncher's nighttime activities, he uses that very phrase. The novel is short enough, and this episode memorable enough, so that when Sydney Carton, two hundred or so pages later, begins his "I am the resurrection and the life" litany, we cannot help but hear the echo from Cruncher. (In the concluding pages of the novel, Jerry Cruncher confesses to Miss Pross, without quite specifying the nature of his past crime. He is readily forgiven by Lorry later, and presumably by the reader.)

If we accept Montaigne's observation about the function of his essays—"I no more made this book than this book made me"—as a supreme truth of creative writing, then *A Tale of Two Cities* cannot be said to have been made by more than a shadow of Charles Dickens. Yet the novel has important bearing on our dominant theme. In his depiction of Jarvis Lorry, Dickens has adduced a rationalization for keeping secrets. Through this character, we are shown (not without the equivocation offered by Cruncher, however) that a closed person can succeed to affection—though not a family. The keeper of secrets, that is to say, need not be murdered or condemned or humiliated. The time has arrived for Jaggers-Wemmick.

The moral scheme of *Great Expectations* is, in outline, remarkably simple if one compares it to the other late novels. The polarities are denoted early in the story and quite unambiguously. Joe Gargery embodies perfect good, Orlick primordial evil (the novel, we note, opens on Christmas Eve). Normally, these two powerful men work together at Joe's forge (a wonderfully fertile figure, this, illuminating much that is to follow). But when they are provoked into direct conflict, Orlick is speedily vanquished: "Without so much as pulling off their singed and burnt aprons, they went at one another, like two giants. But if any man in that neighborhood could stand up long against Joe, I never saw the man. Orlick, as if he had been of no more account than the pale young gentleman [whom Pip had recently fought and defeated], was very soon among the coal-dust, and in no hurry to come out of it" (107–8). A few minutes after the fight, however, Joe and Orlick are quietly composed and even sharing a pot of beer. In the fallen world of *Great Expectations,* good and evil, though distinct and incompatible, work at their tasks together, often shoulder to shoulder. Their figurative proximity at this early point alerts the reader to the careful discrimination that will be necessary in making moral judgments henceforth.

How much easier to judge behavior in *The Old Curiosity Shop,* to choose from Dickens' earlier novels, where Nell's angelic goodness and Quilp's demonic evil are untouching polarities. The moral axis in that novel runs well beyond the human page at both ends, allowing the reader ample room to locate the values on one side or the other. Nell's transcendent virtue is rewarded by an early release from all suffering; at the other extreme, Quilp is buried with a stake through his heart. In *Great Expectations,* however, though it is a Christmas story, good and evil have the same shape and share some of the same work in the world (neither Joe nor Orlick, we note, dies at the novel's end).

Joe Gargery is not angelic but a perfectly good being who endures both the querulousness of Mrs. Joe and the ingratitude of Pip. Joe's selflessness and natural dignity enable him to withstand unhappy circumstances; he is ultimately rewarded with Biddy's love. Orlick, part of the malignant growth of the marshes, is vengeful and cruel. He exists on some edge of elemental darkness ("from the ooze"), yet his evil, like Joe's good, is short of sublime. His assaults are vicious but not monstrous; his habits and attitudes seem low and mean but not really diabolical. Orlick and Joe Gargery represent the high and low points of human potential; their natures circumscribe the range of behavior we are called upon to judge in *Great Expectations.*

If the moral delineations in *Great Expectations* were not so complex, the first meeting between Pip and Jaggers could be read in its elementary sense: "We [Pip and Estella] went on our way up-stairs after the episode; and, as we were going up, we met a gentleman groping his way down" (77). The implication is formed by darkness as well as the contrasting directions, Pip and Estella rising, Jaggers descending. As the novel unfolds, we come to appreciate both aspects of this symbolic encounter. The young people's rise in the world, we learn, is hedged round with ironies; Jaggers' descent has been somewhat obscured by cynical realities. The darkness, however, settles round Jaggers alone. Here is the full scene.

> We went on our way upstairs . . . and as we were going up, we met a gentleman groping his way down.
> "Whom have we here?" asked the gentleman, stopping and looking at me.
> "A boy," said Estella.
> He was a burly man of an exceedingly dark complexion, with an exceedingly large head and a corresponding large hand. He took my chin in his large hand and turned up my face to have a look at me by the light of the candle. He was prematurely bald on the top of his head, and had bushy black eyebrows that wouldn't lie down, but stood up bristling. His eyes were set very deep in his head, and were disagreeably sharp and suspicious. He had a large watch-chain, and strong black dots where his beard and whiskers would have been if he had let them. He was nothing to me, and I could have had no foresight then, that he ever would be anything to me, but it happened that I had thus opportunity of observing him well.
> "Boy of the neighborhood? Hey?" said he.
> "Yes, sir," said I.
> "How do *you* come here?"
> "Miss Haversham sent for me, sir," I explained.
> "Well! Behave yourself. I have a pretty large experience of boys, and you're a bad set of fellows. Now mind!" said he, biting the side of his great forefinger as he frowned at me, "you behave yourself!"
> With these words he released me—which I was glad of, for his hand smelt of scented soap—and went his way down-stairs. (77)

In his introduction to the Macmillan edition of *Great Expectations,* R. D. McMaster shrewdly observes that Dickens encourages, indeed taunts, the reader to fathom Jaggers. Our difficulty in doing so, if I might venture an answer, is Dickens' own: the lawyer (completed by Wemmick) is part of the final formulation of that dominant, troubling theme of secrecy. At no point could the novelist be other than deeply ambivalent about its expression. But in *Great Expectations* we do, I believe, come closest to reading the keeper of secrets as an unwelcome if not evil man. Jaggers, a downstairs man, must finally be rejected by Pip. Those critics who interpret the lawyer as a God-like figure, an artist, or even a valuable teacher for Pip, are misreading Dickens' melancholy reflections for the bitter ironies of a Kafka.

Jaggers' variety of gestures is new to us and requires discussion. Unlike Tulkinghorn, he is not a silent figure, yet his words are invariably impersonal and weighty with assumed authority. Unlike Lorry, Jaggers has no apparent affection or human vulnerability. His cynical detachment and bullying manner suggest strength of a sort, it is true, but also the expense of such strength. His bullying is the first clue to his dark meaning: the man is ruthless (like Tulkinghorn, he is often sadistic). He threatens Pip in their first meeting, though he has neither cause nor excuse. Shortly after, in Chapter xviii, we are given a detailed instance of Jaggers' attitude and effect. We are with Pip and the locals in the Three Jolly Bargemen. Mr. Wopsle, in his splendid ignorance, is holding forth—one should say "performing"—inspired by a murder trial as reported in a newspaper. In his nonsensical rendering of the report, Wopsle implies to his auditors that the suspect is surely guilty. Jaggers, a stranger to one and all, is part of the audience; so mercilessly does he attack Wopsle's notion of things that everyone is made doubtful of the "verdict." The point of this episode is certainly not to recast Wopsle as a fool: the reader has already been shown that. We can also grasp the importance of Jaggers' legal point about presumed innocence. But the scene we have been reading and enjoying is one characterized by the tone of rustic delight. "He [Wopsle] enjoyed himself thoroughly, and we all enjoyed ourselves, and were delightfully comfortable." Pip's words here capture the appropriate mood and understanding. But no sooner does he notice Jaggers than Pip sees how the lawyer listens to Wopsle with "an expression of contempt on his face" (126). It is a look characteristic of Jaggers (and we should note that no God or artist, in Dickens' view, is likely to sneer). All that Jaggers succeeds in doing in this scene is destroying the inconsequential pleasure of the rustics in the public house. We find far less to admire in the lawyer's defense of presumed innocence than we do to dislike in his intemperate and uncalled-for interference.

Pip is the single, excited witness to the one encounter between Jaggers and Joe, and though he does not explicitly comment on its out-

come, the rest of the novel assures us that its importance was not lost
on the boy. Joe Gargery proves himself able to withstand Jaggers' bullying and, indeed, bears down in turn on the lawyer. In another of the
symbolic conflicts which outline the moral shape of this novel, Jaggers
is entirely routed by Joe. The lawyer is endeavoring to convince Joe
that he should take payment for giving up his apprentice, Pip. Offered
in Jaggers' characteristic professional manner of bullying, the money is
refused because it would make the transaction morally dubious.

> "Now, Joseph Gargery, I warn you this is your last chance.
> No half measures with me. If you mean to take a present that I
> have it in charge to make to you, speak out, and you shall have
> it. If on the contrary you mean to say—" Here, to his great
> amazement, he was stopped by Joe's suddenly working round
> him with every demonstration of a fell pugilistic purpose.
> "Which I meantersay," cried Joe, "that if you come into my
> place bull-baiting and badgering me, come out! Which I mean-
> tersay as sech if you're a man, come on! Which I meantersay
> that what I say, I meantersay and stand or fall by!"
> I drew Joe away, and he immediately became placable,
> merely stating to me, in an obliging manner and as a polite ex-
> postulatory notice to anyone whom it might happen to concern,
> that he were not a-going to be bull-baited and badgered in his
> own place. Mr. Jaggers had risen when Joe demonstrated, and
> had backed near the door. (134)

Jaggers comprehends the grounds of Joe's refusal here: he is not morally blind but deeply cynical. The lawyer's power over high and low
alike is his assumption that everyone has a price and will at some time
accept payment. That is to say, he is himself compromised—and therefore astonished that anyone like Joe could maintain his virtue. Later in
the novel, Pip—who is well short of Joe's stature—will have his own
confrontation with Jaggers. The young man will knock Jaggers off
guard, though not rout him; but even his small measure of victory over
Jaggers emphasizes the novel's distinction between light and dark ways.

However striking, Jaggers' gesture of repeated handwashing is finally ambiguous. By some readers, it is accepted as a sign that the lawyer recognizes the sordid work he must do; the washing then represents disapproval and releases Jaggers from blame. Yet he is seen to
wash his hands after virtually *all* human intercourse: after he entertains
Pip and his friends (205), even after being with Pip alone (277). As well
as erasing the dirt of corruption and criminality, Jaggers seems to
cleanse himself from the touch of any human presence, as though the
innocent and guilty were equally unwelcome: the gesture, then, is am-
biguously associated with Jaggers' cultivated detachment. Our problem

in interpretation at this point is added to by the issue of professionalism as it is practiced in Little Britain (and, by contrast, in Wemmick's Walworth home). When proper conduct is enforced in the legal office, sentiment of any kind is proscribed. Jaggers invariably sets the tone, in and out of his office, by avoiding the least expression of personal opinion or interest. Untouched by curiosity or sentiment, Jaggers, like Tulkinghorn, is aloof and apparently imperturbable. The reader's interest is engaged, though never clearly satisfied, in determining the gulf between professional (or artistic) impersonality and antisocial attitudes. The willed solitude of both Tulkinghorn and Jaggers suggests that both have retreated from the world and their own best selves. My own reading here is that for both lawyers a professional concern for secret information has grown to a baleful way of life (contrast Jarvis Lorry): the two are now possessed by the very secrets they guard. That Jaggers makes such a pretense of never judging others is the lawyer's professional disguise, not a human virtue: the truth is that he does not wish to have to judge himself. His own cynicism betokens grave self-doubt.

Estella tells Pip that she believes Jaggers to be "more in the secrets of any place" than anyone she had ever known. This dark man who never laughs, with his "sharp suspicious eyes" causes immediate discomfort almost everywhere he sets foot because his authority is "expressive of knowing something secret about every one of us." In a world where Joe Gargery represents the highest good, Jaggers' air alone would serve to condemn him. We are, moreover, given substantial cause to think badly of Jaggers—yet we are never able to decide that he is evil (or, for that matter, good). Understandably, Dickens would not pass simple or direct judgment on men who are secretive.

In Chapter xx, Pip comes to London for the first time: his childhood is now completed, and henceforth he must be entirely responsible for his behavior. Joe has been left behind, as has Orlick. In London, it is Herbert Pocket, on the one hand, who befriends Pip and instructs him— a young man with "a natural incapacity to do anything secret or mean" (167). But as well as Herbert, Jaggers is to have some authority over the hero—Jaggers, who, on Pip's twenty-first birthday, makes him feel that "coming of age at all seemed hardly worth while in such a guarded and suspicious world as he made of it" (278). Before we leave this instructive twentieth chapter, we are shown a side of Jaggers that is as extraordinary as it is important: the man is criminal. That is to say, one aspect of his secrecy and impersonality is now illuminated as the source of his own guilt.

The chapter opens with a persuasive sign of Jaggers' vast power, for his name alone is sufficient to make the coachman charge Pip an honest fare. We then follow Pip into Jaggers' dismal office, rendered unbearable to the youth on account of the two death masks. When Jaggers does at length appear, he is shown to march past and over putative clients with a blunt arrogance. The last supplicant, a lisping, importunate Jew, is said to be thrown off "with supreme indifference." At this point in his lordly progress, Jaggers reaches his office—where he immediately sets about looking over a would-be false witness. Jaggers rejects this willing perjurer only because the man looks disreputable; the lawyer, we conclude, prefers that his false witnesses look trustworthy. Pip records the incident without further comment, just as he had recorded the earlier moments when Joe had routed Orlick and Jaggers; but these revelations are not lost on Pip.

We perhaps recall Bumble, the simpleton of *Oliver Twist,* whose memorable reflections about the ways of the world included the notion that "the law is a ass—a idiot." The author of *Bleak House* and *Great Expectations* knew much better than that. Like literature itself, the law is an expression of morality abstracted and formalized: it offers an essential text for any man who seeks truth in phrases. The serious literary artist, he who takes immense pains to discover genuine meaning, rightly suspects that those men who debate law are his rivals and potential betrayers. All too often, it must seem to the writer, the man of law deliberately obscures or even falsifies true meaning.

Knowing what we do of Jaggers to this point in the novel, our reflections, now that we see his criminality, perhaps recall Dodson and Fogg or Samson Brass or some of the wicked legal types in *Bleak House.* Indeed, before we have finished *Great Expectations,* we shall learn details of several other doubtful practices on Jaggers' part: how he connives at the illegal return of Magwitch to England; and how, long past, he deliberately misled a court of law about the guilt of a gipsy murderess (Wemmick is implicated in all of these deeds). Yet this last-mentioned charge, whose secret is so carefully guarded, reminds us of the complex delineations demanded if we are to make judgments in this novel. The guilty woman is Molly, Estella's mother; Jaggers' assistance to the mother, dubious as it itself was, has allowed the child to have a name and a chance in life. Perhaps the keeping of secrets can be excused.

The surest evidence we have for thinking well of Jaggers comes late, in Chapter li. It is to be the second-last time we shall see Jaggers at all, and a memorable moment in the story: Pip now gains his small but significant victory over the dark figure. The hero, this time unabashed by the routine impersonality or the death masks in Little Britain, relates the facts about Estella's parentage; he concludes by appealing to Jaggers' buried humanity: "Be more frank and manly with me," Pip pleads. Caught off-guard by Pip, Jaggers for the second time in the novel (the first, his symbolic defeat by Joe) loses control of events, and, though he does not physically retreat, speaks words he had not planned to utter—he confesses. Preserving only the defense of a sup-positional form ("put the case that . . ."), Jaggers allows Pip to under-stand the means he had used in order to protect the mother and her infant daughter. After his narration, we are left to infer that his de-tachment is not a result of blindness or indifference to "the atmosphere of evil" (his phrase) which surrounds him. He kept secret the truth of Molly's crime at least in part because he wished to save her child from the "certain destruction" he knew awaited the child had her mother gone to prison.

If we take these two incidents together, that of Jaggers suborning a witness and that of Jaggers misleading a court in order to save Estella, we form a paradox which is something of a key to this novel. The first act implies gross dishonesty, the second a sympathetic moral aware-ness: each follows from that doctrine of survival in a fallen world—that the ends justify the means. In the simple moral universe of *The Old Cu-riosity Shop,* we are not made to appreciate the urgency of this doctrine: Nell and her forces are good, Quilp and his evil. But in *Great Expecta-tions,* where Orlick and Joe Gargery labor at the same forge, we must appreciate the necessary ends for which secrets *should* be preserved.

Pip's first adventure, in which he meets Magwitch on the marshes, precipitates his great moral crisis. His stealing of food and the file are not blameworthy, for the boy acted out of understandable fear and some compassion as well. Afterward, however, when all threat is re-moved, Pip fails to confess the deed to Joe. His rationalization, as he, now an adult narrator, realizes, was a precocious ends-justify-means argument:

> I do not recall that I felt any tenderness of conscience in refer-ence to Mrs. Joe, when the fear of being found out was lifted off me. But I loved Joe—perhaps for no better reason in those early days than because the dear fellow let me love him—and, as to him, my inner self was not so easily composed. It was much upon my mind (particularly when I first saw him looking about for his file) that I ought to tell Joe the whole truth. Yet I did not, and for the reason that I mistrusted that if I did, he would think me worse than I was. The fear of losing Joe's con-fidence, and of thenceforth sitting in the chimney-corner at night staring drearily at my for ever lost companion and friend, tied up my tongue. I morbidly represented to myself that if Joe knew it, I never afterwards could see him at the fireside feeling his fair whisker, without thinking that he was meditating on it. That, if Joe knew it, I never afterwards could see him glance, however casually, at yesterday's meat or pudding when it came to today's table, without thinking that he was debating whether I had been in the pantry. . . . In a word, I was too cowardly to do what I knew to be right, as I had been too

cowardly to avoid doing what I knew to be wrong. I had had no
intercourse with the world at that time, and I imitated none of its
many inhabitants who act in this manner. Quite an untaught
genius, I made the discovery of the line of action for myself. (37)

That he can write these words now tells us how "good" Pip has become
(and, of course, that *he* can write these words for his character Pip tells
us how insistent Dickens' dominant theme had become). Jaggers' ethic
would have so easily accommodated Pip's deceit that no such confession
need have been uttered. Indeed, had Jaggers' rather than Joe's influence finally prevailed, *Great Expectations* would have had no more autobiographical *raison d'être* than *David Copperfield* (the work Dickens
reread before he began writing of Pip).

The end-justifies-means argument is embodied in the narrative by
its most sympathetic practitioner, Wemmick. His strictures about "portable property" are given freely to Pip on several occasions, and thus
the worldly ethic is particularized reasonably enough—in a fallen
world. Those critics who read Jaggers and Wemmick as teachers for
Pip must consider the way in which their principle, "Get hold of the
portable property," is followed in the story.

At the conclusion, after the attempted escape is thwarted, Wemmick lectures Pip: "I do not think he could have been saved. Whereas
the portable property [that is, Magwitch's money] certainly could have
been saved. That's the difference between the property and the owner,
don't you see?" (428). Pip at that point "sees" not only the sense of
Wemmick's argument but its worldliness as well. He is not Joe Gargery
and thus will not express outrage. In truth, he has little sure ground
from which to rebuke Wemmick, for the complexity of the novel stems
from Pip's own imperfect values. We know that Pip did not deliberately
refuse Magwitch's money at the end (he did once, earlier—in Chapter
xl) but in the speed of events forgot to think of it. To say even so much,
however, if we bear in mind Jaggers and Wemmick as they insist on
payment down to the last "farden," is to say a great deal in Pip's favor.

The hero, then, is compromised in the dubious matter of portable
property only insofar as he looks on without comment at Wemmick's
sly ways: at the fact that Wemmick's ladylove, Miss Skiffins, receives as
gifts articles of "portable property" (282); and at the fact that Wemmick makes bashful boasts about accepting tangible "thanks" for certain
legal favors done (193). Certainly not reprehensible behavior—among
worldly men! But we are not meant to forget that, after all, *Great Expectations* is a Christmas story, and that despite its ironic turns, the moral is
not to be apostate. Our judgment of Pip is, eventually, one of commen-
dation—for not trading on the ethic which sanctions such doctrines as
that of "portable property."

But were all the other issues left in doubt, Pip's confession of his past, his acknowledgment of Magwitch, makes it perfectly clear that he, not David Copperfield, is Dickens' genuine autobiographical hero. The unwritten pages of the 1846 confession are completed here, in *Great Expectations*. Dickens' creative conscious was surely aware of this, for there is a touchstone symbol in both *David Copperfield* and *Great Expectations* which cannot be coincidental. I refer to Dickens' use of Australia, that distant, dreadful island on the far side of a nineteenth-century Englishman's conscience.[6] In both novels, Australia is used as a potential prison for one's past, a place to which unwelcome ghosts are transported. The Micawbers are sent there and allowed to flourish, for in that distant prosperity the Micawbers preserve David from his shameful but now happily secret past. Magwitch is even more emphatically banished to that remote land, and he also prospers there (allowing Pip to prosper in England). But Dickens now forces his autobiographical hero to painful self-knowledge. The harsh and ugly man who embodies Pip's secret returns to England.

Jaggers and Wemmick know the circumstances, and Pip thereby is humiliated; Orlick learns of the relationship, and Pip is thereby endangered (the incident on the marshes). But Pip survives both threats, and in publicly accepting Magwitch, accepts his past; he is thereby freed from Jaggers' power.

That conclusion written, Dickens can very nearly succeed, in *Our Mutual Friend,* in burying the past beneath piles of rubbish—and after a while carting it all away. It is now mere dust; there is nothing more to be raked up. We therefore laugh at Silas Wegg's efforts to uncover some riches—until he in fact finds a will that no one had known of (wills are instruments fashioned in the past so that they can have power in the present). But with a determined stroke of his narrative pen, Dickens invalidates Wegg's discovery, and the man who digs through yesterday's trash is dumped into a passing scavenger's cart (headed toward Australia?). Finally, the darkly talented John Jasper, a man evidently hiding the most horrendous of secrets: what would *he* have expressed of the author's dominant theme? We can do no more than speculate, of course, about his unfinished role, but the prominence and complexity of this character indicate to what degree Dickens' pen continued to be driven by a deeply troubled conscience.

Lawrence Frank

THE INTELLIGIBILITY OF MADNESS
IN *OUR MUTUAL FRIEND* AND
THE MYSTERY OF EDWIN DROOD

> It might be worth while, sometimes, to inquire what Nature is, and
> how men work to change her, and whether, in the enforced distor-
> tions so produced, it is not natural to be unnatural.—*Dombey and Son*

THE MYSTERY of Edwin Drood fascinates, in part, *because* of its very in-
completeness. Since the publication in 1870 of the six monthly parts
Dickens lived to complete, generations of readers have been tempted to
concoct solutions to the various riddles posed by the novel. Both the
common reader and the literary critic succumb: they puzzle over the
identity of the theatrical Mr. Datchery; try to determine whether Edwin
Drood is alive or dead; take their heated stand on the innocence or
guilt of John Jasper. There are no answers to the riddles. If he had
decided on the final shape of his mystery, Dickens' death has forever
cut us off from any sure knowledge of his plans. Reports by his son,
Charles Dickens, Jr., on the confident claims made by John Forster, in
his role as literary executor and biographer, will satisfy no confirmed
"Droodian," with his own theories about the logical conclusion to the
novel. There exists enough evidence—in articles, books and "continua-
tions" of *Edwin Drood*—to indicate that the discussion will never end,
the ingenious resolutions of the plot will continue to appear: each of us
is determined to finish, if not to finish off, the work of the Inimitable.

Yet, this thoroughly enjoyable preoccupation with *Edwin Drood* as
whodunit, finally, ceases to be harmless. All this speculation obscures
the integrity of the fragment as it stands. It ignores Dickens' systematic
critique of the fictive world of *Edwin Drood*. The failure to acknowledge
the novel's autonomy only feeds that compulsion to complete it, or
leads to the illuminating wrongheadedness of the two Leavises in
Dickens the Novelist.

> The last novel, *Edwin Drood,* shows that though unfinished it
> was working up to a merely melodramatic exposure scene.

. . . There is certainly an undercurrent of heightened feeling in every part of the novel concerned with Jasper. This is associated . . . with the tension set up between his public rôle of respectable choirmaster . . . and his secret life in the underworld of opium-addiction and his privately fostered murderous enmity to his nephew. . . . The suggestion of moral interest here is minimal but what possibilities it had are not explored in the novel as it develops, we can see. Such a set-up can be only melodramatic in its working out and *dénouement,* and there is no reason to suppose that we have lost anything of value by *The Mystery of Edwin Drood*'s not having been revealed to us.[1]

But melodrama, as the Leavises surely know, is an inherent part of Dickens' major novels. It becomes a characteristic element of that Gothic vision by which Dickens orders an otherwise bewildering urban landscape.

The London through which Dickens' characters move threatens a terrible isolation; it harbors its own monsters in a gallery of grotesques and Gothic villains for whom the city is their natural setting. In this context John Jasper should not be seen as the conventional villain of romance whose "moral interest" is, in the Leavises' words, "minimal." Neither the central situation nor the central character of *Edwin Drood* can be so easily dismissed. *Edwin Drood* and John Jasper involve the logical culmination of a lengthy process, Dickens' urbanization of the Gothic. His novels attest to the continuity of Dickens' preoccupation with the Gothic. *Bleak House* is, on one level, Dickens' most satisfying reassessment of the "dead" forms of the Gothic novel. But Dickens never turned away from his reliance on those forms. He continued to work within them and to transform them into something new. The Gothic, with its emphasis on a sense of the foreignness of the world in which its characters appear, provides the novelistic frame Dickens needs.

Dickens' "London" has its antecedents in De Quincey's *Confessions,* in the haunted castle through which De Quincey, like a hero in a Gothic romance, searches for Ann of Oxford Street: "If she lived, doubtless we must have been sometimes in search of each other, at the very same moment, through the mighty labyrinths of London; perhaps even within a few feet of each other—a barrier no wider in a London street, often amounting in the end to a separation for eternity!"[2] De Quincey's rendering of the city is suggestive and Dickens exploits it, responding as early as *Oliver Twist* to historical London and to that metropolis of the imagination which is his special realm. In the Memorandum Book Dickens used from 1855 to 1865 there appears a series of entries which help to isolate, and to crystallize, the issue.

The character of the real refugee—not the conventional; the real.

English landscape. The beautiful prospect, trim fields, clipped hedges, everything so neat and orderly—gardens, houses, roads. Where are the people who do all this? There must be a great many of them, to do it. Where are they all? And are *they*, too,so well kept and so fair to see?

Suppose the foregoing to be wrought out by an Englishman—say, from China—who knows nothing about his native country.[3]

The entries I have quoted appear in the midst of other memoranda clearly referring to *Little Dorrit:* several of them are followed by the bracketed words, "Done in Dorrit." But perhaps not just in *Little Dorrit* alone. The entries reveal that Dickens has only begun to explore in his own imagination De Quincey's opposition of the exoticism of Eastern realms, for which the Malay of the *Confessions* stands, and the conventional English landscape. Dickens thrusts into the essentially urban world of his novels a "foreigner," often from the East, who finds himself confused and alienated in the Gothic labyrinth of London.[4]

In *Little Dorrit,* Arthur Clennam returns to England after twenty years in China. His experience is that of the "real refugee" because he discovers his own alienation from the social and religious values of his nominal native land. He undergoes a process of disorientation like that of Charles Darnay upon his return to France in *A Tale of Two Cities.* Dickens' concern lies not with the literal refugee, but with the spiritual refugee lost in a landscape he no longer unquestioningly accepts. It is in *Our Mutual Friend,* through a figure like John Harmon, that Dickens most conspicuously picks up again the motif of the "real refugee." There is a much quoted passage in the Memorandum Book which suggests how the quiet rebellion of an Arthur Clennam becomes the curious stratagem of a John Harmon: "LEADING INCIDENT FOR A STORY. A man—young and eccentric?—feigns to be dead, and *is* dead to all intents and purposes external to himself, and for years retains that singular vein of life and character." [5] Harmon, "anathematized" by his father, flees and returns to England fourteen years later, after his father's death. Disguised as Julius Handford, Harmon is literally and figuratively "lost": a stranger in the city he has not seen for years; a stranger to his own self, which he is in the process of reconstructing, first as Julius Handford, then as John Rokesmith. This feigned death, a motif central to *A Tale of Two Cities,* suggests the radical nature of the refugee's plight and the extremity to which he resorts to salvage himself.

But, in the novels written in the last two decades of his life, Dickens deals with those refugees of the spirit who have never left the apparently familiar streets of London, or the deceptively reassuring English countryside. They experience exactly that disorientation afflicting Arthur Clennam and John Harmon. They awaken to a new vision of a world they have previously failed to question. What Dickens wants to capture appears in yet another entry in the Memorandum Book, another testament to the centripetal force of his imaginative concerns: "Representing London—or Paris, or any other great place—in the new light of being actually unknown to all the people in the story, and only taking the color of their fears and fancies and opinions—*so* getting a new aspect and being unlike itself. An *odd* unlikeness of itself." [6]

Once more the emphasis is upon the state of foreignness: the city is a mystery, perhaps permanently unintelligible. The ambiguous word in the passage is the adverb, "actually." Dickens may be musing about the situation of the literal stranger. Capturing the city through the experience of someone new to it reveals the subjective state of the character and illuminates the city itself in new ways. In *Great Expectations* Pip, wandering in Smithfield on his first day in London, turns into a street and sees "the great black dome of Saint Paul's bulging at [him] from behind a grim stone building which a bystander said was Newgate Prison." The moment reveals Pip's state of mind, the characteristic sense of guilt and imminent punishment with which he lives. But it also tells us something crucial about the paradox which is London: Saint Paul's and Newgate merge into a single entity, an image of a brutalizing society masked by religious rectitude.

Pip is understandably bewildered and threatened by the London to which he is introduced. But London may be "actually unknown" even to those most habituated to it. There is a sense in which the city never exists independently of the consciousness of each of its denizens. The passages in the Memorandum Book, taken as a "cluster" of ideas, indicate Dickens' lively awareness of this. He knows that a sudden wrenching of perspective can create that sense of foreignness he wants to depict. A character awakens to a city he has never "seen" before. In *Our Mutual Friend* Fascination Fledgeby encounters the crippled Jenny Wren in Riah's rooftop garden. Ignorant of the world he thinks he knows, and controls, Fledgeby meets someone who has experienced London in a "new" way. He is deaf to Jenny's cry, "Come up and be dead! Come up and be dead!" He returns, unthinkingly, to the "close dark streets" in which "you hear the people who are alive, crying, and working, and calling to one another" (281). He descends into those narrow streets, the communal grave of those Londoners caught in the stasis of death-in-life.

Fascination Fledgeby accepts his condition. Others in *Our Mutual Friend* do not. They may not achieve Jenny Wren's clarity of vision, leading to the complete inversion of conventional notions of life and death. But they resist, chafe, pursue strategies for survival in a world whose hostility they sense, however vaguely. In the process they, too, become Dickensian refugees: "not the conventional; the real." Their situations lead—I would like to claim, inexorably—to the kind of isolation in which John Jasper exists in *Edwin Drood*. But, with the evidence available to us both in the Memorandum Book and the novels, it is reasonable to argue that in the last completed novel, *Our Mutual Friend*, Dickens has moved at least to the threshold of *Edwin Drood*. Both in Eugene Wrayburn and Bradley Headstone, Dickens captures the disorientation accompanying an emerging estrangement from one's society and oneself. Wrayburn first appears in the novel, "buried alive in the back of his chair," at the Veneerings' preposterous dinner party. He has adopted a second self, languid and bitterly self-ironic, in response to a father who seems intent on choosing both a career and a wife for him. He responds to John Harmon's story and to the coercive intent of the Harmon Will because he sees in the situation a variation of his own. But in the society in which he and his friend, Lightwood, live, they dare not show their feelings.[7]

Instead, Wrayburn adopts the role of the bored parasite, and embraces paralysis. He scorns conventional notions of "Energy," because energetic commitment involves risk, especially to his carefully cultivated "second nature" of "lassitude and indifference." He may echo Lightwood's claim that if *he* is shown "something really worth being energetic about," he will "show you energy" (20). But this is a ruse, a communal fiction the two sustain to hide from themselves the state of despair in which they contrive to live. At best, Wrayburn and Lightwood, like the corpses in the Thames, "float with the stream." They preserve a fragile sense of integrity by disowning the masks they turn to society: yet the mask effectively subverts any real life they may still possess.

Wrayburn's counterpart in *Our Mutual Friend* is Bradley Headstone. The two inhabit different social worlds. Wrayburn's studied nonchalance seems the antithesis of Headstone's habitual self-repression which affects his demeanor, his every movement. But the two establish a peculiar bond whose basis is more than their attraction to Lizzie Hexam. Wrayburn and Headstone are two versions of that condition R. D. Laing has called the "unembodied self": *"The body is felt more as one object among other objects in the world than as the core of the individual's own being.* Instead of being the core of his true self, the body is felt as the core of a *false self,* which a detached, disembodied "inner,' 'true' self looks on at with tenderness, amusement, or hatred as the case may be."[8]

Headstone, whose decent and conventional clothing is worn with a total "want of adaptation between him and it" (217), *is* the unembodied self. As such he becomes, like Wrayburn, an "onlooker at all the body does, [engaging] in nothing directly." [9] Headstone has suppressed whatever vitality he does possess, but he has not extinguished it. Lizzie Hexam threatens Headstone's detached, inner self which remains vulnerable to the sexual and imaginative depths within even Headstone. Headstone is confronted with a loss of self-control as he opens himself up to the influence of another human being.

Headstone—Dickens originally toyed with the name "Deadstone"—has figuratively turned part of himself into a monument to his suppressed self.[10] Wrayburn, in his own way, is buried alive in his proto-Wildean stance. Each has created a bulwark behind which they hide from an alien world. But the self behind the bulwark becomes increasingly impoverished. Wrayburn and Headstone long for fulfilled lives through genuine relationships with others: each fears the exposure of his inner need. Headstone reacts uneasily when Charley Hexam speaks of his sister's habit of staring into the fire, "full of fancies." Wrayburn has become an "embodied conundrum" to himself. His perplexity intensifies as he wavers indecisively between seducing Lizzie Hexam and establishing her as his mistress, or courting her in a manner which acknowledges the value of her sexual and personal integrity.

The "secret, sure perception" which passes between the two during their first encounter in the room shared by Wrayburn and Lightwood involves more, then, than an acknowledgment of sexual rivalry. It reveals, at the same time, each man's dimly felt awareness that his "second nature" is crumbling under the pressure of the need each feels for Lizzie. Wrayburn taunts Headstone with his "perfect placidity" until "Bradley [is] well-nigh mad" (289). He looks at Headstone "as if he found him beginning to be rather an entertaining study" because Headstone is a version of himself: someone driven to madness or despair by a passion he cannot control. Through that "curious monomaniac," as he calls Headstone, Wrayburn can study himself. It is the mark of Wrayburn's dislocation that he remains indifferent to Headstone's pain. Wrayburn has not, as he claims, ceased toying with that "troublesome conundrum long abandoned" (295), the riddle posed by his self. Rather, he determines to experiment upon Headstone, to discover through him to what frenzied ends a commitment to Lizzie Hexam may lead.

Out of their shared malaise emerges one of the remarkable achievements of *Our Mutual Friend:* that "chase" in which Wrayburn and Headstone participate as hunter and hunted, victim and victimizer. Their roles are not static. They shift and vary as each man tries to lay to rest forever that "unspeakable desire" to track out Matthew Arnold's "buried life" which still exists within each man. It stirs, it possesses an ambiguous life of its own. But it apparently cannot express itself through love, through a commitment to Lizzie Hexam. Rather, the buried self emerges in the ritual of the "chase." Wrayburn's account of it reveals how each man invests it with meaning, however perverse.

"Then soberly and plainly, Mortimer, I goad the schoolmaster to madness. I make the schoolmaster so ridiculous, and so aware of being made ridiculous, that I see him chafe and fret at every pore when we cross one another. The amiable occupation has been the solace of my life. . . . I do it thus: I stroll out after dark, stroll a little way, look in at a window and furtively look out for the schoolmaster. Sooner or later, I perceive the schoolmaster on the watch. . . . Having made sure of his watching me, I tempt him on, all over London. One night I go east, another night north, in a few nights I go all round the compass. Sometimes, I walk; sometimes, I proceed in cabs, draining the pocket of the schoolmaster, who then follows in cabs. I study and get up abstruse No Thoroughfares in the course of the day. With Venetian mystery I seek those No Thoroughfares at night, glide into them by means of dark courts, tempt the schoolmaster to follow, turn suddenly, and catch him before he can retreat. Then we face one another, and I pass him as [if] unaware of his existence, and he undergoes grinding torments. . . . Night after night his disappointment is acute, but hope springs eternal in the scholastic breast, and he follows me again to-morrow. Thus I enjoy the pleasures of the chase, and derive great benefit from the healthful exercise." (542–43)

These are the words of a man driven to a final act of desperation. Balked and confused by Lizzie's disappearance, Wrayburn lives out his despair in this Gothic novel of his own making. London, as in De Quincey's *Confessions,* becomes a haunted castle of labyrinthine mazes, subterranean cells, dungeons without means of egress. Wrayburn peoples it with Headstone and himself. Together they seem to be engaged in the eternal quest for the inviolable maiden of Gothic romance. In fact, they become the Gothic hero and his mysterious double discovering their kinship to each other.[11] Wrayburn's disorientation expresses itself in this compulsive patterning of his nocturnal existence: he lives out the nightmare which would otherwise disturb his sleep. In creating the labyrinth for Headstone, in seeking out so consciously the No Thoroughfare which permits him to goad Headstone "to madness" and revenge, Wrayburn constructs his own dead end. The artistry employed in his creation of his own "Venetian mystery" becomes ultimately self-destructive.

The high point of the chase, for both men, occurs with their face-to-face confrontation, in which Wrayburn refuses to acknowledge

Headstone's existence. And Headstone, undergoing "grinding torments," acquiesces in the act. Wrayburn confirms Headstone's own sense that he is socially and psychologically a nullity. But, as he wields the Medusa's head of his own consciousness, turning Headstone more truly into stone, Wrayburn reveals his own potential nothingness.[12] Behind the languid mask of the careless solicitor there may be no authentic self at all: there may be only perversity or a void. The "chase" reveals how fully Dickens anticipates the intersubjective psychology of the twentieth century. In *The Divided Self* R. D. Laing, writing within that tradition, claims that *"the sense of identity requires the existence of another by whom one is known;* and a conjunction of this other person's recognition of one's self with self-recognition."[13] Both Wrayburn and Headstone have tentatively pursued this sense of identity in their unsatisfactory relationships with Lizzie: and both have pulled back. In "the chase" they act out the consequences of their failure. Wrayburn withholds that recognition by another which Headstone needs and fears. And Wrayburn's gesture exposes the fragility of his own sense of himself. He withholds himself from Lizzie and from Headstone. In his chosen isolation, Wrayburn consolidates his sense of defeat: he will not participate in that dialectic which admits that one's own identity is necessarily grounded in *"the existence of another by whom one is known."* In the words of J. Hillis Miller, "When God vanishes, man turns to interpersonal relations as the only remaining arena of the search for authentic selfhood. Only in his fellow men can he find . . . a presence in the world which might replace the lost divine presence."[14]

When Wrayburn and Headstone pass in the night, we see two crippled selves, each encountering its mirror image. The London they now inhabit has taken on "the color of their fears and fancies and opinions—so getting a new aspect and being unlike itself." The maze Wrayburn has created, out of his imagination, possesses a Minotaur at its center which is a version of Wrayburn himself. Wrayburn's "healthful exercise" demonstrates that whatever level of himself he studies in Bradley Headstone is not to be denied. His recurring act of denial becomes a plea to Headstone to rise up against his oppressor and destroy him. The depersonalization of the self, which both men practice, wreaks its own havoc. Wrayburn and Headstone are involved in a process of self-annihilation. The fragile, and dishonest, structure of their lives, based on Wrayburn's lassitude and Headstone's self-repression, has crumbled. The final refuge for each is the ease of death, and the chase is subtly devised, by both, to assure it.

This implicitly suicidal pact between the insulted and the injured leads to the explicit doubling of Headstone that has always been inherent in the precarious organization of his self. The "performance of his routine of educational tricks" becomes unbearable: "Under his daily restraint, it was his compensation, not his trouble, to give a glance to-wards his state at night, and to the freedom of its being indulged" (546). Headstone eagerly awaits that "perverse pleasure akin to that which a sick man sometimes has in irritating a wound upon his body." He consciously prepares for the moment when he will no longer acqui-esce to "being made the nightly sport of the reckless and insolent Eugene." Headstone becomes a haggard, disembodied head, sus-pended in air "like the spectre of one of the many heads erst hoisted upon neighbouring Temple Bar." The murder of Eugene Wrayburn will answer Wrayburn's own deep longing to die; and it will lead to Headstone's own inevitable execution. The moment in which, under the eyes of Rogue Riderhood, Headstone erases his name from the blackboard, and ceases to possess a name, has been long in the making. Headstone has been seeking dissolution, and release, before Riderhood appears to haunt him.

Dickens' own sure perception of the function of the chase is dra-matized on one of those nights when Riderhood encounters Headstone on watch outside Wrayburn's chambers. Riderhood knows neither Wrayburn's name nor Headstone's: for him Wrayburn is the "T'other Governor" and Headstone the "T'otherest Governor." For Riderhood, for us, the nameless two become one. Headstone's wraithlike face floats through the London streets or up the stairs to the door of Wrayburn's chambers: two heads become, as is so often the case in dreams, super-imposed upon a single body. Headstone, like Sydney Carton, becomes a "Double of coarse deportment" to Wrayburn's Charles Darney. They coexist in the same dream, the shared nightmare of their despair.

Dickens' own description of Headstone, in the public house with Riderhood, becomes strangely inappropriate. Headstone enters the tav-ern where "fowls of a beery breed, and certain human night-birds flut-tering home to roost, were solacing themselves after their several man-ners; and where not one of the night-birds hovering about the sloppy bar failed to discern . . . in the passion-wasted night-bird with respect-able feathers, the worst night-bird of all" (554–55). The sudden mora-lizing is out of place, because Headstone cannot be equated with those other derelicts of the night. Dickens here does violence to his own precisely rendered psychological study of Headstone and Wrayburn. He has shown the two engaged in a dance of death. Its horror and its power lie in the reality of the human waste involved. Eugene Wray-burn, like the Steerforth of whom he is a diminished echo, possesses the capacity to achieve creative integration. The paralysis which now torments him has been engendered by a society indifferent to the in-tegrity of those within it. And Bradley Headstone, slow-witted as he seems to be, has, or had, an animal vitality within him that could have found expression in a life of physical exertion and challenge. In the tangled fates of the solicitor and the schoolmaster we see Dickens' indictment of a society whose primary concern is "Dust," the pursuit of the filthy lucre of the pound in the barren landscape of the urban desert.

— 2 —

Although *The Mystery of Edwin Drood* is not simply a continuation of *Our Mutual Friend,* it does clearly emerge out of those recurring concerns revealed in the Memorandum Book and especially in the last completed novel. One thing is crucial. The chase sequence of *Our Mutual Friend* becomes internalized within the consciousness of John Jasper. Wrayburn and Headstone, the T'other and the T'otherest, are collapsed into a single figure who reenacts an even more bizarre version of their shared malaise. Wrayburn and Headstone come to live for the pleasures of the chase, however perverse. John Jasper lives for his expeditions to London or for those opium journeys in his own chambers when he "lights his pipe, and delivers himself to the Spectres it invokes at midnight." [15] Those spectres are curiously akin to the ritual engaged in by Wrayburn and Headstone. As Jasper explains to the Princess Puffer, each opium dream involves "a hazardous and perilous journey, over abysses where a slip would be destruction" (207). The journey involves, always, an unsuspecting fellow traveller who has no awareness he *is* a fellow traveller. It culminates in an act performed "hundreds of thousands of times," indeed, "millions and billions of times," an act which, when done in fact, seems hardly worth the doing. Yet, this obscure act which may involve the unwitting fellow traveller serves, in the dream if not in life, as the necessary prelude to some kind of release, followed by "changes of colors and . . . great landscapes and glittering processions," the exotic dream-scape with which the novel begins. The fate, even the identity of the fellow traveller who "went the journey, and never saw the road" (208) remains unknown, part of those many riddles whose solutions were lost to us with the death of Dickens on 9 June 1870. But the dream and its structure recall the "Venetian mystery" so carefully orchestrated by Eugene Wrayburn. For the chase, like Jasper's dream journey, ends in an act of violence and potential release: Headstone's attack upon Wrayburn. The "time" and the "place" of Jasper's dream suggest just such a moment; the "fellow traveller" seems just such a potential victim.

Jasper's conscious decision to resort to opium and to indulge in the reveries it produces is based in the same need for escape from himself and his circumstances that has driven both Wrayburn and Headstone to what Wrayburn calls their "healthful exercise." Jasper, early in the novel, advises his nephew that he has "been taking opium for a pain—

an agony—that sometimes overcomes [him]" (10). He tells the Princess Puffer, "Yes, I came on purpose. When I could not bear my life, I came to get the relief, and I got it. It WAS one! It WAS one!" (208). It is "the relief" so consciously sought out by Jasper that links him, as much as the texture of the dream itself, to the self-destructive activities of those trapped within the claustrophobic London of *Our Mutual Friend*. But the fact that the dream journey *is* an internalization of the chase is significant. Wrayburn and Headstone exist as distinct, in some ways antithetical figures, united by a common despair; they are further evidence of the degree to which Dickens relies upon and exploits the *Doppelgänger* relationship. In *Edwin Drood* Dickens chooses to collapse Wrayburn and Headstone into a single figure whose solitary consciousness becomes the focal point of the novel. There occur fewer temptations to acquiesce to the possibilities for circumspection, if not outright contradiction, which the use of the double, at least in Dickens' hands, seems to offer. In its initial conception *Edwin Drood* does not appear to be locked into the structure of *A Tale of Two Cities* in which Sydney Carton bides his, or Dickens', time until he can step forward to die for Charles Darnay, resolving complex psychological and moral issues with the fall of the guillotine's blade.

Doubles continue to appear in *The Mystery of Edwin Drood:* in many ways the novel offers a proliferation of double relationships unusual even in Dickens' novels. But John Jasper, although he seeks out, and even creates, his own counterpart, needs none. The fellow traveller of his dreams may be Edwin Drood or himself. No other character necessarily exists to embody that part of himself with which Jasper, like Wrayburn or Headstone, must contend. Yet, in *Edwin Drood,* self-division, which the *Doppelgänger* can so fully explore, especially as a form of extreme dislocation, has become almost the norm.[16] The pressures of Victorian civilization compel Wrayburn, Harmon, Headstone, and others to become "unembodied," cut off from themselves and their activities, living in the presence of an alien being who has come to occupy the same body. The characters who inhabit the Cloisterham and London of *Edwin Drood* seem, rather, to have accepted the psychological bifurcation urged upon them by their milieu. It is John Jasper, the opium addict, who has rejected as inadequate the conventional ways by which those who surround him have adapted to their world.

Jasper takes refuge neither in the pious calisthenics of the Reverend Septimus Crisparkle nor in that state of mind which seems applicable only to Miss Twinkleton, as headmistress of the Nuns' House, but which, in fact, is the psychic stratagem to which so many in the novel turn.

> As, in some cases of drunkenness, and in others of animal magnetism, there are two states of consciousness which never clash,

but each of which pursues its separate course as though it were continuous instead of broken (thus if I hide my watch when I am drunk, I must be drunk again before I can remember where), so Miss Twinkleton has two distinct and separate phases of being. Every night, the moment the young ladies have retired to rest, does Miss Twinkleton smarten up her curls a little, brighten up her eyes a little, and become a sprightly Miss Twinkleton whom the young ladies have never seen. Every night, at the same hour, does Miss Twinkleton resume the topics of the previous night, comprehending the tenderer scandal of Cloisterham, of which she has no knowledge whatever by day. (15–16)

Readers determined to solve the novel's "mystery" have seized upon this apparently lighthearted passage either to convict or acquit Jasper of what is, at best, a hypothetical murder: whatever has occurred following the Christmas Eve dinner has taken place, according to various theories, while Jasper has given himself to the demons of opium. In his daylight role as choirmaster of Cloisterham Cathedral, he is unconscious either of his guilt or his innocence. The passage cries out for speculations like these because of its similarity to a passage in Wilkie Collins' *The Moonstone* which had appeared in serialized form in Dickens' own *All the Year Round*. Collins devises a rather clever expedient by which to recover the Moonstone. He returns Franklin Blake to an opium-induced state of unconsciousness in which he reenacts the theft he has unknowingly committed.[17] But *Edwin Drood* is far too ambitious a work to rely upon a plot device already exploited by someone so closely associated in the imagination of the reading public with the Master himself. Neither the exoticism nor the psychological theorizing which abounds in *The Moonstone* contributes to the kind of integrated social and psychological insight of which Dickens had proved himself capable in even his earliest novels. Collins' implicit allusions and explicit references to De Quincey, to Sir John Elliotson, and to W. B. Carpenter's *Principles of Human Physiology* remain at best useful indications of the sophisticated psychological theorizing which intrigued both Dickens and Collins. But what for Wilkie Collins is psychological dabbling in a vacuum becomes for Dickens a rich and suggestive substratum upon which to erect the world of Cloisterham and London in *Edwin Drood*. Dickens perceives in *The Moonstone* potentialities of which Collins seems unaware. In the mysterious Ezra Jennings, Wilkie Collins settles for De Quincey's most obvious contribution to the literature of the age: the opium-addicted pariah. But Dickens does not. He is far too aware of the origins of that addiction which De Quincey explores in the *Confessions,* and he pursues the implications of the figure of the "opium-eater" in John Jasper.

One of the sources of Jasper's discontent, the "pain" for which he has been taking opium, is his very inability to maintain Miss Twinkleton's "two states of consciousness" which seem to exist in total separation. Jasper suffers because his two states of consciousness have collapsed into a single, anguished entity. Only the greatest act of will and his ambivalent devotion to his nephew permit him to maintain, for ever shorter periods of time, the separation between his two selves. As the successor both to Bradley Headstone and Eugene Wrayburn, he shares their fate: once his self-command is weakened, each yearns for the freedom yielded him by the night. However, most of the characters in *Edwin Drood,* like Miss Twinkleton, are protected from the violent collision between their two states of being, the conventional public self and the other, "truer" self to which even Miss Twinkleton harmlessly turns at night. They exist apparently without the need to seek some kind of reunification of their halved beings. Within each character a dialogue of sorts, implicit or explicit, is established. The dialogue is sometimes objectified through the existence of another character representing one half of the divided self. Always the states of being interact, impinge upon each other. But for Jasper the interaction is more violent and sustained, in part because it is more clearly within him: and, finally, as in the cases of Wrayburn and Headstone, it proves uncontrollable.

Even within the context of the fragmentary *Edwin Drood,* John Jasper, then, is never a "horrible wonder apart," as Rosa Bud comes to perceive him. He is another Dickensian refugee. His isolation and his suffering proclaim a twisted expression of his integrity; they are the inevitable consequences of a society which refuses to acknowledge the expression of that ambiguous "Energy" haunting Wrayburn and Lightwood in *Our Mutual Friend.* This energy can be sublimated into art: as a choirmaster Jasper is an artist of sorts. But the sanctioned channels for human energies, amorphous and self-contradictory as they are, only heighten the frustration of Jasper, so acutely aware of the inadequacies of the society in which he finds himself. His musical art is as mechanical as his relationships with those around him. Jasper, like Headstone before him, pursues an essentially lifeless activity which he manages only to endure. Forced to deny at least one half of himself, possessed of energies far more intense than those influencing the lives of all others but the Landlesses, he turns to opium and the fantasies which provide temporary relief from the paralysis of his life.

The opium dream with which the novel opens reveals at once the fragmented consciousness of Jasper and the ambiguities inherent in his situation.

An ancient English Cathedral Town? How can the ancient English Cathedral town be here! The well-known massive grey square tower of its old Cathedral? How can that be here! There is no spike of rusty iron in the air, between the eye and it, from any point of the real prospect. What IS the spike that intervenes, and who has set it up? Maybe, it is set up by the Sultan's orders for the impaling of a horde of Turkish robbers, one by one. It is so, for cymbals clash, and the Sultan goes by to his palace in long procession. Ten thousand scimitars flash in the sunlight, and thrice ten thousand dancing-girls strew flowers. Then, follow white elephants caparisoned in countless gorgeous colors, and infinite in number and attendants. Still, the Cathedral tower rises in the background, where it cannot be, and still no writhing figure is on the grim spike. (1)

Within this highly erotic fantasy Dickens initiates us into an awareness of the inevitable conflict between Miss Twinkleton's two states of consciousness, into the underworld of vitality upon which the Cathedral Town erects itself. And within it the two, perhaps illusory, halves of John Jasper are "fantastically pieced" together in a Blakean revelation, in an irrefutable marriage of Heaven and Hell. The generalized Eastern setting, with its Sultan and his harem, coexists with the intimidating massiveness of the grey tower of Cloisterham Cathedral which is the emblem of that most representative of English institutions, the Anglican church and all the values for which it stands. Jasper, the dreamer, is caught, suspended, between two worlds. The sinister spike, in reality a rusty spike upon a bedpost, is simultaneously a part of both worlds. It belongs to the world of the Sultan, to that erotic realm in which conventional restraints become meaningless: the Sultan is as savage in his defense of his harem as the "Turkish robbers" who seem intent upon ravishing the dancing-girls swirling through the dream. But, as an instrument of punishment, the spike also suggests the dreamer's consciousness that the world to which the tower belongs punishes, just as remorselessly, those who defy its mores and conventions. The massive tower has been erected to deny the legitimacy, even the existence, of impulses sustained by an energy quite different from the conventional energy from which Lightwood and Wrayburn have recoiled.

Within and beyond the context of this dream, John Jasper plays many, clearly contradictory, roles. He is at once the Sultan jealously guarding his female chattels from the robbers, eager to see them die "one by one" upon the spike. He is also the potential intruder, the "writhing figure," soon to be impaled upon the waiting stake. The dream reflects Jasper's confusion about his relationships to society, to his nephew Edwin Drood, and to himself. Jasper experiences a version of that disorientation which De Quincey describes in an account of one of his dreams in the *Confessions of an English Opium-Eater*. De Quincey speaks of the "unimaginable horror which these dreams of Oriental imagery, and mythological tortures, impressed upon me. . . . I brought together all creatures, birds, beasts, reptiles, all trees and plants, usages and appearances, that are found in all tropical regions, and assembled them together in China or Indostan" (333). Both dreams make use of "Eastern" landscapes, both fix the dreamer in a condition of excruciating disorientation in which he is by turns "the idol . . . the priest . . . [the] worshipped . . . [the] sacrificed" (333). For Jasper the disorientation is rooted in his attitudes toward Edwin Drood. In his dual role as Drood's legal guardian and his sexual rival, John Jasper is the father and the son, the Sultan and the Turkish renegade. He is guilty of that desire at which even the creatures encrusted with De Quincey's "Nilotic mud" might tremble.

The true nature of the relationship between the uncle and the nephew becomes almost casually defined in their chatty interchange in the early pages of the novel which conclude with Drood's casual outburst, " 'And some uncles, in large families, are even younger than their nephews. By George, I wish it was the case with us!' " (8). The opium dream and Drood's comment define Jasper's personal and social predicaments: the two reflect each other. In his relationship with Drood, Jasper is torn by the conventional affection of an uncle for a nephew and by his hatred of the youth who would, in his own words, prefer to be older than his own uncle. Simultaneously, Jasper is at war with the society in which he finds himself. That bizarre and elusive relationship between Eugene Wrayburn and Bradley Headstone, with its muted Oedipal implications, recurs here. To rebel against society is always, metaphorically, to rebel against the father, or someone who replaces the father in the rebel's imagination. Bradley Headstone's determination not to strike until he sees Lizzie and Wrayburn together in a moment of ambiguous intimacy, his vision of Wrayburn as a paternal specter come to haunt him, so close to Wrayburn's vision of his own "M.R.F.," suggest the nature of Headstone's motives. Drood's whimsical desire to be older than "Jack" ironically coincides with one of the ways in which Jasper, in his fantasy, perceives *him;* for "Ned" is the Sultan, the father, of the opium dream, as well as the son seeking to displace the father.[18]

Out of the Oedipal center of the dream landscape, which serves to disclose the multiplicity of his "criminal" desires, emerges Jasper's need to punish and be punished: he both fears and desires the stake. Jasper's rebellion involves his rejection of the values of Cloisterham and his conscious pursuit of those fantasies he finds in the liberating influence of opium. But he has already been led to a punishment more terrible than the physical torture of the dream. The spike is embedded in Jasper's consciousness, itself; it produces a relentless sense of guilt and anxiety. Ironically, the title of Bazzard's unproduced "tragedy," *The*

Thorn of Anxiety, becomes a not-so-comic parody of Jasper's situation. The thorn of anxiety exerts its pressure upon Jasper; he writhes because of its existence.

The opium dream has revealed the extent to which Jasper's consciousness is no longer safely compartmentalized into autonomous and discrete parts. He may flee the opium den, and London itself, with the coming of the dawn, but he cannot leave behind the fantasies of his dreams. Dickens is now consciously working with a Romantic conception of the mind like that which De Quincey describes in his *Confessions.*

> Of this, at least, I feel assured, that there is no such thing as *forgetting* possible to the mind; a thousand accidents may, and will interpose a veil between our present consciousness and the secret inscriptions on the mind; accidents of the same sort will also rend away this veil; but alike, whether veiled or unveiled, the inscription remains for ever; just as the stars seem to withdraw before the common light of day, whereas, in fact, we all know that it is the light which is drawn over them as a veil— and that they are waiting to be revealed, when the obscuring daylight shall have withdrawn. (328–29)

Those stars which shine at night with such intensity, like the red glow of the Princess' opium pipe, continue to exert their influence: "There is no such thing as *forgetting* possible to the mind." Jasper may return to the Cathedral world of Cloisterham, but he brings with him the dreams which no longer remain in another realm of experience. The veil of sunlight, that fragile illusion obscuring "the secret inscriptions on the mind," waits only to be torn by the "accidents" of life, by the oppressive atmosphere of the Cathedral town which denies the existence of the night and its stars and yet forever reminds us, and Jasper, of its enduring presence.

When he dons his sullied white robes, Jasper reenters the world which grates on his ever more irritable nerves. Once again he must cope with the obsequiousness of a Crisparkle; he must endure the enervating boredom of the "Alternate Musical Wednesdays," that obligatory gesture to polite culture which Cloisterham routinely makes. This is the mundane reality pressing in upon him, compelling him to reveal his hopelessness to the surprised Drood.

> "I hate it [my life]. The cramped monotony of my existence grinds me away by the grain. How does our service sound to you?"
> "Beautiful! Quite celestial."
> "It often sounds to me quite devilish. I am so weary of it!"
> (11)

Jasper's opium dreams reflect the confinement that he feels, the searing awareness that the art which he pursues is neither a true vocation nor an authentic expression of his private self. The gargoyles which decorate the old Cathedral at least provided release for the wretched monks. Victorian England denies Jasper even that outlet. In response to such a world a Eugene Wrayburn adopts, if unsuccessfully, a "second nature" of lassitude. For Jasper that is not enough. He furtively turns to opium and the fantasies it offers as a substitute for the open acknowledgment of the repressed energies of his life. He has been deprived of that unified life of self-fulfillment which exists, at best, as a hypothetical norm in the novel. Jasper, in "carving [demons] out of [his] heart," has become, as his name and manner suggest, a living gargoyle.

Jasper's consolation, and his punishment, lies in his twisted love for Rosa Bud, who is so alien to the life of intensity of which he, apparently, was once capable. The unfinished portrait of Rosa, endowed by Drood with a "beauty remarkable for a quite childish, almost babyish, touch of saucy discontent, comically conscious of itself" (7), presides over Jasper's chambers like the image of an impish, secular madonna. Dickens' allusion to Matthew Lewis' *The Monk,* to Ambrosio's reverence of the portrait of Matilda as the Virgin Mary, seems explicit. Ambrosio and Jasper share a common fate: they are reduced, one unconsciously, the other consciously, to the futile worship of the inviolable virgin as a direct consequence of their entombment within a dead institution. They have both experienced a process of repression which leads, in Matthew Lewis' words, to a separation between the "real and [the] acquired character" so that "the different sentiments with which education and nature had inspired him [Ambrosio in this case], were combating in his bosom: it remained for his passions, which as yet no opportunity had called into play, to decide the victory." [19] Matilda, the temptress in league with the devil, arouses those passions, seduces Ambrosio and decides the battle in passion's favor.

Dickens' re-creation of a situation so recognizably analogous to that in *The Monk* reveals again his debt to the Gothic tradition. It also further illuminates the new use of the Gothic in Dickens' hands, the new vision of the traditional villain. The change in language alone is significant. The "passions" of Matthew Lewis, and the eighteenth century, have become the "energy" of Dickens' late novels. The words are not simply synonymous. "Passion" immediately suggests its traditional antithesis, "reason"; the psychic battle is essentially bipolar. We are in the realm of Doctor Johnson's *Rasselas,* in which the ascendance of reason over passion is the norm. "Energy," the term to which Dickens, George Eliot, and other nineteenth-century novelists turn so often, suggests an amorphous reservoir of vitality, perhaps the source of consciousness itself. In such a perspective the psyche becomes at once more complex, less easily defined in reductive moral language. But Dickens modifies eighteenth-century Gothicism in other ways. He rejects, as he has in previous novels, a central Gothic tactic: the use of an explicitly Roman Catholic setting, distant in time and place. The Gothic novel ordinarily titillates the curiosity of a Protestant audience and moderates implicit challenges to contemporary mores. In *The Monk,* Matthew Lewis chooses Madrid in the time of the Inquisition as his setting, and panders to the voyeuristic interests of his audience, to that itch to know what *must* go on behind monastic and conventual walls. He, also, protects himself from the outrage of people who might see in his tale of terror an embryonically coherent critique of English society in the 1790s. In *The Monk* even Lewis' own obsessions undermine any claim to seriousness the novel might pose. The exotic, Poe-esque elements of *The Monk*—the necrophilia, the fetishism, the barely concealed homosexuality—threaten to reduce the novel to the status of a clinical document.

In *The Mystery of Edwin Drood* the diversionary tactics are gone. The critique of conventional rationalism and bourgeois society ceases to be disguised and intermittent. Dickens exploits the Gothic, not to obscure the thrust of his critique, but to establish causal relations between the individual predicament and the environment. The London of *Bleak House* and *Our Mutual Friend* is a Gothic castle haunted by incubi and grotesques of various kinds, expressing the social and psychological terrors of Victorian society. The Cloisterham of *Edwin Drood* is that analogue of the haunted castle, the monastery of the Gothic tradition. But it is the monastery transformed. There is no evasive distinction between the suspect values of the cloister and the saner values of a secular society. Instead, the secular world becomes permeated with the values which repress and destroy Matthew Lewis' Ambrosio. And although the concern with repressed sexuality remains a predominant issue in *Edwin Drood,* the novel encompasses, often indirectly and by implication, the full complexity of the indivudual's situation in nineteenth-century England: the quest for the unified self is the core of the novel. The spirit of Silas Wegg, in pursuit of his amputated leg, presides over both *Our Mutual Friend* and *Edwin Drood.* His anxious complaint to Mr. Venus is a credo, of sorts, for both novels: "I shouldn't like—I tell you openly I should *not* like . . . to be what I may call dispersed, a part of me here, and a part of me there, but should wish to collect myself like a genteel person" (82). It is a moment of high comedy and terrible seriousness. The dispersal of the self seems the inevitable fate for the inhabitants of London and Cloisterham.

At last, London, "the great black city [which casts] its shadow on the waters, [with] its dark bridges [spanning] them as death spans life" (197), merges into the superficially distinct world of Cloisterham.

There is no longer the seemingly inviolable separation between the city and the serene Canterbury of *David Copperfield*. The provincial Cathedral town, in the green garden of the countryside, becomes undeniably an extension of the city of death. The Cathedral itself is sepulchral, rising above the crypts beneath it. The town's inhabitants are strangely cut off from nature and change: for them time has stopped. Although Cloisterham "was once possibly known to the Druids by another name, and certainly to the Romans by another," and to the Saxons and Normans by even other names, the townspeople "seem to suppose, with an inconsistency more strange than rare, that all its changes lie behind it, and that there are no more to come" (14). The reality of past change and the violence which has preceded the current peacefulness have disappeared from the collective consciousness of those in Cloisterham. For Dickens, the recognition of change is not designed to celebrate continuity, but to assert the need for that necessary change which the town of Cloisterham resists as if it were its *raison d'être*. This, in spite of the fact that daily "the Cloisterham children grow small salad in the dust of abbots and abbesses, and make dirt-pies of nuns and friars; while every ploughman in its outlying fields" grinds the bones of "once puissant Lord Treasurers, Archbishops, Bishops and such-like" to make his bread (14). The past does not contribute as it should to the enduring life of the town, providing the dust in which to fertilize new life. Instead, the past reinforces the "oppressive respectability" of the town. Its weight lies heavy upon the people of Cloisterham, imposing upon them the outmoded values of another time: "In a word, a city of another and a bygone time is Cloisterham." The town *is* the past. It impinges upon the present architecturally by incorporating its "fragments" into surviving buildings. But it has also insinuated itself into the consciousness of its inhabitants. The past exists through those "jumbled notions . . . incorporated into many of its citizens' minds" (14).

The Cathedral is the dominant landmark, the ultimate emblem of the sway of the past. And another landmark of bygone days remains in use to remind us that apparently long-forgotten atrocities are even now perpetrated upon unwitting victims: "In the midst of Cloisterham stands the Nuns' House; a venerable brick edifice whose present appellation is doubtless derived from the legend of its conventual uses" (15). But the Nuns' House, now a Seminary for Young Ladies, serves the same unnatural functions it once served. The zealous abbess out of the pages of *The Monk* has been replaced by the innocuous Miss Twinkleton. Her scrupulous observation of existing proprieties makes her the unconscious spokesman of notions persisting from an age supposedly less enlightened than that of Victorian England. The Nuns' House is clearly a pale, but very real, reflection of a severer time: "Whether the nuns of yore . . . were ever walled up alive in odd angles and jutting gables of the building for having some ineradicable leaven of busy mother Nature in them which has kept the fermenting world alive ever since; these may be matters of interest to its haunting ghosts (if any), but constitute no item in Miss Twinkleton's half-yearly accounts" (15). Miss Twinkleton may forget the past and its relevance to the present, but Dickens cannot. John Jasper is the Ambrosio of *Edwin Drood:* he has taken "to carving demons" out of his own psyche. The girls of the Nuns' House are its trapped novitiates, direct descendants of Agnes in *The Monk.* Agnes, in her time, succumbs to that "ineradicable leaven of busy mother Nature" in her and, like the storied nuns of Cloisterham, is "walled up alive" amidst the decaying corpses in the vaults beneath the abbey of Saint Clare. The students of the Nuns' House remain metaphorically buried alive, encircled by the chaste admonitions of a Miss Twinkleton, who inevitably refrains from the use of the all-too-suggestive word, "bosoms," substituting in its place the far more delicate and genteel euphemism, "hearts." Even as she reads aloud to Rosa Bud from the romantic novels fashionable in the thirties and forties, Miss Twinkleton bowdlerizes them in a way initially comic, but finally grotesque (201–2). The romantic drivel which she finds so offensive is no less untrue to human realities than the "interpolated passages" she creates to celebrate the "pious frauds" of a bourgeois conception of domestic bliss in a "suburban establishment," sanctioned by the consent of "papa" and "the silver-haired rector." The sterility of Miss Twinkleton's, and society's, vision of marriage is as stifling as the religious asceticism of old. The domestic arrangement of which she speaks sentences even someone like Rosa, still a child, yet possessing potentialities for sexual and emotional fulfillment, to a version of that ancient punishment reserved for the nuns who would not deny their own natures.

Ultimately, no one in *The Mystery of Edwin Drood* remains untouched by obsolete values and conventional expectations which perpetuate themselves almost unchallenged. Edwin Drood, with his condescending and proprietary attitude toward Rosa, with his airy confidence in his ability "to wake up Egypt a little," epitomizes the conventional self. His predicament, of which he seems so unconscious, is another version of John Harmon's and Eugene Wrayburn's in *Our Mutual Friend.* All three must contend with fathers, living or dead, who try to control the shape of their sons' lives. Rosa Bud has been willed to Drood, in the words of Bella Wilfer, "like a dozen of spoons, with everything cut and dried beforehand, like orange chips" (37). But Drood, Miss Twinkleton and society as a whole acquiesce without question to the absurdity of the will which shapes, or distorts, both his life and Rosa's. Drood, young English gentleman that he is, accepts the stifling role that society and a dead father have fashioned for him. He is not even stirred by the sense of uneasiness that Eugene Wrayburn responds to in analogous circumstances.

In this context, Jasper's revelation to Drood that he hates "the cramped monotony of [his] existence," makes his accompanying warning particularly ambiguous. Drood should realize that "even a poor monotonous chorister and grinder of music—in his niche—may be troubled with some stray sort of ambition, aspiration, restlessness, dissatisfaction, what shall we call it?" (12). Jasper relishes his own ironic use of the word, "niche." In using Drood's own phrase, Jasper implies Drood is implicitly responsible for *his* suffering. And, yet, his avowal of his discontent is to be taken "as a warning." In part, Jasper implies that even the confident Drood may find himself forced to "subdue" himself to a career and a life that have become a yoke. It is Drood's youthful lack of imagination which makes it impossible for him to conceive that he, too, might awaken one day to a sense of his life's meaninglessness. His uncle's suffering is his first exposure to a certain potentiality within himself.

Nor can Drood possibly understand the more insidious warning, that Jasper's "ambition, aspiration, restlessness, dissatisfaction," may involve a direct threat to his own life. He cannot imagine that he stands between his uncle and Rosa Bud. The ambiguity of this warning is not the conscious dissembling of a Gothic villain. It expresses Jasper's own confusion about his motives and intentions, for his commitment to his nephew is a real one. The look that Jasper ordinarily casts upon Drood is necessarily enigmatic: "Once for all, a look of intentness and intensity—a look of hungry, exacting, watchful, and yet devoted affection—is always, now and ever afterwards, on the Jasper face whenever the Jasper face is addressed in [Drood's] direction" (7). The "Jasper face" is more than an allusion to the gargoyle Jasper has become. The phrase points to the mask of stone which conceals Jasper's deeper feelings. The intensity of his look as it feeds upon Drood suggests the latent homosexuality which has become another element in his already complex relationship to him.

Jasper's consuming interest in his nephew's well-being, rooted in his own conflicting desires, is an acknowledged fact of his life. The diary which Jasper keeps is, as he admits to Crisparkle, "in fact, a Diary of Ned's life too." What he records there are not simply the events of his routine life or the conventional milestones in Drood's. The entries reveal his internal struggle, his ongoing debate about himself and Drood: they become a dialogue between the conventional self and its rebelling counterpart. Jasper is full of love and concern for his "dear boy," now almost a man; he is, simultaneously, jealous, perhaps murderous, in his lust for Rosa Bud. When he warns Drood and is reassured to learn that Drood "can't be warned," Jasper has not yet made the choice between his nephew and Rosa Bud. So, on one night of many such nights, John Jasper stands with a "peculiar-looking pipe," filled with something that is *not* tobacco, and gazes into one of the two bedrooms in his set of chambers where " his nephew lies asleep, calm and untroubled." He contemplates the sleeping Drood, that avowedly "shallow, surface kind of fellow" who has not yet responded to the violation of his own integrity which his engagement to Rosa poses. Jasper passes from Drood's room to his own, from a shallow realm to the depths inhabited by "Spectres" which have yet to disturb Drood's sleep (38). He has discarded an obsolete part of himself and slipped into the kingdom of dreams incessantly whispering to him.

It is no accident that Dickens moves from this nocturnal scene to the daylight world and the Reverend Septimus Crisparkle performing his daily calisthenics. Cloisterham's world of walls, gates, and locks now has *its* Minotaur in the form of John Jasper. The oppressiveness of the Cathedral town produces the need for the affirmation of some norm which embodies a compromise between the claims of human energy and the entrenched proscriptions of society. Crisparkle would seem to be living proof of a viable accommodation between "oppressive respectability" and the fermenting vitality of the human spirit. But just as the city of London casts its shadows on the waters of the Thames, the past and present cast their shadows upon the life of the Minor Canon. Like so many characters in Dickens' novels who seem to be offered as moral and psychological touchstones, Crisparkle provides no real alternative to the predicament of John Jasper. His association with the Anglican Church and his dependence on the patronage which has led to his present position compel us to take an ironic view of what he does and what he stands for. For Crisparkle's "contented and boy-like" satisfaction with "his present Christian beat" is based all too clearly on his total incapacity for entertaining an ironic vision of himself or others. Jasper, so acutely sensitive to the affectations of those around him, inevitably smiles when the ingenuous Crisparkle pointedly emphasizes that he is inquiring about the choirmaster's health at the express wishes of the Dean: he, at least, is aware of the Dean's hypocrisy and patronizing manner, if Crisparkle is not.

But it is primarily the exaggerated physical well-being and self-satisfaction of Crisparkle, and the ways in which they are achieved and at what cost, that Dickens knowingly dwells upon. To come upon Crisparkle in the midst of his morning exercises is to learn the nature of his limitations. We find Crisparkle, after "having broken the thin morning ice near Cloisterham Weir with his amiable head," in the act of "assisting his circulation by boxing at a looking-glass with great science and prowess" (38). While John Jasper grapples with his private demons,

Septimus Crisparkle is free to feint and dodge before his own benevolent reflection, enjoying his skill and his mastery over a nonexistent op-
ponent. His limitations are his blessing: he is as innocent of any knowledge of the depths that Jasper has plumbed as he is of the glaring
pomposity of the Dean. His "soft-hearted benevolence" is the fruit of a
naïveté initially as appealing as his "radiant features." But the looking-
glass suggests the superficiality of his achievement. Crisparkle, like the
Veneerings and Podsnaps of *Our Mutual Friend,* mirrored in the two-
dimensional realm of "the great looking-glass," dwells upon the surface
of life. This is the basis of his health, mental and physical. The domestic arrangements in Minor Canon Corner, the very nature of the tranquillity which reigns there, reveal the extent of Crisparkle's retreat from
life. The Mrs. Crisparkle with whom he lives is, as Dickens rather too
pointedly observes, the "mother, not [the] wife, of the Reverend Septimus." As the old lady stands to say the Lord's Prayer before their
breakfast, the Minor Canon also stands "with bent head to hear it, he
being within five years of forty: much as he had stood to hear the same
words from the same lips when he was within five months of four" (39).

Time has stopped for Septimus Crisparkle, much as it seems to
have stopped for Cloisterham and for Minor Canon Corner.

> Swaggering fighting men had had their centuries of ramping
> and raving about Minor Canon Corner, and beaten serfs had
> had their centuries of drudging and dying there, and powerful
> monks had had their centuries of being sometimes useful and
> sometimes harmful there, and behold they were all gone out of
> Minor Canon Corner, and so much the better. Perhaps one of
> the highest uses of their ever having been there, was, that there
> might be left behind, that blessed air of tranquillity which per-
> vaded Minor Canon Corner. (39)

The passage, which reads like a burlesque of evolutionary platitudes,
teems with an animus barely under Dickens' control. The old savagery,
brutality, and energy appear to be gone, banished from the earth, "and
so much the better." They seem expressly to have become extinct to
make way for a higher order of existence, for that fragile, dainty world
inhabited by the "china shepherdess" and her compliant son. The
"blessed air of tranquillity," the "serenely romantic state of . . . mind,"
which is theirs to enjoy is the product of volcanic eras of violence and
suffering. Implicitly, the passage asks why these two people, harmless,
perhaps even generous and kind, should be the beneficiaries of those
centuries of turbulence. They have not quelled the violence and engendered order; they have only inherited it. But the bitterness of Dickens'
vision lies finally in the reference to the past as "a sorrowful story that
is all told, or a pathetic play that is played out" (40). The ramping, the

raving, the drudging, the dying are not things of the past. John Jasper haunts the quiet of Cloisterham and Minor Canon Corner. The young Deputy, with the peculiar "object" Durdles has provided him as a channel for his energies, roams the streets of Cloisterham, as do other young present-day savages, victims of ignorance and neglect. As the Reverend Septimus Crisparkle benevolently walks his Christian beat, Cloisterham seethes with Jasper's frustrated passion and the malignant, but justified, resentment of ferocious boys, like Deputy, who are destroyers for want of what Durdles calls "an enlightened object." The value of Crisparkle's benevolence and the validity of the conventional wisdom for which he stands are circumscribed by the reality of his limitations. The world of Minor Canon Corner becomes a fragile ark in a sea of dark and unacknowledged forces.

There is, in fact, no one to whom the reader can imaginatively turn in the opening pages of *Edwin Drood*. Dickens has created a hypothetical No Thoroughfare in which each of the major figures of the novel exists. The individual and the social predicament is one of acute crisis, awaiting only one of those De Quincean "accidents" to rend the veil of normality. With the appearance of Helena and Neville Landless the veil is torn: the exotic and savage Orient erupts upon the illusory tranquillity of Cloisterham. John Jasper no longer indulges his fantasies in furtive and guilt-ridden isolation. The world of his dreams manifests itself, alive and undeniable, in the forms of the two youths, incongruous in the midst of the Cathedral and the monastery ruins, "much as if they were beautiful barbaric captives brought from some wild tropical dominion," as Crisparkle observes to himself. They pose a striking contrast to the shallowness of Drood, to the domesticated vitality of Crisparkle and to the distorted energies of a Deputy or a Jasper: "An unusually handsome lithe young fellow, and an unusually handsome lithe girl; much alike; both very dark, and very rich in color; she, of almost the gipsy type; something untamed about them both; a certain air upon them of hunter and huntress; yet withal a certain air of being the objects of the chase, rather than the followers" (44).

These splendid creatures, as yet untouched by the "oppressive respectability" of Cloisterham, possess intact that elusive and indefinable vitality which the walls of the Cathedral, the monastery, and the Nuns' House have been built to channel into the narrowest of conduits. Their very presence in Cloisterham serves to remind us, once again, that the psychic and physical qualities they possess cannot be walled in without disastrous consequences for the individual and society. The Landlesses, "slender, supple, quick of eye and limb; half shy, half defiant," suggest undifferentiated energy itself, reasserting its primacy, challenging the jumbled notions of a culture which has tried to turn away from the human questions such energy poses.

In a stroke the brother and sister reassert the continuity between *Edwin Drood* and De Quincey's *Confessions*. For Dickens, the Landlesses and the Ceylon from which they come possess that aura of mystery, revelation, and potential terror which echoes De Quincey's ambivalent response to those Eastern images which finally dominate his dreams. The Malay, real or imaginary, who appears at De Quincey's cottage in the Lake Region eventually represents everything that is alien and un-English in De Quincey himself, everything that is somehow taboo and to be denied at all costs. Within the *Confessions* the incident has far-reaching consequences. The Malay becomes the physical manifestation of De Quincey's guilt, the living expression of those desires which, in the elaborate mythology of opium addiction, are unleashed through the agency of the drug. The Malay, by reappearing in his dreams, becomes the medium through whom De Quincey is initiated even further into a knowledge of the unspeakable.

> The Malay has been a fearful enemy for months. I have been every night, through his means, transported into Asiatic scenes. I know not whether others share in my feelings on this point; but I have often thought that if I were compelled to forego England, and to live in China, and among Chinese manners and modes of life and scenery, I should go mad. The causes of my horror lie deep; and some of them must be common to others. Southern Asia, in general, is the seat of awful images and associations. (332)

Through his identification with the Malay, De Quincey can express the horror, and the appeal, of those potentialities which southern Asia, "as the cradle of the human race," holds for him. The feeling of abhorrence is intensified by the undeniable lure of "the ancient, monumental, cruel, and elaborate religions of Indostan" (333). The "barrier" of terror which protects De Quincey from the savagery and fecundity of the Orient is far more fragile than he would like to admit.

The Ceylon from which Dickens brings the Landlesses is deeply rooted in this De Quinceian vision of the East, "the seat of awful images and associations," as well as of "a dim and reverential feeling." It possesses a special charge because of the literary tradition to which it belongs. The Landlesses, like De Quincey's Malay, are from "the cradle of the human race"; they, too, are De Quincey's "antediluvian man renewed," dark but beautiful emissaries from a realm fermenting with life, savagery, and passion. There man loses his very individuality: he becomes a "weed," only one more manifestation of life in its bewildering variety. Neville and Helena Landless assert the enduring presence of the violent centuries which only seem to be of the past. They are the warning, and the promise, that the creative potentialities of such energies have not forever been lost to the people of the sepulchral Cathedral town. The Landlesses, however mysterious and volatile, are the harbingers of life in the midst of unambiguous death. The question remains whether such exotic and sensuous beings, who even communicate by a mysterious process of intuition or telepathy, will be permitted to survive intact, or whether they will be so directed and improved by the well-meaning Crisparkle that they will lose the vitality they possess.

The Landlesses introduce alternative, and alien, modes of being into Cloisterham. They also act as catalytic agents, like the opium Jasper smokes. Their presence tends to break down the elaborate social and psychic barriers which have, so far, provided that illusory separation between Crisparkle's innocuous daylight world and the midnight world into which Jasper flees for refuge and release. With their appearance Jasper's already disintegrating command of himself undergoes further erosion. He begins to communicate more explicitly and urgently his repressed desires.

Rosa Bud is already troubled by Jasper's passion for her. She is woman enough to have felt the intense sexual desire he expresses through his music and his singing. However, she does not understand that her fear is also based on some vaguely stirring response to Jasper within herself. On the night of the Crisparkles' dinner party, which welcomes the Landlesses to Cloisterham, Rosa finds herself submitting to the inevitable performance required of a young lady at such a party. Jasper accompanies her on the piano: "The song went on. It was a sorrowful strain of parting, and the fresh young voice was very plaintive and tender. As Jasper watched the pretty lips, and ever and again hinted the one note, as though it were a low whisper from himself, the voice became a little less steady, until all at once the singer broke into a burst of tears, and shrieked out, with her hands over her eyes: 'I can't bear this! I am frightened! Take me away!' " (51).

Of all those in the drawing room only Helena, Rosa, and Jasper understand what lies behind the girl's outcry. The intense eroticism of the proceedings, the subtle violation of Rosa, as Jasper "[hints] the one note, as though it were a low whisper from himself," has gone unnoticed by the others. But Helena, who possesses a sexual awareness banned from the respectable parlors of respectable people, understands the implications of Jasper's attentiveness. She stands beside Rosa, "intent" upon Jasper. While Edwin Drood unperceptively assumes that "Jack's" conscientiousness has intimidated Rosa, Helena knows the real basis of Rosa's terror. And knowing it, possessing the knowledge of that sexuality Victorian society denies, she would not be afraid of Jasper "under any circumstances."

In Helena Landless, Rosa finds her antithesis. Rosa calls herself a "mite of a thing," while Helena is "womanly and handsome," with "resolution and power enough to crush" the less confident Rosa (52). Her own remarks suggest that Rosa, "wonderfully pretty, wonderfully childish," has willed her innocence and passivity, as well as her denial of her own sexual nature. Characteristically, when she and Edwin Drood agree to break their engagement, Rosa wants to think of him as a brother. But Helena Landless inhabits a different psychic realm. She has already seen that Jasper lusts after Rosa. She even understands the deception underlying Rosa's idea of herself as a helpless victim of a force thoroughly beyond her control: "He has made a slave of me with his looks. He has forced me to understand him, without his saying a word; and he has forced me to keep silence, without his uttering a threat" (53). The act of compulsion, from Rosa's perspective, seems all on the part of Jasper, yet Rosa's susceptibility to his presence, to his every gesture, reveals the extent to which she is not merely a slave to her music master but an unconscious partner in an intensely charged exchange. There is a certain thrill behind her confession that on this night, "It was as if he kissed me, and I couldn't bear it, but cried out" (54). Her shame and terror do not proceed only from Jasper's violation, as Drood's "uncle," of the primal taboo against incest. In a milieu in which Miss Twinkleton must speak of "the future wives and mothers of England" in a lowered voice, lest the company be shocked by even the most veiled allusion to the sexual act, Rosa has been denied the capacity to accept her own sexuality. She is, necessarily, drawn to a Helena Landless who can ask, quite directly, "You do not love him [Jasper]? . . . You know that he loves you?" (53), because she has not yet fallen victim to Cloisterham's crippling inhibitions. But in embracing Helena, Rosa has turned to someone whose vision of her plight must be different from her own. Helena's "wild black hair [falls] down protectingly over [Rosa's] childish form": "There was a slumbering gleam of fire in the intense dark eyes, though they were then softened with compassion and admiration" (54). Here Rosa is lost in an embrace as potentially sexual as any Jasper might offer. One wonders what can be the source of Helena's compassion or admiration for this childish creature, unless it is pity for Rosa's weakness and curiosity in her lack of self-knowledge.

But the evening is not over. The gates of the Nuns' House close upon Rosa and Helena, but the forces that have been released have not yet played themselves out. As Rosa and Helena are brought together by the fascination which opposites hold for each other, Edwin Drood and Neville Landless are drawn together, not by the power of love, but by that of mutual contempt, even hatred. Drood has already been moved by the sensual intensity of the dark-complexioned Helena, just as Landless has responded to the fragile, childlike beauty of Rosa. Each seeks out, intuitively, an opposite to complement his own nature. Their un-expressed desires help to create the antagonism they feel for each other. It is intensified by that casual sense of superiority which Drood exudes as the anointed Westerner ready to bring the wonders of tech-nology to Egypt, and as Rosa's fiancé with his infuriatingly proprietary attitude. Landless' own feeling of racial inferiority, his acute sensitivity to the most casual slight, adds the final measure of provocation. He lacks that easy ability to mask his emotions Drood has inherited, as he has inherited Rosa, without that all-important knowledge that his man-nerisms are at best only a fragile veneer. Drood's genteel composure has so maddened Landless that only the sudden intervention of Jasper prevents a violent quarrel. He appears, as it were, out of the darkness, to lay a "startling right hand" on Drood's shoulder and to stand be-tween the two, at once separating and joining them, as he places his left hand on the "inner shoulder" of Landless. In the darkness of the tran-quil Cloisterham night John Jasper has encountered the externalized manifestation of his own warring states of mind.

The following scene in Jasper's chambers reveals the extent to which Jasper's private dreamworld now impinges more and more upon the world of conventional reality. As Eugene Wrayburn finds in Brad-ley Headstone an "entertaining study" and incorporates the schoolmas-ter into a version of his own Gothic novel through "the chase," John Jasper presides over the dramatic reenactment, before his very eyes, of the conflicts dominating his dreams. He casually calls attention to the unfinished portrait of Rosa Bud, hanging in its central place over the chimneypiece. This act, alone, rekindles the quarrel he has apparently tried to halt. When he turns his back upon the two young men to prepare a jug of "mulled wine" before the fire, "it seems to require much mixing and compounding" (58). On this evening Jasper has found an intriguing substitute for his usual means of escape. If he has, in fact, drugged the wine, he has created the conditions under which all that he has so long repressed can be exposed without risk to himself. In the opium den of the Princess Puffer and in his own bedchamber, Jasper has repeatedly undertaken, in the company of an unsuspecting fellow traveller, that perilous dream journey, "over abysses where a slip would be destruction." Jasper has before him, now, Drood and Land-less, each a "traveller," each a potential threat to the other. As a specta-tor, he momentarily possesses even that illusion of distance and self-command which enables Eugene Wrayburn to sleep so soundly after the healthful rigors of the chase.

As he goads Landless to renewed fury, Jasper participates in the frustration and envy lying behind it. He speaks of Drood's prospects, of the world before him, of the marriage which is his legacy, and then ex-poses his own resentment, carefully screened by his bantering manner:

"You [Landless] and I have no prospect of stirring work and interest, or of change and excitement, or of domestic ease and love. You and I have no prospect . . . but the tedious, unchanging round of this dull place" (58). Under other circumstances Jasper has revealed his sense of alienation and frustration to Drood; he has seemed to understand that his nephew might well find himself in a "niche" like his own. But now he is free, under the aegis of Landless' presence, to express obliquely that envy of his nephew that has become inextricably bound to his own discontent. Drood justifiably protests that his situation is not as comfortable, as free of restraints, as it seems: both he and Rosa have begun to perceive the absurdity of their engagement, the element of coercion behind the benevolence of two dead fathers and the unthinking acquiescence of society. But Drood's emerging awareness of the violation of his integrity by the will lies temporarily beyond the comprehension of either Landless or Jasper. Neither can understand Drood's apparent lack of commitment, his maddening indifference to the tempting "golden fruit that hangs ripe on the tree for him" (58). Drood's pose, so akin to the adopted languor of Eugene Wrayburn, is his muted protest to the circumstances into which he has been born. But his "air of leisurely patronage and indifference" as he speaks of the unfinished portrait of Rosa as a "joke, sir, a mere joke" is enough to madden Landless and Jasper. Jasper has identified himself with Landless: both are dark, alien young men, with "no prospect[s]," taunted by Drood's easy self-assurance. The man who stands before them is not simply a sexual rival: he represents a state of consciousness the two abhor.

Jasper's self-possession throughout the intensifying quarrel resembles the passivity of the dreamer who observes the landscape and the flow of events passing before him. But, like the dreamer, Jasper participates in all that happens, for without him there is nothing. His consciousness is the ultimate ground of this scene; all the characters are versions of his multifaceted self. Throughout the dreamlike quarrel which follows Jasper plays many roles. Through Landless he is the enraged son rebelling against Drood, the patronizing father. In his efforts to calm Landless and Drood, he becomes the father intervening to protect the son he loves. Even through the words of Drood, a part of Jasper reveals itself.

When he responds to Drood's annihilating condescension with the observation, "I said that in the part of the world I come from, you would be called to account for it" (59), Landless unwittingly expresses Jasper's own sense of foreignness. Both belong to the *same* part of the world, a metaphorical Ceylon like De Quincey's southern Asia, that "seat of awful images and associations." Drood's contemptuous response to Landless is his confession that he has acquiesced more than he knows to his conventional world: "Only there? . . . A long way off,

I believe? Yes; I see! That part of the world is at a safe distance" (59). But *that* "part of the world" is in Jasper's chambers this night, in defiance of the walls of Cloisterham and the social taboos designed to exclude it.

Drood's claim that Landless is "no judge of white men" is the final thrust. Like Wrayburn's calculated denial of Headstone's existence, Drood's comment exiles Landless, and the dark Jasper, from the civilized island world of England, from that socially defined reality to which the two men pose a challenge. Drood's racism is only another version of the enduring attempt of society to shut out alternative visions of reality. At this point, only Jasper's intervention prevents a struggle between two modes of being. The nightmare has almost worked itself out to its logical conclusion, but Jasper's intercession imposes, once again, the barriers separating not only Landless and Drood, but the conflicting parts of Jasper's own consciousness. The two apparently distinct states of mind reassert their primacy. Landless finds himself in the dark, standing "with a bare head in the midst of a blood-red whirl, waiting to be struggled with, and to struggle to the death" (60). But the time, place, and fellow-traveller of Jasper's endlessly repeated dream journey are not yet at hand. At this moment Jasper is prepared for the "struggle to the death" neither with Drood nor with himself. The crisis has not come; the choice between who is to live and who is to die, if only figuratively, is still to be made. And Jasper, speaking to Crisparkle of the events of the evening, reveals more completely than he realizes his own confusion and anxiety: "I shall never know peace of mind when there is danger of those two coming together with no one else to interfere" (62). The two parts of the divided self are held, literally and figuratively, at arms' length by an interceding agent. For the moment Jasper himself is the agent. Even in his desperation he cannot as yet contemplate the destruction of the nephew who is like a son to him, because he is a part of himself. But that separation of the two bedrooms, reflecting the artificial compartmentalizing of Jasper's psyche, has run its course as a strategem for survival.

His urgent need to reconcile, if possible, the fragmented parts of his own consciousness impels Jasper to turn to Septimus Crisparkle. The diary entry he shows Crisparkle, expressing his concern over "the demoniacal passion of this Neville Landless, his strength in his fury, and his savage rage for the destruction of its object" (86), is a confession of guilt and a plea for help. Jasper accepts Crisparkle's efforts to affect a reconciliation between Landless and Drood because it raises the possibility of some resolution to his own anguish. The Christmas Eve dinner party for three offers a chance for that reunification of his own psyche which Jasper still seeks.

The prospects for an enduring reconciliation, either between

Drood and Landless or within Jasper himself, are undermined from the start by the fact that it is Crisparkle who has taken the initiative in the affair. Crisparkle, far more than Drood, remains the voice of conventional morality at its most blatant throughout the novel. He continues to present its positive qualities and its inherent inadequacy. When he comes upon Helena and Neville Landless in their usual solitary walk beside the river, Crisparkle's attempts to pacify Landless' intensity reveal once more how alien and incomprehensible real energy and intensity are to him. To ask Landless to take the first step and to apologize to Drood is a violation of Landless' integrity. He almost pleads with Crisparkle, "My nature must be changed before I can do so, and it is not changed" (82). But this is precisely Crisparkle's intent: to alter the nature of Neville Landless, to draw over his intensity the veil of social convention. Crisparkle *is* the social conscience in its most gentle and attractive form. But beneath the gentleness it remains unrelenting in its determination to reduce other modes of being to its own constricted state. So Crisparkle gently rebukes Landless for his clenched hands and responds with deadening gravity to Landless' open admission of his admiration for Rosa Bud. As he reminds Landless that Rosa is "shortly to be married" and that his "admiration" for her is "outrageously misplaced," Crisparkle reveals his acceptance of the bizarre situation in which Drood and Rosa find themselves. He defends the socially sanctioned, if anachronistic, betrothal with a solemnity worthy of the Dean himself. He proves himself less imaginative, less compassionate, than even that most angular of men, Mr. Grewgious. For Crisparkle the antidote to emotions which defy socially acceptable limits is a regimen of physical fitness or an exhausting walking tour: he is the quintessential headmaster of a boys' school.

With this perspective, Crisparkle lapses into a condescension which exposes his willingness to play unthinkingly with Landless' life. He chooses to treat Landless' response to Rosa as a mere infatuation, a "fancy of the moment." This is a classic instance of the invalidation of another's experience. There is no mistaking Crisparkle's conviction that he knows the true state of Neville's feelings: his tone exudes it. Crisparkle tells Landless what he ought to feel, what others in similar situations have felt. He imposes upon the orphaned twins a conception of individual experience sanctioned by the conventional wisdom of which he is a spokesman. He subverts Landless' experience in the name of social stability. Crisparkle performs his social obligation with a sense of complete benevolence. It is his duty to deny the validity of Landless' "world," his Ceylon, and to assert the conventional claims of those in Cloisterham.[20]

Surprisingly, Helena and Neville Landless humble themselves before Crisparkle. Suddenly, neither has the ability to penetrate Crisparkle's self-satisfied façade. Even Helena, who has understood at once the relationship of Jasper to Rosa, accepts Crisparkle's advice. As the three separate, Helena takes the hand Crisparkle offers her "and gratefully and almost reverently [raises] it to her lips" (85). It is an outrageous gesture on the part of both. It seals the first stage in the socialization of the Landlesses, that moment in which they are, in the words of Laing, "tricked and [have] tricked [themselves] out of [their] minds, . . . out of [their] own personal worlds of experience, out of that unique meaning with which potentially [they] may endow the external world." [21] The only "Heaven" a Crisparkle can offer the Landlesses is the secular sterility of Minor Canon Corner. The brother and sister, so like "beautiful barbaric captives brought from some wild tropical dominion," have bowed before the civilizing touch of the Minor Canon: they have violated all that has made them "slender, supple, quick of eye and limb." When he acquiesces to the pledge of silence exacted by Crisparkle, Landless accepts, at his sister's urging, what for him may prove to be a death sentence. He has been asked to do the impossible: to erase from his consciousness not just a specific feeling for Rosa, but also the sources of that feeling. He is now alienated from himself, potentially another John Jasper.

But Crisparkle has affected at best a temporary, if not altogether illusory, restoration of peace to Cloisterham. He lacks the power to heal the disorder from which Jasper and the Cathedral town suffer. The novel moves toward Christmas Eve and that violent storm which is to dissipate forever the aura of tranquillity in which Cloisterham takes refuge. There are omens warning that some final eruption of long suppressed forces must take place. In spite of the "veil between our present consciousness and the secret inscriptions on the mind" which Crisparkle tries to reestablish, the "obscuring daylight" of which De Quincey speaks in the *Confessions* will withdraw to reveal the ineradicable nature of those inscriptions. Under the aegis of the red light burning steadily in his gatehouse chambers, the chaotic forces within John Jasper are released from their habitual bondage on that Christmas Eve: they are free to rage without the threat of restraint. In the midst of the turbulent darkness of the storm, the persistence of the steady burning of Jasper's lamp assumes a sinister significance. John Jasper presides over the violence that thunders along the empty streets at midnight, "rattling at all the latches, and tearing at all the shutters, as if warning the people to get up and fly with it" (130). He is, figuratively, the source, if not the master, of all that is released. For the same red light glowed throughout Jasper's midnight ramble with Durdles and the confrontation with Deputy. It has burned during all the lonely vigils when Jasper has delivered himself to his midnight "Spectres." And its reflection has appeared in the cupped hands of the Princess Puffer as she nurses the "red spark of light" emanating from the bowl of the opium pipe. The red light unifies Jasper's existence: it is the spark of consciousness.

The storm whose ground is Jasper's consciousness succeeds in obliterating time itself on this most un-Dickensian of Christmas Eves. On the Christmas morning which follows the storm, "it is then seen that the hands of the Cathedral clock are torn off; that lead from the roof has been stripped away; . . . and that some stones have been displaced upon the summit of the great tower" (130). But the tower remains, the hands of the clock will be replaced. As in Jasper's recurring dream, the tower seems indestructible. Perhaps time has been momentarily denied, or transcended. But the moment of transcendence passes. With the return of day, the obscuring veil of light returns. The storm, "like a wounded monster," finally drops, sinks, and dies. The Minotaur has had its moment of ambiguous freedom; now time and the values of society reassert themselves, as they always must.

The storm manifests the violence behind Jasper's self-conscious constraint. It also obscures forever those events which occur while it rages on. The vexing impenetrability of events remains an inherent part of *Edwin Drood*. Jasper, like De Quincey, might well claim adherence to "the doctrine of the true church on the subject of opium: of which church I acknowledge myself to be the only member—the alpha and the omega" (299). But as a communicant in that church which inverts the values of a Christianity he only routinely observes, John Jasper writhes in the power of a god beyond his control. He cannot know whether the ritual he performs has culminated only in his erotic, narcissistic visions or in an act of perverse religious devotion, the sacrificial murder of his nephew, and necessarily, of part of himself. Nor can we.

Jasper's behavior after the disappearance of his "dear boy" is intelligible only within this context of pure ambiguity. In the last chapter of the fragment as we have it, "The Dawn Again," Jasper returns to the opium den of the Princess Puffer. For months he has been preparing his own opium in spite of the hag's proud claim that only she has "the real receipt for mixing it" (205). The possibility exists that the effects of the drug upon Jasper's consciousness have become unpredictable. The glowing red lamp visible during the storm suggests that he has once again taken refuge in his visionary world before Drood's return from the river bank: he has prepared himself to meet the "fellow-traveller" of the dream journey. But the complexity of Jasper's psychological situation becomes as labyrinthine as the novel itself. If a murder has been committed, it may have been assimilated into the journey Jasper has relived "millions and billions" of times. But the "murder" may be only a dream, a dream taking on the appearance of reality. Jasper's ravings in the presence of the Princess only reveal his total disorientation. The enigmatic "it" which "comes to be real at last," but which "is so short that it seems unreal for the first time" (208), need not be the act itself. Dickens offers no clues as to whether it is a real or a visionary murder which has failed to satisfy Jasper. There is only Jasper's conviction that the enigmatic "it" must have occurred because his dreams now offer "no struggle, no consciousness of peril, no entreaty," because some ill-defined *"that"* has appeared for the first time in the panorama of the dream-scape (208).

In either case the confused and shaken Jasper moves more than ever under the sway of conflicting and elusive motivations. The disappearance of Drood is a wrenching blow to the uncle who has taken an almost womanish interest in him: "It would be difficult to determine which was the more oppressed with horror and amazement: Neville Landless, or John Jasper" (135). If Edwin Drood is dead, Jasper must struggle with the remorse which overwhelms him, for he has lived through Drood in spite of his envy and resentment of him. At the same time, on some level of his wracked consciousness, his jealousy of Drood—his nephew, his "son"—asserts itself, and he is tormented by an excruciating guilt. But it cannot be directed toward himself. In his diary Jasper has evaded the full impact of his own feelings by concentrating upon the tableau of violence, involving Drood and Landless, which he has so artfully contrived. Once again his guilt is displaced onto Landless, who conveniently embodies both the creative and destructive potentialities of his oppressed self. The mechanisms of the dreamworld usurp the order of reality. Innocent or guilty of the enigmatic act itself, John Jasper will pursue a murderer because he must: he stalks himself in the form of Neville Landless. Like Oedipus, he proclaims judgment on himself. Deputy's defiant challenge, "I'll blind yer, s'elp me! I'll stone yer eyes out, s'elp me! If I don't have your eyesight, bellows me!" (110–11), suggests the validity of the analogy. In this complex way Dickens remains true to the psychological bonds established between the uncle and the nephew who has become his double.

— *3* —

The *Doppelgänger* is a figure appearing repeatedly in the Gothic tradition and in Dickens' novels. The *Doppelgänger* relationship becomes an inherent part of Dickens' mature novels: it often determines their structure and the complicated, and apparently artificial, ways in which they characteristically end.[22] With the dragging of the river and the futile search along the riverbanks, *Edwin Drood* returns to familiar images and motifs, to *David Copperfield, Great Expectations,* and *Our Mu-*

tual Friend, and to the recurring theme of death-by-water: "All the live-long day, the search went on. . . . Even at night, the river was specked with lanterns, and lurid with fires; far-off creeks, into which the tide washed as it changed, had their knots of watchers, listening to the lapping of the stream, and looking out for any burden it might bear; . . . but no trace of Edwin Drood revisited the light of the sun" (136). The quintessential Dickens ritual has begun anew. The living may recoil from the dead, with that "innate shrinking of dust with the breath of life in it, from dust out of which the breath of life has passed" (105), but they struggle to retain their hope that an individual can defy death's power. As those who watch and yearn for Rogue Riderhood's return to life become a part of his solitary struggle in *Our Mutual Friend,* the inhabitants of Cloisterham participate in the search for Drood. They listen and they gaze with that same rapt suspense which possesses those who gather at the foot of Eugene Wrayburn's sickbed after he has been attacked by Bradley Headstone: "This frequent rising of a drowning man from the deep, to sink again, was dreadful to the beholders" (740). The watchers at the bedside are held there by that almost involuntary denial of the reality of death which makes life possible.

The fate of Edwin Drood is never clearly revealed within the uncompleted novel. In *Our Mutual Friend* Eugene Wrayburn's psychological dilemma is far more severe than Drood's. But Wrayburn, convinced of the necessity of his own death, as he confesses to Lizzie, is reprieved and undergoes a process of rebirth. Wrayburn's marriage to Lizzie has its analogy in Drood's decision to break the engagement with Rosa Bud. Both Wrayburn and Drood defy their fathers, living or dead, and challenge the seemingly inflexible demands of the past. Wrayburn does so with an almost miraculous impunity from the usually formidable sanctions of the father and society. When he releases Rosa from her engagement, Drood shows the promise that has only been latent in him until that moment. For him to die, in a Dickensian state of grace, would seem implausible. He has made the choice both John Harmon and Eugene Wrayburn have made before him: he has refused to acquiesce in outmoded notions, to the view of an "other" as his rightful property. Edwin Drood, too, has chosen life.

The rhythm of the novel, of all Dickens' later novels, almost dictates Drood's survival of whatever ordeal he has experienced, as well as his inevitable return to Cloisterham. The river fails to yield its burden to the watchers, not because Drood's corpse is hidden in the Cathedral crypt or the Sapsea monument, but because there may be no burden to yield. If he *is* alive, Drood has, like other Dickensian heroes, experienced a life-renewing, baptismal ritual. Mr. Peggotty's words, spoken at the foot of Barkis' deathbed in *David Copperfield,* inform this novel as they have earlier ones: " 'People can't die, along the coast,' said Mr. Peggotty, 'except when the tide's pretty nigh out. They can't be born, unless it's pretty nigh in—not properly born, till flood' " (445). Edwin Drood may have been plunged into the waters of the river and delivered back to life through its transforming power: out of the potent mud of the river, as opposed to the sterile dust of Cloisterham and the grit of London, comes life. The storm which objectifies Jasper's destructive energies may serve to heal the dislocation of Drood, as Headstone's attack upon Wrayburn serves to resolve the "crisis," the state of indecision, in which Wrayburn finds himself just before "the reflected night [turns] crooked, flames [shoot] jaggedly across the air, and the moon and stars [come] bursting from the sky" (698).

Edwin Drood's fate must remain a matter for speculation. So must John Jasper's, although his role as nemesis, like Bradley Headstone's, suggests what may lie in store for him. He, too, is one of the avid searchers, cruising the river in barge and boat, "or tramping amidst mud and stakes and jagged stones in low-lying places." The foreign, muddy world of the Thames calls to him, also. He returns to his gatehouse, "unkempt and disordered, bedaubed with mud that had dried upon him, and with much of his clothing torn to rags" (136). He has emerged from the primal ooze, like Fagin, Magwitch, and Gaffer Hexam, like Pip, John Harmon, and Eugene Wrayburn. He is the archetypal Dickens father who haunts his son; the son who must acknowledge a stratum of human consciousness forever subject to abuse, forever undeniable; the recurring *Doppelgänger* who descends into the depths, like Steerforth, Carton, and Headstone, never to return alive, but to die in the violence of a storm off Yarmouth or "under the ooze and scum behind one of the rotting gates" of a Plashwater Weir Mill Lock. Jasper has made his own descent into the regions of the godlike river. His reemergence from it indicates that, like Riderhood or Wrayburn, he has been granted the opportunity to deny or to accept the potentiality for change within him.

It is in this state of exhaustion and disorientation that Jasper must encounter the calculated insensitivity of Mr. Grewgious as he persists in his slow, provoking revelation of the broken engagement. The solicitor's callousness suggests that he already suspects Jasper of something. He remorselessly puts Jasper to the test and watches the "ghastly figure throw back its head, clutch its hair with its hands, and turn with a writhing action from him," until at last Jasper utters his shriek of horror and is reduced to "nothing but a heap of torn and miry clothes upon the floor" (138). Jasper undergoes a process of total disintegration. His identity, fragile and confused as it is, has been defined by the bizarre triangle uniting Rosa, Drood, and himself, just as Headstone has defined himself in his relationship to Wrayburn and Lizzie. With

the disappearance of Drood and with the breaking of his engagement
to Rosa, the entire construct, so inverted, fantastic and self-destructive,
collapses. Jasper's apparently guilt-revealing collapse proves that without both Drood and Rosa his own existence is imperiled. With the loss
of those relationships by which he has defined himself, Jasper becomes
a nullity, a heap of clothes upon the floor, and no more. What the un-
moved, and unmoving, Grewgious gazes upon is the remnant of Jasper's extinguished self, like that "cinder of a small charred and broken
log of wood sprinkled with white ashes, or is it coal," which is the only
remnant of the spontaneously combusted Krook in *Bleak House.*

The failure of the attack upon Wrayburn and the marriage of Wrayburn and Lizzie lead to Bradley Headstone's willed self-extinction.
When he erases his name from the blackboard, he accepts his own
dissolution and prepares for the suicidal struggle with Rogue Riderhood, at best a poor substitute for the one he sought to have with
Wrayburn. But the closing chapters of *Edwin Drood* as we possess them
constitute, in part, Jasper's attempt to reconstruct an identity. It is not,
as it might have been, a Carlylean rebirth. Jasper, caught in a No Thoroughfare at least partially of his own making, chooses stasis, not
growth. He seeks to recapture a state of being not unlike the one he
has known for so long. That multifaceted, but fixated, role he has
forged for himself in response to an oppressive society has made him
its captive. Unerringly, he begins to reconstruct another version of that
fantasy which has sustained, and tortured, him. Drood may not be the
real barrier which separates him from Rosa Bud. There may be a part
of Jasper which withholds itself from a final commitment to the girl.
In the fantasy, then, Drood plays the convenient role of son and father,
just as Rosa becomes both maiden and mother; doubly tempting, doubly inviolable, because of her contradictory status in the choirmaster's
distorted scheme of things.

This explains Jasper's eager grasping at the fact of the broken engagement, once he has recovered from the original impact of
Grewgious' news. He is free to reassure himself that Drood is not dead,
that he has chosen to disappear. But in the process of spinning out this
hypothesis, Jasper traps Crisparkle into revealing Landless' infatuation
with Rosa. If he has not already sensed this, Jasper receives from the
Minor Canon the hint he has needed. With the recovery of Drood's
watch and shirt-pin, Jasper begins to weave anew the old fantasy by
which he has managed to live. The diary which was to have been destroyed upon the New Year, and which Jasper has called a record of
Drood's life, also has a new use. For Jasper himself has a new "life," a
new reason for living, and another person who can become the object
of Jasper's obsessive attention: "I now swear and record the oath on
this page, . . . that I will fasten the crime of the murder of my dear

dead boy, upon the murderer. And that I devote myself to his destruction" (146). Jasper has had to disguise, even from himself, his attitude toward Drood, "[his] dear dead boy." But he feels no such constraint in the case of Neville Landless, who, like the convenient
stepparent in the fairy tale, can be loathed without remorse, without
guilt. And by fastening his attention upon Landless, Jasper does not
have to forego the dream journey, the exquisite thrill of destroying the
fellow-traveller as the prelude to the moment of erotic release. The
original dream begins to lose at least some of its ambiguity. Unlike
Bradley Headstone, who works on obsessed with the idea that the "instrument might have been better, the spot and the hour might have
been better," Jasper creates another opportunity to strike: he begins to
shape another time, another place, another fellow-traveller.

When he finds Rosa Bud in the garden of the Nuns' House, John
Jasper, as in the opening dream of the novel, is once again in the process of piecing together his scattered consciousness. In the midst of
summer and renewed life, Jasper obeys his old impulses by forcing
himself upon Rosa. The course of action he pursues, consciously or
not, terrifies the girl and causes her to recoil with repugnance. Love,
apparently, is no longer what Jasper needs, if he has ever sought it. He
finds other emotions more pleasing, and less immediately threatening,
however sterile and self-destructive they may prove to be. He now
prefers the illusory pleasures of the dreamworld, just as Headstone
comes to relish the masochistic pleasures of the chase. Jasper's words
and actions frustrate any possibility of satisfaction within the context of
reality; and they protect him from a rejection he would find intolera-
ble. He will be driven back to the world of opium, away from the living.
But the fantasy, with the Sultan and the dancing-girls, relies on images
incorporated into the dream landscape, static images of real persons.
Jasper has returned to the enduring triangle, to the dreamlike figures
locked in yet another dance of death.

Behind the melodramatic words and gestures of Jasper in the interview with Rosa lies this psychological reality. As he leans so casually
upon the sundial, another emblem of that time he is trying to deny,
Jasper engages in a remarkable *tour de force.* He directs his performance both at anyone who might glance out from the windows of the
house and at Rosa, who finds herself once again within his power,
compelled by the intensity of his voice to listen, transfixed, to a confused torrent of love and hate: "In the distasteful work of the day, in
the wakeful misery of the night, girded by sordid realities, or wandering through Paradises and Hells of visions into which I rushed, carry-
ing your image in my arms, I loved you madly" (170–71). The melodramatic cadences of the speech obscure the insinuations with which it is
charged. If Jasper has been false to Drood, so has Rosa in her inability

to love him "quite in the right way." If Drood has been unworthy of her, Rosa has proved unworthy of the "Paradises and Hells" into which Jasper has rushed for her sake. Any guilt which Jasper feels must be shared by Rosa: her indifference to his devotion and to Drood makes her a secret partner in whatever crimes Jasper has committed or has dreamed of committing. And Rosa, however appalled, must respond to this man, apparently in spite of herself: "Her panting breathing comes and goes as if it would choke her; but with a repressive hand upon her bosom, she remains" (171).

The conventionalized language, the predictable gestures of the Gothic villain, and the responses of the immaculate virgin in this scene cannot dissipate the reality of the energy produced in their confrontation. As Rosa is reduced, perhaps through the pressure of literary convention, to calling Jasper "a bad, bad man," the futility of Jasper's attempts to incorporate Rosa into the visionary Paradises and Hells of which he speaks becomes apparent. Rosa may unwillingly respond to Jasper's intensity as she has done "that night at the piano," she may fail in her attempt to deny her own sexuality, but she is not Helena Landless. The disparity between the eroticism of Jasper's dreams and Rosa's bland timidity becomes undeniable. She has no place in such dreams; she has not known the intensity of such feelings as Jasper's. She had become aware of the ethical and psychological absurdity of her engagement to Edwin Drood. But she remains a stranger to man's capacity for frustration and to the refuge offered by perversity. For her Jasper must remain a "horrible wonder apart"; her ignorance is the seal of her innocence.

But the real Rosa Bud has ceased to be the object of Jasper's obsession. He lusts now for the exotic, sensual dancing-girls of his dreams. He may feed upon Rosa's hatred and exultingly claim that Rosa is "more beautiful in anger than in repose," that he wants not her love, but her "pretty rage . . . [and] enchanting scorn" (171). But this is a lie. Rosa is now only the occasion for his feverish reveries. Her abhorrence is the sought-for check: it prevents Jasper from experiencing the emptiness of his vision of her. Rosa becomes the final version of the Dickens heroine; even her name harkens back to Rose Maylie. Through her, Dickens acknowledges the fundamental limitations of the innocent creatures he has so often, and so ambivalently, celebrated. It is Helena Landless, like Sikes' Nancy, who possesses the intensity commensurate with the hunger Jasper feels. But Helena is a dark and alien creature from the East, thrust into the cloistered, suffocating world of England where she cannot flourish. And Jasper can no longer respond to a real woman.

Edwin Drood's disappearance eliminates the barrier to his own desires upon which Jasper has relied. Now Jasper must re-create the eternal triangle of his dreams: Rosa will remain the inviolable object, both desired and hated for her inviolability; Neville Landless will replace Drood and become the necessary barrier to the consummation of his desires. Jasper hopes to fix Rosa in her former role by threatening Landless' life. He offers to relinquish his vindictive pursuit of Landless, and "henceforth to have no object in existence" but Rosa. But the girl cannot submit to such coercion. The savagery of Jasper's words insures her moral revulsion: "There is my past and my present wasted life. There is the desolation of my heart and my soul. There is my peace; there is my despair. Stamp them into the dust, so that you take me, were it even mortally hating me!" (173). Jasper has not made a proposal. He has suggested a twisted compact designed to fix himself and Rosa in a timeless and mutually destructive hell. The scene is a far darker version of the one in which Bradley Headstone proposes to Lizzie Hexam in *Our Mutual Friend*. Headstone sees Wrayburn as a real rival whom he cannot hope to defeat. Jasper creates a fictive rival in the form of Neville Landless. Both men succeed in driving the women they "love" into flight. In Headstone's case this leads to the suicidal chase. In Jasper's it affects his final isolation from everything, from everyone, around him. The revulsion he has so artfully, compulsively, aroused in Rosa is a reflection of his own self-abhorrence: he has become the outcaste, the De Quinceian pariah, he has long felt himself to be.

John Jasper has reached that narcissistic cul-de-sac which has been his aim from the first. The windows of the Nuns' House, looking out upon the garden, become mirrors as well as windows. Jasper is acutely aware of them as such: " 'I do not forget how many windows command a view of us,' he says, glancing towards them. 'I will not touch you again, I will come no nearer to you than I am. Sit down, and there will be no mighty wonder in your music-master's leaning idly against a pedestal and speaking with you, remembering all that has happened and our shares in it. Sit down, my beloved' " (170). The windows protect both Jasper and Rosa. They are his pretext for his immobility, his pose of idleness. The intensity of his voice, the workings of his features and hands, complement his attitude of ease to reveal the completeness of Jasper's division from himself. But he revels in this moment of stasis, although it exposes the untenable nature of his situation. Jasper is aware of his consummate performance, of the incongruity of his ferocity masked by his languid posture: it is an artistic achievement, however inverted. He smiles and folds his hands upon the sundial "so that his talk would seem from the windows (faces occasionally come and go there) to be of the airiest and playfullest" (172). This incredible self-consciousness leads to the playing of a role within a role; it exposes the condition to which Jasper's life and art have been reduced. He has become the unembodied self for whom there are no authentic gestures, but only further means of disguising the real self, hidden behind layers of posturing.

The novel has come full circle; to some extent it has never left the opium den of the opening pages. The spike which fused the world of the Town with that of the Sultan reappears in the form of the sundial upon which Jasper has impaled himself. He has not transcended his situation, or time. He has made a futile gesture to perpetuate an impasse, to stop time. He is fixed, in De Quincey's words, at the summit: *he* is the idol, the priest, the worshipped, and the worshipper. He shrinks from reciprocal commitments to others. His only "object" in life has become himself and his dreams. He fails to lock Rosa Bud into the narcissistic fantasy sustaining his precarious identity: but he has successfully fixed himself within it. In the season of growth and maturation, with its natural movement toward the harvest, Jasper has chosen to deny his own participation in the process of change. He leaves the garden of the Nuns' House "with no greater show of agitation than is visible in the effigy of Mr. Sapsea's father opposite" (173). He has fulfilled the omen inherent in his name: he has become an effigy of himself, a stone man. It is to this state that the Dickens "hero" has been reduced.

With Rosa's flight to London, a disquieting, and familiar, movement begins in the novel. *The Mystery of Edwin Drood* has moved from the start toward the dead end in the garden scene. Now, the inevitable gathering together of the good-of-heart usurps the rhythm of the fragment. With the appearance of Tartar we confront a figure from the realm of fairy tales, the bronzed and healthy ruler of a "beanstalk country" which he has created in the heart of gritty, begrimed London. His presence in the novel is a far more serious threat to its integrity than the element of melodrama which has been so central to it. Tartar reveals an attempt to retract what has been acknowledged, to erase that volatile energy which expresses itself through Jasper. Tartar presides over his "garden in the air" in a set of chambers described in language which could be a self-parody of an earlier style: his "chambers were the neatest, the cleanest, and the best ordered chambers ever seen under the sun, moon, and stars" (188). Dickens himself openly points to the Shandean quality of Tartar's domestic arrangements: "When a man rides an amiable hobby that shies at nothing and kicks nobody, it is always agreeable to find him riding it with a humorous sense of the droll side of the creature" (189). Apparently, Tartar's ironic awareness of himself is akin to Dickens' ironic stance toward his own character. But however fanciful in conception Dickens recognizes him to be, Tartar still exists as the figurative antidote to the darkness of Jasper. The sunburned, blue-eyed Tartar and his man, Lobley, "the dead image of the sun in old woodcuts," are to penetrate the walls of Cloisterham and

London with the light and the life that have been systematically excluded.

But there is no place for fairy tales, even "Jack and the Beanstalk," in the world of *Edwin Drood*. The incongruity of Tartar and Lobley in the midst of the other characters emphasizes Dickens' success in capturing the repressive atmosphere pervading England. Even Helena and Neville Landless belong to this world in a way that Tartar and Lobley do not. Their fierce beauty and their instinctive knowledge of primal states of consciousness dramatize the fascination and terror generated in others who may, or may not, possess the untamed life of the orphaned twins. They pose, as much as John Jasper, the dilemma of man in society: they explain the walls as they defy them. Tartar presents the recurring efforts of civilizations, and of authors, to deny a fundamental implacability within the irrational. He stands for man's efforts to convince himself there are no inner demons to conquer, no wild spirits to tame and domesticate. Tartar's shipshape chambers, immaculately neat, ingeniously organized, become the highest expression of man's use of his own energies. He is civilization without its discontents.

In one sense Tartar is not the complete intrusion I have claimed him to be. He is an integral part of those foreshadowings of rebirth and renewal so central to all of Dickens' later novels. From the beginning the promise of regeneration has been implicit in *Edwin Drood*. In the first chapter John Jasper returns from the opium den in time for evening service which begins when the "intoned words, 'WHEN THE WICKED MAN—' rise among groins of arches and beams of roof, awakening muttered thunder." The verse is from Ezekiel 18:27, "Again, when the wicked *man* turneth away from his wickedness that he hath committed, and doeth that which is lawful and right, he shall have his soul alive." [23] The Christian perspective implicit in the allusion stands in tension with the subversive vision of the Gothic. The Cathedral with its "massive grey square tower" is repeatedly juxtaposed to a vital world of nature beyond its sepulchral interior, a nature quite different from the exotic landscape of Jasper's dreams. Mr. Grewgious, looking into the Cathedral on an autumn afternoon, can only sigh, "It's like looking down the throat of Old Time" (73). The Cathedral, sign of a bankrupt Christianity and of repressive, life-denying institutions, is always distinguished from "the free outer air, the river, the green pastures, and the brown arable lands, the teeming hills and dales . . . reddened by the sunset" (73). The Cathedral still stands, still holds sway. It subdues the "sea of music" which "rose high, and beat its life out, and lashed the roof, and surged among the arches, and pierced the heights of the great tower." The resurgent sea of sound, of human aspiration, presses rhythmically, persistently, against unyielding Cathedral walls. There is a question of how long the Cathedral can defy time and the cycles of the seasons. The novel opens upon an autumnal day presaging winter and death. It ends, in its fragmentary form, upon a summer day on which the sun shines, trees wave in the balmy air, birds sing, and "scents from gardens, woods, and fields—or, rather, from the one great garden of the whole cultivated island in its yielding time—penetrate into the Cathedral, subdue its earthy odour, and preach the Resurrection and the Life" (215). The island pulsates with harbingers of life. But the harvest toward which the novel seems to move must also exact its ritualistic sacrifices.

For John Jasper the Resurrection and the Life preached by "the whole cultivated island" are unattainable illusions. His psychic terrain has become that of the Landlesses, a Ceylon indebted to De Quincey's southern Asia, cut off from the pastoral order of rural England. He must writhe upon the spike of which he has dreamt, impaled there both by a world hostile to a version of "nature" alien to its own and by his own obsessive seeking out of that triangular constellation which constitutes his identity. He reeks of the taint of the eternal scapegoat, a role he compulsively pursues. If Deputy's words are oracular, if he is a diminutive Tiresias to Jasper's Oedipus, the blight which has fallen upon this garden of England will be removed only with the eradication of its apparent source. But Jasper is not a source, a cause. He is the logical culmination of a far too narrow vision of human potentialities, rejecting multiplicity of expression in the name of order and "cultivation." Nevertheless, Jasper seems doomed to the ritualistic death of a Bradley Headstone and a Rogue Riderhood.

In *Our Mutual Friend* Dickens imagines an impasse like Jasper's in *Edwin Drood*. The pose which has become Eugene Wrayburn's imprisoning "second nature" is not easily cast off. It is so much a part of himself that, if it is to die, the whole man must risk death too. The second nature is not to be shrugged off like a knapsack nor is it to be amputated like a diseased limb so that the organism as a whole may live. It is because it is so deeply intertwined with the authentic self that Wrayburn has remained for so long, even to himself, an "embodied conundrum." As the "T'Otherest," as the most prominent of the repressed, unembodied selves in *Our Mutual Friend,* it is Bradley Headstone, Wrayburn's double, whose death will save Wrayburn as George Radfoot's saved John Harmon.

In *Our Mutual Friend,* as in *Edwin Drood,* Charles Dickens seeks to integrate his major characters into the society he has been criticizing. He consigns Headstone and Riderhood to the depths of the river, to the primal ooze from which all life comes. He purges the world of the novel of their twisted expressions of human potentialities. In the process, a force, a power, an energy, is forever lost. Both John Harmon and Eugene Wrayburn come to grips with the past; both exorcise the power their fathers' wills have seemed to possess. John Harmon finds a new father in the form of Mr. Boffin: he accepts his inheritance not from the dead father, but from a surrogate who removes the tarnish from the Harmon gold so that it may be used creatively. Eugene Wrayburn confronts his living father, to find that the man who has seemed such a tyrant "is a much younger cavalier" (811) than Wrayburn himself. This is a new version of M.R.F., previously more incubus than father, who has supposedly attempted to dictate the shape of his son's life. Once Wrayburn is convinced that his father, in his unique way, has offered what is "tantamount—in him—to a paternal benediction on our union, accompanied with a gush of tears," his ghost can be forever laid to rest, like that of Old Harmon. M.R.F., a comic version of the ghost of King Hamlet, "will continue to saunter through the world with his hat on one side," unperturbed by his son's unconventional marriage. Wrayburn is free at last to become himself. The state of paralysis and despair has passed. Wrayburn has been freed from the straightjacket of his acquired self as Bradley Headstone has escaped, if only through death, from his respectable suit of clothes and his respectable life.

In this manner *Our Mutual Friend* affirms the viability of the integrated self and its participation in a meaningful communal life. It involves a turning back to *A Tale of Two Cities* and to the death of Sydney Carton. Bradley Headstone, like Sydney Carton, becomes the traditional scapegoat. They share the same shadowy past, freeing each of them from any specific history which might undermine their usefulness as vicarious atoners for collective and individual guilt. The death of each involves an attempt on Dickens' part to evade the very psychological and moral dilemma he has posed; he banishes it from the world of the novel. Just as Carton's execution is inadequate as a means of restoring Charles Darnay to the condition of happiness he enjoys at the end of the novel, for Darnay *has* been guilty of crimes against the French people, Headstone's death cannot miraculously restore Wrayburn to the psychic wholeness he possesses at the end of *Our Mutual Friend*. Regeneration involves personal loss as well as gain. Neither Harmon nor Wrayburn should be expected, within the boundaries of the fictional worlds they inhabit, to escape so totally unscarred by the past which has almost destroyed them. Bradley Headstone's own failure to achieve the personal and social integration of Harmon and Wrayburn should not be forgotten. It exists to remind us how tenuous and fragile such integration has become within the confines of a society perceived in the image of the haunted castle of the Gothic tradition.

The Mystery of Edwin Drood is also resonant with echoes of these works which have preceded it. The recurrent patterns of Dickens' imagination operate strongly within the novel as we have it. The willed urge for integration which controls the conclusion of *Our Mutual Friend* has been an inherent part of all the great novels. It is present in this last, uncompleted work, but it should not blind us to the implications of John Jasper's dilemma. The thorn of anxiety is deeply imbedded in his consciousness. His discontent with his sense of confinement in the "dull place" of Cloisterham which offers no prospect "of stirring work and interest, . . . of change and excitement, . . . of domestic ease and love" becomes an indictment of a civilization. It leads to that awful moral and psychological isolation which cuts him off from "accordance or interchange" with anything around him.

Through Jasper, the full nature of discontent becomes coherently articulated. His confession to Edwin Drood, that he hates "the cramped monotony of [his] existence," is the cry of a suffering and cornered human being whose alienation from himself and society is a mark of his humanity.[24] His death alone will neither heal the society in general, nor implement, even ritualistically, the rebirth of a few isolated individuals. There can be no redemption even for the few, through the death of the Minotaur: the labyrinth which created him must fall, the walls of Cloisterham must crumble in some cataclysmic moment akin to the upheaval in *A Tale of Two Cities*.

John Jasper, superficially beyond the pale of sympathy, reveals the extent to which human energy may be twisted and inverted. He lives out before our eyes that desperation of which Dostoevsky's underground man speaks with such grotesque eloquence. Jasper has created his own underground world which dramatizes, implicitly, what Dostoevsky's antihero, with his infinite capacity for talk, chooses to tell us.

> We are all divorced from life, we are all cripples, every one of us, more or less. We are so divorced from it that we feel at times a sort of loathing for real "living life," and so cannot bear to be reminded of it. Why, we have come almost to looking upon real "living life" as an effort, almost as hard work, and we are all privately agreed that it is better in books. And why do we fuss and fume sometimes? Why are we perverse, and why do we ask for something else? We don't know what ourselves.[25]

The essence of Jasper's challenge to those around him who have accepted the self-division inherent in Miss Twinkleton's "two distinct and separate phases of being" which never clash lies in the claim of the underground man: "So that perhaps, after all, there is more life in me than in you." Jasper's rebellion takes the form of perversity and self-absorption. He has chosen this as the only mode of self-expression appropriate in a world whose values, as perpetuated by Miss Twinkleton and

Septimus Crisparkle, are so inadequate to man's psychological and moral predicament. In creating John Jasper, Dickens explores the ambiguities of human consciousness denied by a society no longer understanding itself or the human beings for whom it exists. Dickens' Gothicism becomes essential to the expression of this vision.

In his hands the Gothic vision forges the link between an Ambrosio, John Jasper, and the underground man. Once Byronic rebellion ceases to be possible and self-consciousness leads to the impasse in which one does "not know how to become anything: neither spiteful nor kind, neither a rascal nor an honest man, neither a hero nor an insect" (181), a John Jasper becomes inevitable. He turns, as a last resort, inward upon himself, carving demons out of his own soul. In the words of the underground man, "it is just in that cold, abominable half-despair, half-belief, in that conscious burying oneself alive for grief in the underground, . . . in that acutely recognized and yet partly doubtful hopelessness of one's position, in that hell of unsatisfied desires turned inward, in that fever of oscillations, of resolutions determined forever and repented of again a minute later—that the savor of that strange enjoyment of which I have spoken lies" (188). This impasse is part of Dickens' multifaceted legacy to the twentieth century. His Gothicism becomes the means of exploring the nature of unconscious forces and their elusive, often indefinable, manifestations in the ultimate Gothic castle, modern consciousness itself. This is the realm Charles Dickens understood: it is the realm he charted so well and bequeathed to us who still inhabit it.

NOTES
INDEX

LEONARD F. MANHEIM: *Dickens' HEROES,* heroes, *and heroids*

1   Otto Rank, *Der Mythus der Geburt des Helden,* with an Introduction by Sigmund Freud (Leipzig: F. Deuticke, 1909), p. 161 (translation mine). There is another and fuller synthesis of these persistent fantasies by Karl A. Menninger: see the conclusion of this study. A similar synthesis, with a nonpsychoanalytic orientation—its author averred that he had not even heard of Rank's study, published over twenty years earlier than his—is to be found in Lord Raglan's *The Hero* (1937; rpt. New York: Oxford University Press, 1956). The fantasy in one of its applications is discussed with great brilliance and economy by Alan Dundes in "The Father, the Son, and the Holy Grail," *Literature and Psychology* 12, no. 1 (1962), 101–12.

2   Thomas Mann, *Essays of Three Decades,* trans. H. T. Lowe-Porter (New York: Alfred A. Knopf, 1947), pp. 12–13. The most recent comprehensive treatment of multiple projection (psychological decomposition, doubling) is that of Robert Rogers, *A Psychoanalytic Study of the Double in Literature* (Detroit: Wayne State University Press, 1970).

3   *American Imago* 9, no. 1 (April 1952), 21–43.

4   *DSA,* vol. 1 (Carbondale and Edwardsville: Southern Illinois University Press, 1970), pp. 225–37, 295–96.

5   *Studies in the Novel* 1, no. 2 (Dickens Centenary Number, 1970), 189–95.

6   *Texas Studies in Literature and Language* 7, no. 2 (Summer 1965), 181–200.

7   *Psychoanalysis and the Psychoanalytic Review* 47, no. 4 (Winter 1960–61), 2–16; reprinted in *Hidden Patterns,* ed. Leonard and Eleanor Manheim (New York: Macmillan, 1966), pp. 113–31.

8   *American Imago* 12, no. 1 (Spring 1955), 17–23. All of these studies have as their source and point of departure my Columbia University doctoral dissertation, *The Dickens Pattern: A Study in Psychoanalytic Criticism* (microfilm only, University Microfilms, 1950). I am indebted for aid in the documentation of the present paper to the former assistant editor of *Hartford Studies in Literature,* Mr. Robert M. Como.

9   Percy Fitzgerald, in *The Life of Charles Dickens: As Revealed in His Writings* (London: Chatto and Windus, 1905), pointed out Dickens' identification of his own early trials with shoe-blacking by the quotation given in the text, and also in Mrs. Jarley's conversation with Slum, her versifying publicity man; in the emphasis on boot-blacking at Dingley Dell and in

Fagin's den; in Tim Linkinwater's reference to "hyacinths . . . in blacking bottles"; in Krook's inclusion of blacking bottles in the "inventory" of his warehouse of junk; in Bumble's issuing medicine in blacking bottles; and in the mention by one of the Barnacles of blacking as an important article of British commerce. André Maurois, in *Un essai sur Dickens* (Paris: Grasset, 1927), tells about Dickens' incomprehensible reference during a game he was playing with his children late in life: he referred to "Warren's Blacking, No. 30, Strand." Thus we have what amounts to a private symbolism of the hero's boyhood trauma.

10   See John R. Harvey, *Victorian Novelists and Their Illustrators* (New York: New York University Press, 1971); John R. Reed, "Emblems in Victorian Literature," *Hartford Studies in Literature* 2, no. 1 (1970), 19–39; Reed's review of the Harvey book, *Hartford Studies in Literature* 3, no. 3 (1972), 209–12. Steig may be represented, *inter alia*, by "Martin Chuzzlewit's Progress by Dickens and Phiz," *DSA*, vol. 2 (1972), pp. 119–44, especially pp. 143 ff. where there is a descriptive analysis of the *Chuzzlewit* frontispiece which has much in common with my description. I had no access to Steig's paper at the time (quite a long time ago) when my description was written. I am happy to

find that our minds independently ran in the same direction, and I acknowledge with gratitude Steig's notations as to Dickens' instructions to Phiz.

11   J. B. Priestley, *The English Comic Characters* (New York: Dodd, Mead and Co., 1931).

12   Of course, since Michael Steig set us right in the *Dickens Studies Newsletter* 4, no. 2 (1973), 40, we cannot call him "Old Trent" any longer. But is it not evidence that he is clearly a father-figure, pushed ahead into old age, with a "daughter" who is pushed back into prepuberty, that so many commentators have assumed that his name *had* to be Trent?

13   For interesting new light on Quilp, see Branwen Pratt's "Sympathy for the Devil: A Dissenting View of Quilp," *Hartford Studies in Literature* 6, no. 2 (1974), 129–46.

14   Stephen Leacock, *Charles Dickens: His Life and Work* (New York: Doubleday, Doran, 1933), p. 166.

15   In the Houghton-Mifflin edition (1894) it appears at pp. 331–35 and bears the number XXXIV. In another edition it bears the number XXXVI, and in still another edition I consulted it does not appear at all. I leave this problem to the textual investigator.

16   Karl A. Menninger, *The Human Mind* (New York: A. A. Knopf, 1930), p. 251.

JAMES E. MARLOW: *Dickens' Romance*

1   See especially Monroe Engel, "Dickens on Art," *Modern Philology* 53 (1955), 25–38, and P. A. W. Collins, "Keep *Household Words* Imaginative," *The Dickensian* 52 (1956), 119–23, and "Queen Mab's Chariot among the Steam Engines: Dickens and 'Fancy,' " *English Studies* 42 (1961), 78–90.

2   "In Memoriam," *Cornhill Magazine* 9 (February 1864), 130.

3   Quoted by Harry Stone, *Charles Dickens: The Uncollected Writings from*

Household Words 1850–1859 (Bloomington: University of Indiana Press, 1968), II, 468.

4   George H. Ford, *Dickens and His Readers* (New York: Norton Library, 1965), p. 23.

5   John Forster, *The Life of Charles Dickens* (London: Chapman and Hall, 1872–74), III, 349.

6   Mamie Dickens, *My Father As I Recall Him* (New York: P. Dutton, 1897), p. 57.

7 Quoted by Engel, "Dickens on Art," pp. 25–26.

8 Collins, "Keep *Household Words* Imaginative," p. 120, n.

9 "A Preliminary Word," *Household Words* 1 (1850), 1.

10 *Letters from Charles Dickens to Angela Burdett-Coutts 1841–1865,* ed. Edgar Johnson (Boston: Little, Brown, 1952), hereafter referred to as *to Coutts. The Letters of Charles Dickens,* ed. Walter Dexter (London: Nonesuch Press, 1938), will be referred to as *NL; The Letters of Charles Dickens,* ed. Mamie Dickens and Georgina Hogarth (London: Chapman and Hall, 1880), as *Letters; Letters of Charles Dickens to Wilkie Collins,* ed. Lawrence Hutton (New York: Harper Bros., 1892), as *To Collins.*

11 "Shakespeare and Newgate," *Household Words* 4 (October 1851), 25. This article is attributed by Stone to Dickens (I, 343).

12 This term of Kierkegaard's— whom we sometimes forget was Dickens' contemporary—is admirably suited to describe the predicament of many of Dickens' characters.

13 Leigh Hunt, "On the Realities of Imagination," chap. xxxi of *The Indicator* (London, 1825).

14 Ford, p. 129.

15 Forster, III, 319–20.

16 Engel, "Dickens on Art," p. 35.

17 William Hazlitt, *The Spirit of the Age* (1825; rpt. London: Scholar Press, 1971), p. 14.

18 T. E. M. Boll, "The Plotting of *Our Mutual Friend," Modern Philology* 42 (1944), 113.

19 Earle Davis, *The Flint and the Flame* (Columbia: University of Missouri Press, 1963), p. 30.

20 William Hazlitt, *The Round Table* (London: J. Templeman, 1841), p. 288.

21 Wayne C. Booth, *The Rhetoric of Fiction* (Chicago: University of Chicago Press, 1966), pp. 125 ff.

22 Ford, p. 140.

23 A. A. Mendilow, *Time and the Novel* (1952; rpt. New York: Humanities Press, 1965), pp. 96–97.

24 Ernst Cassirer, *An Essay on Man* (Garden City, N.Y.: Doubleday and Co., 1955), p. 191.

25 Mendilow, p. 101.

26 Cassirer, p. 190.

27 Forster, III, 344.

28 Alain, "Imagination in the Novel," *The Dickens Critics* (Ithaca, N.Y.: Cornell University Press, 1961), p. 172.

29 Suzanne K. Langer, *Feeling and Form* (New York: Scribner's Library, 1953), p. 369.

30 *The Spirit of the Age,* p. 11.

31 See "By Rail to Parnassus," *Household Words* 11 (1855), 477–80, in which a poor clerk, after reading Leigh Hunt's *Stories in Verse,* is able to accomplish in the world what, but for that literary respite, he could not otherwise have done. This simple story clearly bears Dickens' approval, if not his hand (See Anne Lohrli).

32 "A Paper-Mill," *Household Words* 1 (1850), 531.

33 William Hazlitt, *An Essay on the Principles of Human Understanding* (1805; rpt. Gainesville: University of Florida Press, 1969), p. 3.

34 William Hazlitt, *The Plain Speaker* in *The Complete Works,* ed. P. P. Howe (London: J. M. Dent & Sons, 1931), XII, 47–48. See Hazlitt's essay on Godwin in *The Spirit of the Age* for an example of the failure of higher standards of morality.

35 Ford, p. 113.

36 *The Plain Speaker,* p. 193.

37 R. D. Laing, *The Divided Self* (London: Penguin, 1970), p. 83.

38 Stone, II, 665.

39 Langer, p. 262.

40 Mrs. Langer says: "The first thing is to estrange it [the form of the work] from actuality, to give it 'otherness,' 'self-sufficiency' " (p. 59). Her point is that the articulated form must be clearly distinguished from the usual meanings associated with its constituents, that is, it must be divorced from

all instrumental values. For Mrs. Langer the resulting "otherness" enables the audience to see the pure semblance and thus grasp the import.

I have been arguing, on the contrary, that for Dickens the otherness is itself the end.

H. L. KNIGHT: *Dickens and Mrs. Stowe*

[1] Alice C. Crozier lists Dickens as one of the four major nineteenth-century influences on Mrs. Stowe in *The Novels of Harriet Beecher Stowe* (New York: Oxford University Press, 1969), p. 155. She expands on Dickens' influence later in the book, esp. p. 203.

[2] Harry Stone, "Charles Dickens and Harriet Beecher Stowe," *Nineteenth-Century Fiction* 12 (December 1957), 188–202.

[3] This fragment appeared in Catherine Gilbertson, *Harriet Beecher Stowe* (New York: D. Appleton-Century Co., 1937), p. 160.

[4] 18 September 1852, as reprinted in Harry Stone, ed., *Charles Dickens' Uncollected Writings from Household Words* (Bloomington: Indiana University Press, 1968), pp. 433–42. Denman's 1853 pamphlet was compiled from articles in the *Standard,* the first of which antedated this article.

[5] Mrs. Richard Watson. An excerpt from this letter and a detailed discussion of it follow.

[6] *Sunny Memories of Foreign Lands,* 2 vols. (Boston: Phillips, Sampson and Co., 1854). The Dickenses appear primarily in chap. 13, "London—the Lord Mayor's Dinner."

[7] "The True Story of Lady Byron's Life," *Atlantic Monthly* 24 (September 1869), 295–313.

[8] Stone, "Charles Dickens and Harriet Beecher Stowe," p. 202.

[9] *The Letters of Charles Dickens,* ed. Walter Dexter (London: Nonesuch Press, 1938), II, 430–31: hereafter referred to as *NL.*

[10] I am indebted for this information to a personal letter from Professor Harry Stone, California State University at Northridge.

[11] Stone, "Charles Dickens and Harriet Beecher Stowe," p. 193.

[12] For the enormous amount of attention paid Little Nell and her death, in both England and America, see George H. Ford, *Dickens and His Readers* (Princeton, N.J.: Princeton University Press, 1955), chap. 4.

[13] From *The Immortal Dickens* (London: Palmer, 1925), as quoted in Edgar Johnson, *Charles Dickens: His Tragedy and Triumph* (New York: Simon and Schuster, 1952), I, 324.

[14] See Kenneth Lynn's Introduction to his edition of *Uncle Tom's Cabin* for the John Harvard Library (Cambridge, Mass.: Harvard University Press, 1962). A discussion of "the religion of Love" follows.

[15] The Countess Giuccioli, Byron's mistress for the longest period of time during the years after he left Lady Byron—and herself a married woman who left her husband for the poet—published a memoir in which she placed the blame for Byron's troubles at the feet of Lady Byron. It was the popularity and wide acceptance of this memoir which prompted Mrs. Stowe to publish her own account of that marriage.

[16] Gladys Storey, *Dickens and Daughter* (London: F. Muller Ltd., 1939).

[17] Ada Nisbet, *Dickens and Ellen Ternan* (Berkeley: University of California Press, 1952).

[18] Johnson, I, 267.

[19] Stone, "Charles Dickens and Harriet Beecher Stowe," p. 201.

[20] *NL,* III, 416.

[21] Ibid. (6 October 1869).

[22] Unpublished letter in the Pierpont Morgan Library, printed in Stone, "Charles Dickens and Harriet Beecher Stowe," p. 202.

[23] *NL* (24 October 1869).

[24] Stowe, "The True Story of Lady Byron's Life," p. 313.

EDWARD J. EVANS: *The Established Self*

[1]   John Forster, *The Life of Charles Dickens* (London: Chapman and Hall, 1872–74), II, 41–42.
[2]   Ibid., p. 24.
[3]   For example, in her *Domestic Manners of the Americans* (1832), Mrs. Trollope states that one of her principal aims in describing American life is "to show how greatly the advantage is on the side of those who are governed by the few, instead of the many."
[4]   *The Letters of Charles Dickens,* eds. Madeline House, Graham Storey, Kathleen Tillotson (London: Oxford University Press, 1965–74), II, 402 (12 October 1841).

[5]   Ibid., III, 43 (31 January 1842).
[6]   Steven Marcus, *Dickens: From Pickwick to Dombey* (New York: Simon and Schuster, 1968), p. 225.
[7]   J. Hillis Miller, *Charles Dickens: The World of His Novels* (Bloomington: Indiana University Press, 1969), p. 130.
[8]   Barbara Hardy, "Martin Chuzzlewit," in *Dickens and the Twentieth Century,* eds. John Gross and Gabriel Pearson (Toronto: University of Toronto Press, 1962), p. 115.
[9]   Miller, p. 102.
[10]   Harry Stone, "Dickens' Use of His American Experiences in *Martin Chuzzlewit,*" *PMLA* 72 (1957), 464–78.

CHRISTOPHER MULVEY: *David Copperfield*

[1]   Jacob and Wilhelm Grimm, *Tales of Grimm and Andersen* (New York: Modern Library, 1952), p. 244.
[2]   See the first fourteen sheets of the manuscript of *David Copperfield* in the Forster Collection in the Victoria and Albert Museum Library (Pressmark 161.48A.12), and see also John Forster, *The Life of Dickens,* ed. A. J. Hoppé (London: J. M. Dent & Sons, 1966), II, 77–79.
[3]   Harry Stone, "Fairy Tales and Ogres: Dickens' Imagination and *David Copperfield,*" *Criticism* 6 (1964), 324.

NINA AUERBACH: *Dickens and Dombey*

[1]   Quoted in Gladys Storey, *Dickens and Daughter* (London: Müller, 1939), p. 100.
[2]   Angus Wilson, *The World of Charles Dickens* (New York: Viking Press, 1970), p. 59, regrets Dickens' attenuated treatment of sexual relationships, but he does not deplore it, while Kate Millett, *Sexual Politics* (New York: Doubleday, 1970) and Carolyn Heilbrun, *Toward a Recognition of Androgyny* (New York: Knopf, 1973) treat this lack as the central fact about Dickens' novels. Despite Professor Heilbrun's relative dismissal of Dickens, her ideal of a dehumanizing sexual polarity giving way to a healthily reconciling androgyny is, I think, an apt concept to apply to him.
[3]   Patricia Thomson, *The Victorian Heroine: A Changing Ideal, 1837–1873* (London: Oxford University Press, 1956), p. 93.
[4]   Andrew Sinclair, *The Better Half: The Emancipation of the American Woman* (New York: Harper & Row, 1965), p. 164. But recently Dickens has had ample defenders to make his women more palatable to a self-consciously liberated age. Sylvia Manning, in *Dickens as Satirist* (New Haven: Yale University Press, 1971), traces the development in his heroines away from debility to physical strength and

muscular activity; Ellen Moers, in "*Bleak House:* The Agitating Women," *The Dickensian,* 69 (January 1973), 13–24, discusses the plenitude of active, bustling, mobile women in that novel; and Alex Zwerdling, in "Esther Summerson Rehabilitated," *PMLA,* 88 (May 1973), 429–39, subtly exposes to us Esther's neurotic patterns, a "rehabilitation" that would have been desecration in any century but our own.

5   Elizabeth C. Wolstenholme, "The Education of Girls, its Present and its Future," in *Woman's Work and Woman's Culture,* ed. Josephine Butler (London: Macmillan and Co., 1869), pp. 290–330.

6   Dickens' "Violated Letter," published in the *New York Tribune,* 16 August 1858, and reproduced by Ada Nisbet, *Dickens and Ellen Ternan* (Berkeley and Los Angeles: University of California Press, 1952), p. 67. In one of those telling distortions gossip can produce, the English actress Blanche Galton referred to Ellen Ternan in 1928 as "Dickens's god-daughter" (Nisbet, p. 24).

7   Pearl Chesler Solomon, *Dickens and Melville in Their Time* (New York: Columbia University Press, 1975), p. 80.

8   Manning, pp. 46–47. See also Michael Steig, "Iconography of Sexual Conflict in *Dombey and Son,*" *Dickens Studies Annual,* ed. Robert B. Partlow, Jr. (Carbondale and Edwardsville: Southern Illinois University Press, 1970), I, 161–67. Steig traces the pervasive motif of the battle of the sexes in *Dombey,* showing how it surfaces in the smallest details of the text and illustrations.

9   Sarah Lewis, *Woman's Mission* (Boston: J. W. Parker, 1840, "from the English edition"), p. 13.

10   Leonore Davidoff discusses the transition from rural to railroad time-units in *The Best Circles: Society Etiquette and the Season* (Totowa, N.J.: Rowman and Littlefield, 1973), pp. 34–35.

11   John Ruskin, *Sesame and Lilies* (London: Smith, Elder and Co., 1865), p. 146.

12   See Julian Moynahan, "Dealings with the Firm of Dombey and Son: Firmness vs. Wetness," *Dickens and the Twentieth Century,* ed. John Gross and Gabriel Pearson (London: Routledge, 1962), pp. 121–31. This essay is one long and witty shudder at the death Florence carries about with her; Moynahan's insights are brilliant, but his assumption that Dickens is not responsible for his own effects seems needlessly patronizing. Alexander Welsh, in his *The City of Dickens* (London: Oxford University Press, 1971), subtly defines the love and death which Dickens' heroines offer his heroes as a manifestation of "Victorian angelology"; he has a particularly good definition of Florence Dombey.

13   Florence's familiarity with the dying is a perfect education, according to Sarah Ellis, *The Women of England: their Social Duties and Domestic Habits* (New York: Fisher, Son and Co., 1843). According to Mrs. Ellis, female education is bad for the health if it strains the intellect and bad for the soul if it teaches accomplishments: a young girl should acquire only those duties she will need in marriage, of which the foremost is the gentle skill of behavior in a sickroom. Dombey conveniently ignores the cultivation of her mind—she teaches herself enough to teach Paul—and she has no mother to instill in her those accomplishments which "a world of mothers" were inflicting on their marriageable daughters; as far as her education goes, it seems that her family's dexterity in dying or almost dying is the best possible training she could have. Abandoned by a corrupting world, the orphans make the purest of women.

14   Moynahan, p. 126.

15   Sarah Lewis, p. 95.

16   Obviously, I disagree with accounts of the novel such as Grahame Smith's *Dickens, Money, and Society*

(Berkeley and Los Angeles: University of California Press, 1968), pp. 103–20. According to Smith, *Dombey and Son* is too purely personal to rank with Dickens' greatest works: the firm of Dombey and Son lacks the overwhelming symbolic magnitude of Chancery in *Bleak House* or the Circumlocution Office in *Little Dorrit*. To me, the firm is deliberately intangible, Dombey's dream rather than Dickens' reality; the symbolic poles of the novel are the railroad and the sea, both of them very much alive. *Dombey* is not, in my opinion, a failed social anatomy, but an achieved embodiment of a world divided into sexual antinomies. It is not, in other words, a sketch for what Dickens was to do more successfully later, but a work conceived and executed in terms unique in the canon.

[17] Welsh aligns the train with Florence, as a vision of her rises before Dombey on his death-charged journey to Leamington in Chapter xx. But, though *to Dombey* his daughter blends with the train in a vision of death, in the novel's scheme the nature of the train is that of the man.

[18] John R. Reed, *Victorian Conventions* (Athens: Ohio University Press, 1975), pp. 45–46, analyzes at length Hablot K. Browne's illustration of the Edith-Carker confrontation in Dijon, showing 'the wealth of "masculine, almost heroic" associations surrounding Edith, in contrast to Carker's lax vulnerability.

[19] The *Saturday Review*, 25 (14 March 1868), 339–40.

[20] Quoted in John Forster, *The Life of Charles Dickens* (London: Everyman's Library, 1966), II, 197.

[21] Quoted in Edgar Johnson, *Charles Dickens: His Tragedy and Triumph* (New York: Simon and Schuster, 1952), II, 1008.

[22] Mamie Dickens, *My Father as I Recall Him* (Westminster: The Roxburghe Press, 1896), p. 8.

[23] Quoted in Storey, p. 219.

[24] I should like to thank the Gyral Foundation for their generous support during the writing of this article, and Professor Elizabeth Helsinger and Doreen Berger-Green of the University of Chicago for taking time to provide me with seemingly inaccessible material.

JOSEPH BUTWIN: *The Paradox of the Clown in Dickens*

[1] In his famous postscript to *The Great Tradition* ([New York: New York University Press, 1963] pp. 227–48), F. R. Leavis describes the way in which the circus act represents vitality and art for an industrial population starved of both. Leavis cites this passage and more emphatically the exposure of Tom Gradgrind in the circus ring as proof that in *Hard Times* Dickens achieves "a concentration and flexibility in the interpretation of life such as we associate with Shakespearian drama." For a more thorough study of Dickens' judgment of utilitarianism throughout the novel see Michael Goldberg, *Carlyle and Dickens* (Athens: University of Georgia Press, 1972), chap. 6.

[2] For the influence of Grimaldi on the English pantomime see David Mayer III, *Harlequin in His Element:· The English Pantomime, 1806–1836* (Cambridge, Mass.: Harvard University Press, 1969).

[3] For the historical development of Clown see M. Willson Disher, *Clowns and Pantomimes* (London: Constable, 1923). An excellent anthropological, psychological, and literary study of the clown unbound by time or country is William Willeford, *The Fool and His Scepter: A Study of Clowns and Jesters and Their Audience* (Evanston, Ill.: Northwestern University Press, 1969). See also Enid Welsford, *The Fool: His Social and Literary History* (London: Faber and Faber, 1935). Al-

though both of these books appeal to certain English literary sources, neither touches Dickens. In his *Stages of the Clown: Perspectives on Modern Fiction from Dostoyevsky to Beckett* (Carbondale and Edwardsville: Southern Illinois University Press, 1970), Richard Pearce establishes a clownish typology that is only loosely dependent on clowns as performers. In a chapter on *Great Expectations* and *The Trial* he defines Pip and Joseph K. as social intruders based on a classical, comic model. Pearce makes useful allusions to Baudelaire's "Essence of Laughter" and Bergson's "Laughter," essential texts for any study of the clown.

4   Dickens' edition of *The Memoirs of Joseph Grimaldi* has recently been republished (London: MacGibbon & Kee, 1968) with a biographical essay by Richard Findlater. Future citations appear in parentheses in my text. See also Findlater's *Grimaldi: King of Clowns* (London: MacGibbon & Kee, 1955).

5   For a reading of the *Sketches* from the point of view of structural linguistics see J. Hillis Miller, "The Fiction of Realism: Sketches by Boz, Oliver Twist and Cruikshank's Illustrations" in J. H. Miller and D. Borowitz, *Charles Dickens and George Cruikshank* (Los Angeles: William Andrews Clark Memorial Library, 1971), pp. 1–69.

6   William Empson, *The Structure of Complex Words* (Ann Arbor: The University of Michigan Press, 1967), chap. 5.

7   Hans Holbein, *The Dance of Death,* intro. James M. Clark (London: Phaidon Press Ltd., 1947).

8   A curious analogue to the death of Dismal Jemmy's clown is the death of Grimaldi's son which Dickens recorded after he had written *The Pickwick Papers:* "He had died in a state of wild and furious madness, rising from his bed and dressing himself in stage costume to act snatches of the parts with which he had been most accustomed, and requiring to be held down

to die, by strong manual force" (p. 287).

9   See Ellen Moers, *The Dandy: Brummell to Beerbohm* (New York: Viking Press, 1960), chap. 10. Mayer describes the frequent satire of the dandy by the clown (*Harlequin in His Element,* pp. 172–90).

10   Charles Dickens, *The Old Curiosity Shop* (London: Oxford University Press, 1951), pp. 122–32, includes the "Phiz" illustration of the graveyard scene. In a chapter called "Corpses and Effigies" John Carey provides extensive proof of Dickens' preoccupation with dead bodies and anything that might bring them to mind such as masks, waxworks, and artificial limbs. Carey does not mention Punch. *The Violent Effigy: A Study of Dickens' Imagination* (London: Faber and Faber, 1973), pp. 80–104.

11   Mayhew's reports of the street entertainers appeared in *The Morning Chronicle* (May–June 1850) four years before Dickens wrote *Hard Times* in the spring of 1854. They were republished in Volume III of the 1861 edition. In addition to the "Street Clown" (*London Labour and the London Poor* [London: Griffin, Bohn, and Company], pp. 119–20), other testimonies by a "penny-gaff clown," a "canvas clown," and a "penny-circus jester" tell a great deal about actual clownish performance, but they do not develop the pathetic contrast of the performance and the private life. Harland S. Nelson argues convincingly for Dickens' knowledge of Mayhew's articles from the time of their first appearance. ("Dickens' *Our Mutual Friend* and Henry Mayhew's *London Labour and The London Poor*," *Nineteenth-Century Fiction* 20 [December 1965], 213, n. 9.). Dickens would have known Mayhew himself before this when both were associated with the editors of *Punch.* Mayhew's awkward expulsion from that group would explain the pleasure he might take in the clown's rejection of jokes from *Punch,*

cited below. For excellent essays on Mayhew as well as a convenient dating of the articles see Eileen Yeo and E. P. Thompson, *The Unknown Mayhew* (New York: Pantheon Books, 1971).

¹² Mayer quotes a *Times* encomium of Grimaldi which describes the pleasure people take in hearing "such jokes as do not require the fatigue of comprehension." Although Mayer uses this particular article to demonstrate "Grimaldi's part in making this genre respectable," one wonders if it were not written with the tongue lodged part way in the cheek. The

writer goes on to compare the public reception of well-worn slapstick gestures with the timeless attraction of fires, dogfights, overturned coaches, "or the taking of convicts from Newgate in a wagon to Blackfriars-bridge." For such pleasures we "notoriously lay down even the Waverly novel." Dickens might wince. Mayer, pp. 17–18.

¹³ Charles Baudelaire, *Selected Writings on Art and Artists,* trans. P. E. Charvet (London: Penguin Books, 1972), p. 421.

STANLEY TICK: *Toward Jaggers*

¹ Graham Greene, "Henry James: The Private Universe," *Collected Essays* (Harmondsworth: Penguin Books, 1969), p. 21.

² For expressions of each, see G. R. Stange, "Expectations Well Lost: Dickens's Fable for His Time," *College English* 16 (1954), 9–17; Paul Pickerel, *"Great Expectations,"* in *Dickens: Twentieth Century Views,* ed. M. Price (Englewood Cliffs, N.J.: Prentice-Hall, 1967), pp. 158–68; Edgar Johnson, *Charles Dickens: His Tragedy and Triumph* (New York: Simon and Schuster, 1952), II, 988–94; and T. A. Jackson, *Charles Dickens: The Progress of a Radical* (London: Lawrence and Wishart, 1937), p. 111.

³ See John Forster, *The Life of Charles Dickens,* Fireside edition (J. M. Dent & Sons, 1903–7), p. 21.

⁴ Well after I completed my study, I came across K. J. Fielding's "Dickens and the Past," in *Experience in the Novel,* ed. Roy Harvey Pearce (New York: Columbia University Press, 1968). Though he concentrates on *Little Dorrit* and uses a rather different focus, Professor Fielding surveys the later novels with a perspective similar to mine.

⁵ Contemporary reviewers pointed out Tulkinghorn's lack of motivation, and most subsequent commentators have remarked in some way upon this same flaw.

⁶ Consider the haunting expressions of the husband and wife emigrants in Ford Madox Brown's famous *The Last of England* (1855), inspired by the departure of Thomas Woolner to Australia.

LAWRENCE FRANK: *The Intelligibility of Madness*

¹ F. R. Leavis and Q. D. Leavis, *Dickens the Novelist* (New York: Pantheon Books, 1970), pp. 116–17.

² Thomas De Quincey, *Confessions of an English Opium-Eater together with Selections from the Autobiography of Thomas De Quincey,* ed. Edward Sackville-West (London: The Cresset Press, 1950), p. 289. This is the 1822 edition of the *Confessions.* Further ref-

erences to this text will be followed by page number in parentheses.

³ Charles Dickens, "Memoranda." These "Memoranda" are in the Henry W. and Albert A. Berg Collection of the New York Public Library (Astor, Lenox and Tilden Foundations) and are used with the knowledge of the Executive Officer of those Foundations. The notebook was begun in Jan-

uary 1855, according to the date at the front of the book, and seems not to have been continued after 1865. I quote from a series of entries on the same page which have a blue line drawn through them, usually an indication that in Dickens' mind the ideas had been "done," incorporated into a work. The incomplete reproduction of the "Memoranda" in the third volume of the Nonesuch *Letters* is misleading, not only because of its fragmentary nature, but because entries do not appear in their correct order. The passages I quote follow the manuscript of the "Memoranda," which is not paginated.

4   See Chrisopher Herbert, "De Quincey and Dickens," *Victorian Studies* 17 (March 1974), 247–63, for another discussion of the two authors.

5   Dickens, "Memoranda."

6   Ibid.

7   For discussions of *Our Mutual Friend* see: H. M. Daleski, *Dickens and the Art of Analogy* (New York: Schocken Books, 1970) and J. Hillis Miller, *Charles Dickens: The World of His Novels* (Cambridge, Mass.: Harvard University Press, 1958).

8   R. D. Laing, *The Divided Self* (Baltimore: Penguin Books, 1965), p. 69.

9   Ibid., p. 69.

10   See Ernest Boll, "The Plotting of *Our Mutual Friend*," *Modern Philology* 42 (1944), 96–122. The essay includes a reproduction of Dickens' working notes for the novel.

11   My discussion of the function of the *Doppelgänger* both in *Our Mutual Friend* and *The Mystery of Edwin Drood* has been influenced by the following works dealing, in various ways, with this subject: Sigmund Freud, "The 'Uncanny,' " trans. Alix Strachey, in *On Creativity and the Unconscious* (New York: Harper and Row, 1958); Otto Rank, *The Double,* trans. and ed. Harry Tucker, Jr. (Chapel Hill: University of North Carolina Press, 1971); Otto Rank, *Beyond Psychology* (Philadelphia: E. Hauser, 1941); Robert Rogers, *The Double in Literature*

(Detroit: Wayne State University Press, 1970); Mark Spilka, *Dickens and Kafka* (Bloomington: Indiana University Press, 1963); Ralph Tymms, *Doubles in Literary Psychology* (Cambridge: Bowes and Bowes, 1949).

12   See Laing, pp. 48, 76. Dickens uses the image of Medusa in his treatment of Mrs. Clennam in *Little Dorrit;* he anticipates Laing's more systematic use of the myth: "If [Mrs. Clennam] had been possessed of the old fabled influence, and had turned those who looked upon her into stone, she could not have rendered [Arthur] more completely powerless (so it seemed to him in his distress of mind) than she did, when she turned her unyielding face to his" (680).

13   Ibid., p. 139.

14   J. Hillis Miller, *The Form of Victorian Fiction* (Notre Dame, Ind.: University of Notre Dame Press, 1968), p. 33.

15   Charles Dickens, *The Mystery of Edwin Drood,* ed. Margaret Cardwell, The Clarendon Dickens (Oxford: Oxford University Press, 1972), p. 38.

16   See Rogers, pp. 138–60.

17   The passage in *The Moonstone* to which critics refer occurs when Ezra Jennings, a kind of protopsychoanalyst, quotes the work of Dr. Elliotson in an attempt to introduce Blake to the realm of the unconscious.

The passage pointed out to me [Blake], was expressed in these terms:—

"Dr. Abel informed me," says Mr. Combe, "of an Irish porter to a warehouse, who forgot, when sober, what he had done when drunk; but, being drunk, again recollected the transactions of his former state of intoxication. On one occasion, being drunk, he had lost a parcel of some value, and in his sober moments could give no account of it. Next time he was intoxicated, he recollected that he had left the parcel at a certain house, and there being no address on it, it had remained there safely, and was got on his calling for it."

I quote from Wilkie Collins, *The Moonstone* (London: Tinsley Brothers, 1868), III, 125.
18 Dickens' explicit interest in such a configuration of relationships is revealed in his "Memoranda" in entries which are worked out in *Our Mutual Friend:* they suggest situations in *A Tale of Two Cities* and *Our Mutual Friend,* and define some parts of *Edwin Drood.* The clusters of entries in the "Memoranda" reveal clearly the ways in which Dickens' last two novels are part of the same imaginative concerns.
19 Matthew G. Lewis, *The Monk* (New York: Grove Press, 1952), p. 239.
20 This paragraph is indebted to R. D. Laing, *The Politics of Experience* (New York: Ballantine Books, 1967), p. 36; and to J. H. Van den Berg, *The Changing Nature of Man,* trans. H. F. Croes (New York: W. W. Norton, 1961), pp. 224–25.

For where would we be if we granted any individual a right to have a world of his own? A world in which everything looks different, a world in which things have another substantiality? Soon there would be more and more people who would demand the same right. Things must retain their stability, they are the condition of our understanding. Even more than that, they are understanding itself. . . . No one

is allowed to take it away from us, not even [a] patient [under analysis]. If he were, our common existence would fall to pieces.

21 Laing, *Politics,* p. 73.
22 For discussions of the Gothic and the double to which I am particularly indebted see: Leslie A. Fiedler, *Love and Death in the American Novel* (New York: Criterion Books, 1960), pp. 3–212; and Masao Miyoshi, *The Divided Self* (New York: New York University Press, 1969).
23 See Richard M. Baker, *The Drood Murder Case* (Berkeley and Los Angeles: University of California Press, 1951), p. 43.
24 Much of this monograph was written with Lionel Trilling's *Sincerity and Authenticity* (Cambridge, Mass.: Harvard University Press, 1972) in mind. I have clearly been responding to his discussion of R. D. Laing in the final chapter of his book. I only want to emphasize that I have tried not to confuse fictionalized "madness" with the "madness" of real, and suffering, human beings. I am not arguing *for* "madness" as the only authentic response to modern culture, nor am I claiming that there can be civilization without its discontents. But there is a need for remembering that "madness," in fiction and in life, may well be intelligible as a commentary upon the ways in which a culture has failed the individual.
25 Fyodor Dostoevsky, *Notes from the Underground,* in *Three Short Novels of Dostoevsky,* trans. Constance Garnett, rev. and ed. Avrahm Yarmolinsky (New York: Doubleday, 1960), pp. 296–97. Further references to this text will be followed by page number in parentheses.

INDEX